2770

KU-692-760

Behavioral Sciences

PreTest®
Self-Assessment
and Review

Behavioral Sciences

PreTest®
Self-Assessment
and Review

Sixth Edition

Edited by

Evan G. Pattishall, Jr., Ph.D., M.D.
Dean Emeritus and Professor Emeritus of Behavioral Science,
Health and Human Development
College of Health and Human Development
The Pennsylvania State University
University Park, Pennsylvania

McGraw-Hill, Inc.
Health Professions Division/PreTest Series

New York	St. Louis	San Francisco	Auckland
Bogotá	Caracas	Lisbon	London	Madrid
Mexico	Milan	Montreal	New Delhi	Paris
San Juan	Singapore	Sydney	Tokyo	Toronto

Behavioral Sciences: PreTest® Self-Assessment and Review, Sixth Edition

1 2 3 4 5 6 7 8 9 0   DOCDOC   9 8 7 6 5 4 3 2

ISBN 0-07-051996-X

The editors were Gail Gavert and Bruce MacGregor.
The production supervisor was Gyl Favours.
R.R. Donnelley & Sons was printer and binder.
This book was set in Times Roman by Compset, Inc.

Library of Congress Cataloging-in-Publication Data

Behavioral sciences : PreTest self-assessment and review /
    edited by Evan G. Pattishall, Jr.—6th ed.
        p.   cm.—(Basic sciences series)
    Includes bibliographical references.
    ISBN 0-07-051996-X
    1. Psychology—Examinations, questions, etc. 2. Social
sciences—Examinations, questions, etc. I. Pattishall,
Evan G. (Evan Gradick). II. Series.
    [DNLM: 1. Behavior—examination questions.
    2. Behavioral Sciences—examination questions.
    WM 188 B419]
    BF78.B43   1993
    150'.76—dc20
    DNLM/DLC
    for Library of Congess   91-38981
                                                         CIP

Contents

Introduction

Behavioral Sciences: PreTest® Self-Assessment and Review provides students, as well as physicians, with a comprehensive and convenient instrument for self-assessment and review within the field of behavioral sciences. The 500 questions parallel the format and degree of difficulty of the questions contained in Step 1 of the United States Medical Licensing Examination (USMLE) as well as the Foreign Medical Graduate Examination in the Medical Sciences (FMGEMS).

NEW FOR THIS EDITION: To conform with current USMLE guidelines, all K-type (multiple true-false) questions have been eliminated.

Each question in the book is accompanied by an answer, an explanation, and specific page references to current journal articles, textbooks, or both. A bibliography, listing all the sources used in the book, follows the last chapter.

Perhaps the most effective way to use this book is to allow yourself one minute to answer each question in a given chapter; as you proceed, indicate your answer beside each question. By following this suggestion, you will be approximating the time limits imposed by the board examinations previously mentioned.

When you finish answering the questions in a chapter, you should then spend as much time as you need verifying your answers and carefully reading the explanations. Although you should pay special attention to the explanations for the questions you answered incorrectly, you should read *every* explanation. The author of this book has designed the explanations to reinforce and supplement the information tested by the questions. If, after reading the explanations for a given chapter, you feel you need still more information about the material covered, you should consult and study the references indicated.

Behavioral Sciences

PreTest®
Self-Assessment
and Review

Biologic Correlates of Behavior

DIRECTIONS: Each question below contains five suggested responses. Select the **one best** response to each question.

1. All the following endocrine glands are subject to control by the brain EXCEPT the

(A) pancreatic islets
(B) pituitary
(C) parathyroid
(D) thyroid
(E) adrenal

2. In the treatment of psychophysiologic disorders, all the following statements about minor tranquilizers are true EXCEPT

(A) they fail to result in long-term improvement
(B) they reduce interpersonal dilemmas
(C) they produce drowsiness
(D) they result in need for increased dosages
(E) they reduce high levels of stress

3. All the following hormones are recognized as being important in influencing sexual behavior EXCEPT

(A) luteinizing hormone releasing factor
(B) oxytocin
(C) estradiol
(D) testosterone
(E) androstenedione

4. All the following are common forms of psychophysiologic disorders EXCEPT

(A) bronchial asthma
(B) dysmenorrhea
(C) headache
(D) diabetes
(E) neurodermatitis

5. When an axon is cut, all the following events take place EXCEPT

(A) there is a rapid local degeneration of the axon and myelin sheath
(B) macrophages from the general circulation are unable to enter the area to phagocytose axonal debris
(C) proliferation of fibrous astrocytes forms a glial scar around the zone of trauma
(D) scarring can block the course taken by the regenerating axons
(E) degeneration spreads in both directions along the axon from the zone of trauma

6. Clinical features of major depressive disorders suggest a defect in the

(A) frontal lobes
(B) pituitary
(C) hippocampus
(D) hypothalamus
(E) corpus callosum

7. Immunocompetence can be suppressed by all the following EXCEPT

(A) the endocrine system
(B) chronic stress
(C) the central nervous system
(D) the autonomic nervous system
(E) psychosocial factors

8. All the following statements on the influence of environment on brain structure and behavior are true EXCEPT

(A) the structure of the brain is to an important degree specified by genetic and developmental processes
(B) the pattern of interconnections between neurons is influenced considerably by experience
(C) there is very little evidence for the notion of the critical period in the development of normal social and perceptual competence
(D) at certain stages in its development, the integrative action of the brain and its cellular structure are dependent upon the brain's interaction with its environment
(E) the action of the environment on the brain varies with age

9. The pituitary secretion of endorphins is closely linked to the secretion of adrenocorticotropic hormone (ACTH) so that endorphins facilitate the ability to respond to

(A) retarded growth
(B) severe hypertension
(C) stress
(D) chronic pain
(E) tachycardia

10. Antibody titers to latent viruses, e.g., Epstein-Barr or herpes simplex, can be increased at least initially by all the following EXCEPT

(A) relaxation training
(B) immunosuppressive chemotherapy
(C) the stress of academic examinations
(D) loneliness
(E) sustained noise

11. Psychosocial stress increases the secretion of catecholamines and thus induces an increase in a number of cardiovascular pathogenic phenomena. All the following are increased EXCEPT

(A) damage to intima of coronary arteries
(B) blood pressure and heart rate
(C) blood lipids
(D) first-degree AV block
(E) ventricular arrhythmias

12. Hyperventilation from anxiety, threat, or fear results in all the following EXCEPT

(A) reduced CO_2 in the blood
(B) reduced acid level in the blood
(C) increased sympathetic activity
(D) increased risk of cardiac arrhythmia
(E) increased oxygen supplied to brain tissue

13. Studies of the effects of acute and chronic stress in humans indicate that the activity of all the following components of the immune system are decreased EXCEPT

(A) polymorphonuclear granulocytes
(B) lymphocyte T-cell cytotoxicity
(C) production of interferon
(D) latent virus antibody titers
(E) activity of natural killer cells

14. Dream deprivation in humans tends to produce

(A) impaired performance on simple verbal tasks with no emotional content
(B) less total need for dream sleep
(C) major impairment of psychological functions
(D) retardation of formation of memory
(E) integration of emotional material with memories of other experiences

15. Experimental preavoidance stress-conditioning procedures can induce significant increases in all the following EXCEPT

(A) plasma potassium
(B) plasma sodium
(C) plasma aldosterone
(D) blood pressure
(E) heart rate

16. When persons with a type A pattern of coronary-prone behavior are subjected to stressful situations, they exhibit increases in all the following EXCEPT

(A) plasma norepinephrine
(B) systolic blood pressure
(C) heart rate
(D) occipital alpha activity
(E) cortisol

17. The diathesis-stress model of psychophysiologic disorders postulates the presence of which of the following major factors?

(A) Inadequate coping style
(B) Individual response stereotype
(C) Lack of health belief resolution
(D) Adequate homeostatic restraints
(E) Unconditioned stimulus

18. Over time, vigorous exercise results in all the following EXCEPT

(A) increased high-density lipoprotein cholesterol (HDL-C)
(B) decreased low-density lipoprotein cholesterol (LDL-C)
(C) decreased very low-density lipoprotein cholesterol (VLDL-C)
(D) decreased total cholesterol
(E) increased triglycerides

19. Harry Harlow's work with inanimate surrogate mothers for monkeys suggests that the early experience critical to the ultimate development of "love" is

(A) positive reinforcement
(B) protection from danger
(C) contact comfort
(D) need-reduction by nursing
(E) sexual stimulation

20. The left hemisphere of the brain is generally associated with each of the following functions EXCEPT

(A) language acquisition
(B) affective aspects of language
(C) mathematical reasoning
(D) finger dexterity
(E) vocalization

21. The hormone with the greatest role in aggression is

(A) thyroxine
(B) testosterone
(C) estrogen
(D) progesterone
(E) aldosterone

22. Dynorphin, a natural brain endorphin, has all the following characteristics EXCEPT that it is

(A) 50 times more potent than any other known endorphin
(B) 200 times more potent than morphine
(C) able to bind to pain receptors with great specificity
(D) a producer of tolerance and dependence
(E) clinically useful in more severe pain problems

23. A direct pathologic consequence of stress-induced elevation of plasma cortisone is injury to the

(A) neuroendocrine system
(B) immune system
(C) cardiovascular musculature
(D) hypothalamus
(E) central nervous system

24. Consumption of alcohol is associated with all the following EXCEPT

(A) inhibition of mobility of macrophages
(B) inhibition of proliferation of T cells
(C) inhibition of cytotoxicity of T cells
(D) inhibition of production of antibodies
(E) damage to the thymus

25. Which of the following substances is the most responsive to psychosocial stress?

(A) Catecholamines
(B) Growth hormone
(C) Endorphins
(D) Adrenocorticotropic hormone (ACTH)
(E) Insulin

26. The gate control theory of pain assumes all the following EXCEPT that

(A) the substantia gelatinosa is the primary vehicle for gating
(B) the spinal gate mechanism is influenced by nerve impulses that descend from the brain
(C) the activity in the large nerve fibers will tend to facilitate the transmission by opening the gate
(D) motivation, emotion, and cognition modulate the pain experience
(E) the spinal gate mechanism in the dorsal horn modulates the transmission from afferent fibers to spinal cord transmission cells

27. Research on rapid eye movement (REM) sleep patterns shows all the following findings EXCEPT that

(A) a newborn baby spends more than 50 percent of sleep time in REM sleep
(B) under normal circumstances, 80 percent of the adult sleep cycle consists of REM sleep
(C) deep sleep begins to be replaced with longer periods of REM *lighter* sleep after the age of 30
(D) the amount of REM sleep determines the amount of actual rest
(E) when REM sleep is interrupted consistently, tiredness and neurotic tendencies develop

28. The most common organic explanation for a sleep disturbance in a healthy person is

(A) disruption of normal circadian rhythms
(B) accumulation of hepatic enzymes
(C) the inevitable consequences of high activity
(D) suppressed REM sleep
(E) misuse of hypnotics

29. A lesion of the axons of motor neurons that innervate skeletal muscle (lower motor neurons) will result in all the following consequences EXCEPT

(A) paralysis of individual muscles on the side of the lesion
(B) a paradoxical increase in reflex activity
(C) reduction in muscle mass (atrophy)
(D) decrease in muscle tone
(E) sealing off of the axoplasm

30. True statements regarding the gate control theory of pain include all the following EXCEPT that it

(A) allowed for clinical predictions that have proved empirically useful
(B) encouraged the testing of pharmacologic and surgical blocks
(C) reversed emphasis on pain as solely an afferent sensory experience
(D) hypothesized a higher central decoding mechanism for control of pain
(E) postulated that cognitive factors could exert descending control of pain

31. A by-product of the research on the gate control theory of pain was the determination that the pain experience can consist of each of the following components EXCEPT

(A) sensory-discriminative
(B) motivational-affective
(C) cognitive-evaluative
(D) reflex imaging
(E) operant conditioning

32. All the following statements about sleeping pills are correct EXCEPT

(A) they lose their effectiveness in about 2 weeks
(B) barbiturates gradually lead to an increase in hepatic enzymes
(C) patients develop tolerance for benzodiazepines much less rapidly than for pentobarbital
(D) barbiturates enhance REM sleep
(E) there is often a broad cross-tolerance to other hypnotics

33. All the following response patterns will usually accompany dreaming EXCEPT

(A) electroencephalographic desynchrony
(B) more visual imagery during non-REM sleep
(C) rapid eye movements
(D) loss of sternocleidomastoid tonus
(E) cardiorespiratory irregularities

34. The relationship between social and biologic processes in the generation of behavior has historically been classified by which of the following terms?

(A) Classically conditioned
(B) Organic and functional
(C) Genetic and familial
(D) Neuropathologic and socio-pathologic
(E) Psychoanalytic and dynamic

35. All the following statements about the behavioral assessment of alcohol abuse are true EXCEPT

(A) persons with a high degree of acquired tolerance tend to exhibit less evidence of behavioral impairment than those with less tolerance
(B) trained clinical observers are prone to frequent errors when estimating the actual levels of intoxication of alcohol abusers
(C) women attain higher blood levels, absorb alcohol faster, and reach peak blood alcohol levels sooner than men
(D) police officers are more accurate in estimating blood alcohol levels than are social drinkers
(E) in identification of intoxication, the rate of false negative errors is greater than false positive errors

36. The use of relaxation techniques for stress reduction affects diabetic patients by producing

(A) increased levels of plasma cortisol
(B) increased sensitivity to insulin
(C) increased glucose-stimulated secretion of insulin
(D) significant improvement in glucose tolerance
(E) no significant change in requirements for exogenous insulin

37. When one has no sense of control over a stressful situation, all the following physiologic reactions will occur EXCEPT

(A) weaker corticosteroid elevations will develop
(B) an endogenous opioid peptide will be released
(C) a brief endogenous opiate analgesia will be produced
(D) greater suppression of the cytotoxicity of natural killer cells will occur than in controllable stress
(E) a weaker immune response to mitogen stimulation will develop than in controllable stress

38. In attempting to moderate stress, it has been found that lack of sense of control will result in all the following EXCEPT

(A) increased incidence of gastric ulceration
(B) higher levels of catecholamines if a person's job is self-paced
(C) increased excretion of epinephrine under conditions of uncertainty
(D) comparatively lower levels of corticosteroid production if stress is predictable
(E) lower rate of corticosteroid decline after termination of the stress

39. Dream deprivation is most apt to produce

(A) a rebound phenomenon of increased dreaming
(B) an increase in anxiety and irritability
(C) acceleration of memory formation of emotionally toned words
(D) a decrement in intellectual function
(E) a temporary increase in nightmares

40. Which of the following statements about natural killer cells is true?

(A) Their activity increases with the secretion of corticosteroids through the hypothalamic-pituitary-adrenal axis
(B) They play a role in inhibition of tumor growth
(C) They are ineffective in deterring the spread of distant cancer
(D) Their activity increases under conditions of psychosocial stress
(E) None of the above

41. Metabolic changes occurring during exercise include all the following EXCEPT

(A) the rate of glucose removal from the blood and plasma increases
(B) the amount of insulin required for glucose uptake increases
(C) the sensitivity of insulin receptors in skeletal muscle increases
(D) the sensitivity of insulin receptors in adipose tissue increases
(E) metabolic rate remains elevated for some hours after moderate-to-vigorous exercise

DIRECTIONS: Each group of questions below consists of lettered headings followed by a set of numbered items. For each numbered item select the **one** lettered heading with which it is **most** closely associated. Each lettered heading may be used **once, more than once, or not at all.**

Questions 42–46

For each description that follows, select the substance with which it is most closely associated.

(A) Dopamine
(B) Dopamine-β-hydroxylase
(C) 6-Hydroxydopamine
(D) Norepinephrine
(E) Acetylcholine

42. Transmitter that ultimately mediates all overt behavior

43. Substance found to be deficient in the brains of schizophrenic persons

44. Substance that poisons neurons by forming peroxides and has been implicated in the cause of schizophrenia

45. Agent that mediates behavioral reward and is found at high levels in the median forebrain bundle

46. Agent that is a putative transmitter and also a precursor of another transmitter in the brain reward system

Questions 47–52

Match the following descriptions with the appropriate stages of sleep.

(A) Stage 1 REM sleep
(B) Stage 1 NREM sleep
(C) Stages 1 through 4 slow wave sleep (NREM)
(D) Stage 4 delta wave sleep (NREM)
(E) Stage 2 NREM sleep

47. Decline in heart rate, blood pressure, and respiration and increase in gastrointestinal movements

48. Suppression by the benzodiazepines

49. Greatest likelihood of sleeper awakening spontaneously

50. Highest frequency of dream recall

51. Longer duration during the first half of night

52. Continuous decline in the elderly

Questions 53–58

Match the descriptions below with the substances produced by smoking behavior.

(A) Nicotine
(B) Carbon monoxide
(C) Hydrogen cyanide
(D) Both hydrogen cyanide and carbon monoxide
(E) Both nicotine and carbon monoxide

53. Contribution to increased prevalence of fatal and nonfatal cardiovascular disease

54. Promotion of chronic obstructive pulmonary disease, emphysema, and chronic bronchitis

55. Valuable in the discrimination of smokers from nonsmokers

56. Maintenance of pharmacologically satisfying doses by adjusting smoking behavior to titrate intake

57. Decreased oxygen content in fetal blood and subsequent complications in pregnancy

58. Elevated blood levels from exposure to smoke from other people's cigarettes

Questions 59–64

For each description select the biologic system or substance with which it is most closely associated.

(A) Endocrine and autonomic nervous systems
(B) Hypothalamic-limbic-midbrain circuits
(C) Adrenal cortex and thyroid
(D) Neuropeptides
(E) Dopaminergic circuit or system

59. Highly relevant for Parkinson's disease and schizophrenia

60. Active in mediating integrative processes relevant to survival

61. Substantially involved in mediating adaptive functions of memory appraisal and motivational-emotional response

62. Active in "fine tuning" one's mood

63. Especially active when one becomes very upset, angry, or depressed for an extended period of time

64. Coordinated by the hypothalamus

Questions 65–72

For each psychological response, select the biologic system or anatomic region with which it is most closely associated.

(A) Sympatho-adrenomedullary system
(B) Hypothalamic-pituitary-adrenocortical (HPAC) system
(C) Immune system
(D) Endorphin-enkephalin system
(E) Anterior hypothalamus

65. Suppressed by stress

66. Increased metabolic activity in response to stress

67. A "conservation-withdrawal" pattern

68. Reduction of fear and pain in aversive situations

69. Peptic ulceration and clinical depression

70. Implicated in hypertension, angina pectoris, and cardiac arrhythmia

71. Suppressed by increased lympholytic steroid hormones

72. The relaxation response

Biologic Correlates
of Behavior
Answers

1. The answer is C. *(Gatchel, 2/e. pp 18–20.)* Most glands receive either direct neural control from the brain or indirect control from hormones secreted by the hypothalamus. Thus, thyroid secretion is subject to hypothalamic control, whereas insulin secretion depends in part on adrenergic influence from the autonomic nervous system. The parathyroids are notably free of brain control; in regulating calcium metabolism, they in turn are regulated by blood levels of calcium.

2. The answer is B. *(Gatchel, 2/e. p 159.)* Minor tranquilizers have been traditionally a major form of treatment of psychophysiologic disorders. They can be an effective means of lowering high levels of anxiety and stress, especially when combined with some form of behavioral therapy or psychotherapy to deal with the situational or interpersonal factors that are involved. On a long-term basis, however, minor tranquilizers alone have not been very effective because they do not resolve the situational and interpersonal factors, they lead to tolerance with need for increased dosages, and they often have side effects of drowsiness and withdrawal symptoms of insomnia, tremors, and hallucinations.

3. The answer is B. *(Carlson, 4/e. pp 320–338.)* Oxytocin is one of the peptide hormones that apparently is behaviorally inactive. It has an important function in parturition by facilitating contractions of the uterus; the hormone also facilitates ejection of milk during lactation. The gonadal steroids, in contrast, exert profound effects on behavior. They are necessary for appropriate reproductive and parental behavior patterns in any species of mammals. In addition, gonadal hormones mediate many forms of agonistic behavior.

4. The answer is D. *(Gatchel, 2/e. pp 146–152.)* Psychophysiologic disorders were formerly referred to as *psychosomatic illnesses.* They are characterized by physical symptoms from organs of the body that have become dysfunctional through an interaction between psychological, biologic (including genetic), and sociocultural factors. Specifically, the most common psychophysiologic disorders are bronchial asthma, dysmenorrhea, headache, neurodermatitis, and peptic ulcer. Diabetes, along with many other diseases, has a strong psychological component, but is not considered to be a psychophysiologic disorder.

5.   The answer is B. *(Kandel, 3/e. pp 258–262.)* When the axon is cut, the axon and synaptic terminals are deprived of essential metabolic connections with the cell body. Since axonal transport occurs in both directions, the result is a rapid local degeneration of the axon and myelin sheath, with the cell body also being affected. Synapses mediate both electrical signals and nutritive interactions between neurons. Thus, changes occur in the cell body (retrograde changes) and also in subsequent neurons that receive synapses from the damaged neurons. Macrophages from the general circulation enter the trauma area and phagocytose axonal debris, and glial cells (astrocytes and microglia) proliferate to assist in the process. This proliferation of fibrous astrocytes forms a glial scar around the trauma area, which can then block the course of regenerating axons and the reformation of central connections. The behavioral effects of nerve lesions are peculiar to the location of the lesion in the brain and the nerve cell connections, so that the same type of injury will have different behavioral effects depending on its location.

6.   The answer is D. *(Kandel, 3/e. pp 869–880.)* Clinical studies of patients with major depressive disorders indicate that an intrinsic regulatory defect involving the hypothalamus underlies the disorder. It also involves the monoamine pathways. The hypothalamic modulation of neuroendocrine activity has been implicated, as have been the neurotransmitter systems of serotonin and norepinephrine. Recent evidence suggests a major role for the heritability of such neurochemical disorders. The role of behavior in stimulating or triggering such mechanisms is also being explored. While the frontal lobes, the pituitary, the hippocampus, and the corpus callosum are related to the emotions, memory, and neural communications, they do not play as major a role in the depressive disorders as does the hypothalamus.

7.   The answer is B. *(Gatchel, 2/e. pp 121–126.)* *Immunocompetence* refers to the ability of the various components of the immune system to recognize, respond to, and reject elements and antigens that do not belong in the body. The immune system can no longer be regarded as an autonomous system. The autonomic and central nervous systems and the endocrine system have been known to influence and to be influenced by the immune system, and it has now been demonstrated that psychosocial factors can also influence the immune system and affect its ability to respond to invading organisms and antigens. Psychosocial stress can suppress immunocompetence. While acute stress tends to suppress the immune system, chronic stress tends to enhance the immune system, especially over time.

8. The answer is C. *(Kandel, 3/e. pp 945–957.)* All functions of the brain represent an interaction between genetic and environmental factors (e.g., learning). It is also known that the structure of the brain is greatly influenced by genetic and developmental processes. It is not always appreciated that the structure of the brain, specifically the pattern of interconnections between the neurons, also depends on experience with behavior. This influence is established early, in that there are certain critical stages in the development of the brain when the integrative action of the brain and its cellular structure are dependent upon its interaction with its environment. Further, the work of Harry Harlow with isolated young monkeys, the work of René Spitz and others with early human sensory and social deprivation, and the early sensory deprivation perception studies of von Senden, Riesen, Hubel, and Wiesel have soundly established the importance of the critical period concept upon the development of normal social behavior, physical growth, and normal visual perception. The influence and the action of the environment on the brain do vary with age—both normal and abnormal patterns of stimulation have a more profound effect at early stages of development. Environmental stimuli, social experience, and learning and memory also continue to have an influence on adults.

9. The answer is C. *(Kandel, 3/e. pp 217–218, 397–398.)* Under stressful conditions, the organism secretes endorphins and ACTH together. Pro-opiocortin is a common precursor. The close link between endorphins and ACTH suggests that they serve a mediation function for a closely related set of adaptation responses. Thus, they can facilitate one's response to stress and at the same time help one to withstand pain and mobilize for coping activity to deal with the stressful challenge or threat. Almost every physical stress agent increases plasma levels of β-endorphin as well as adrenocorticotropin and corticosterone.

10. The answer is A. *(Gatchel, 2/e. pp 128–129.)* The immune system may control latent viruses such as Epstein-Barr or herpes simplex, but it cannot destroy or eliminate them. If the immune system is weakened so that the virus becomes more active, the antibody titers to the virus will increase. Immunosuppressive drugs will increase antibodies to latent viruses. Kiecolt-Glaser and Glaser, working with medical students and elderly residents of nursing homes, were able to demonstrate that the stress of examinations and loneliness were associated with elevated antibody titers. Sustained noise also causes a rise in antibody titers initially, but after a few days the organism seems to adapt and titers return to normal. Studies have also demonstrated that relaxation training produces decreased antibody titers to latent viruses by generating an increase in natural killer cell activity.

11. The answer is D. *(Lindzey, 3/e. pp 855–859.*) The secretion of epinephrine and norepinephrine (catecholamines), which is accelerated under conditions of psychosocial stress, induces pathogenic states leading to cardiovascular disease—for example, increased blood pressure and heart rate, elevated blood lipids, acceleration of the rate of damage to the inner areas of the coronary arteries, and also the induction or provocation of ventricular arrhythmias. First-degree AV block is a conduction disorder unrelated to stress. The provocation of ventricular arrhythmias is especially important as a potential cause of sudden death.

12. The answer is E. *(Lindzey, 3/e. pp 859–860.*) If a person is agitated, anxious, in a state of panic or near panic, or in a state of hypervigilance to minor or major threat cues, increased breathing (hyperventilation) is a frequent response. Typically, a series of major physiologic, behavioral, and psychological changes is evoked. The reduced CO_2 in the blood lowers the blood's acid level; sympathetic activity, cardiac arrhythmias, and heart rate increase; decreased oxygen is supplied to brain tissue; and cerebral vasoconstriction is heightened. Acute anxiety ensues, generally focused on the threatening situation or somatic complaints, and the sense of fear is heightened. The altered patterns of vascular, neurologic, and cerebral activity are mainly responsible for the psychomotor and cognitive impairments. Such psychological, social, physical, or environmental hypervigilance frequently results in temporary impairment and defective decision-making characterized by excessive vacillation and an impulsive choice of options.

13. The answer is D. *(Ader, 2/e. pp 850–864. Gatchel, 2/e. pp 125–133.*) A number of experimental and clinical studies on the effects of psychosocial stress on the human immune system have demonstrated a decrease in the activity of natural killer cells in healthy human subjects. Likewise, stress was related to a decrease in lymphocyte cytotoxicity and a decrease in the rate of microbe engulfment by polymorphonuclear granulocytes. There was also a depression in the response of T lymphocytes to mitogens. Latent viruses, such as herpes simplex or Epstein-Barr, are generally controlled by the immune system, but when the immune system is suppressed, the antibody titers to the virus will increase. Another study demonstrated that sleep deprivation decreased the ability of blood neutrophil granulocytes to phagocytize *Staphylococcus aureus* and increased the production of interferon by blood lymphocytes. Also, the phytohemagglutinin-induced DNA synthesis of blood lymphocytes was reduced after sleep deprivation of 48 h.

14. The answer is D. *(Carlson, 4/e. pp 273–286.*) More is known about the effects of depriving a person of various kinds of sleep, such as dream sleep, than about the effects of total deprivation of sleep. There appears to be a need for a certain amount of dream sleep. A deficiency produces a "rebound" phenomenon of increased dreaming when uninterrupted sleep is permitted. Contrary to earlier speculations, dream deprivation does not produce any major impairment in psychological functions, nor does it produce any impairment of performance on simple verbal tasks with no emotional content. Dream sleep deprivation, however, does impair the recall of emotionally toned words. It somehow assists the integration of emotional material with memories of other experiences. A major effect of dream deprivation is that it retards formation of memory. An interesting variation is that new learning experiences result in an increase in subsequent dream sleep.

15. The answer is E. *(Weiss, Perspectives, pp 311–317.)* Stress studies using such situations as preavoidance conditioning, postsurgical convalescence, exposure to cold conditions, and other stressful conditions have shown a significant increase in certain physiologic measures. The most recent findings involving the stress of preavoidance conditioning have shown significant increases in systolic and diastolic blood pressure, plasma potassium, and plasma sodium, with decreases in heart rate. These behaviorally induced changes in potassium are significant because they are known to increase the secretion of aldosterone, which is the most potent of the salt-retaining hormones. Behavioral conditioning procedures are also known to produce increases in ACTH and renin-angiotensin, which can vary the levels of aldosterone. The interactions between these behaviorally induced physiologic measures are significantly related to the development of chronic elevation of blood pressure.

16. The answer is D. *(Weiss, Perspectives, pp 31–34, 321–328.)* The incidence and prevalence of coronary heart disease caused by atherosclerosis have been linked to the type A pattern of coronary-prone behavior. Persons considered to be type A are more prone to respond to environmental challenges (social, psychological, or physical) with increased physiologic responses. These behaviorally induced physiologic responses over a lifetime appear to be linked to the development of certain cardiovascular disorders. Laboratory studies of humans have found that type A persons exhibit an increased level of systolic blood pressure, heart rate, plasma norepinephrine, plasma epinephrine, and cortisol and a decrease in occipital alpha activity. Other increases associated with coronary heart disease include those in serum cholesterol, serum triglycerides, platelet aggregation, clotting time, and serum corticotropin.

17. The answer is B. *(Gatchel, 2/e. pp 156–157.)* The diathesis-stress model of psychophysiologic disorders states that individuals are predisposed toward a particular mental or physiologic reaction and that the disorder will become manifest as a reaction to stress. Two major factors are postulated by the model: (1) individual response stereotype, consisting of a predisposition to respond physiologically to various situations and in a particular way; and (2) inadequate homeostatic restraints caused by stress-induced breakdown, previous accident, infection or trauma, or by genetic predisposition. Situational determinants play an important role as does one's perception of the situation, which generates increased or decreased physiologic response. While one's coping style and one's values or attitudes can play a role, they are not considered to be major factors in the diathesis-stress model. The role of learned response can also be important, but is not a major postulate.

18. The answer is E. *(Rosen, pp 114–116.)* Vigorous exercise over time has been shown to increase the high-density lipoprotein cholesterol in the blood while decreasing the low-density lipoprotein cholesterol, very low-density lipoprotein cholesterol, total cholesterol, and triglycerides. Thus, vigorous exercise acts to reduce several established risk factors for coronary heart disease and to promote increased high-density lipoprotein cholesterol, which has an antiatherogenic effect.

19. The answer is C. *(Kaplan, 6/e. pp 123–126.)* In the late 1950s, Harry Harlow discovered that monkeys reared with a substitute "mother" covered with terry cloth were much more likely to engage in effective heterosexual relationships as juveniles than were monkeys raised with a substitute mother made of steel wire. He concluded that the comfort provided by the clothed (or natural) mother was a critical precursor of the feeling of love. He also demonstrated its importance for positive social and emotional development.

20. The answer is B. *(Kandel, 3/e. pp 7–10.)* While the control of certain intellectual functions by the right hemisphere or left hemisphere is not as clearcut and clearly divided as was once thought, there are still general functions related to the right or left hemisphere. The left hemisphere is much more involved in language, smaller muscle movements, vocalization, finger dexterity, and logic. The right is much more involved in large motor programs, great muscles of the limbs, spatial abilities, and "gestalt" thinking. It is important to remember that the hemispheres do interact with each other.

21. The answer is B. *(Carlson, 4/e. pp 357–376.)* In most species, the male tends to be more aggressive than the female. Animal handlers long have taken advantage of the fact that castration, by reducing aggression, makes animals more tractable. Testosterone administered postpubertally to castrated rats can restore aggressiveness to almost normal levels. Similarly, neonatal female mice develop masculine aggressive behavior on receiving androgens. Androgens also promote aggression in humans. Boys are more aggressive than girls at ages 3 to 10, as has been demonstrated in studies of male and female children. Criminals with a history of violence have also been found to have differences in testosterone levels, but it is not yet certain whether the higher androgen levels promote violence or the aggression increases the androgen levels. Probably both mechanisms are active.

22. The answer is E. *(Williams, RB, pp 3–9.)* Research on hypothalamic hormones has led to the discovery of many neuropeptides. The study of endorphins that bind to various opiate receptors in the brain has led to some amazing discoveries. Dynorphin, a natural brain endorphin, is reported to be 200 times more potent than morphine and 50 times more potent than other known endorphins. The high degree of potency indicates that it is able to bind with great specificity to pain receptors, but it also appears to produce tolerance and dependence. While it is highly potent, it is still experimental and not in clinical use. It occurs in the pituitary, other parts of the brain, spinal cord, and adrenal medulla.

23. The answer is B. *(Weiss, Perspectives, pp 371–400.)* Psychosocial stress, whether experimentally or environmentally induced, has been shown to produce increased levels of adrenal corticoids. This is accomplished through neuroendocrine pathways involving the cerebral cortex, the hypothalamus, the pituitary, and the adrenal cortex. The direct effect of such stress-induced elevation of plasma cortisone is injury to various components of the immune system, and this injury results in increased vulnerability to the subsequent action of latent oncogenic viruses, newly mutated cancer cells, or other pathologic processes that are normally prevented by normally functioning mechanisms of immunologic surveillance. As an example, increased blood levels of glucocorticoids over an extended period of time have a lytic effect on lymphocytes and on lymphatic tissues such as the thymus, nodes, and spleen. Thus their depletion enhances various pathologic processes, including that of cancer.

24. The answer is D. *(Gatchel, 2/e. p 133.)* Consumption of alcohol has been shown to affect the immune system, apparently in relation to dose. Macrophages are inhibited and move more slowly toward chemical signals released by the body. Proliferation and cytotoxicity of T cells are also inhibited. Increased doses of alcohol can damage certain bodily tissues, such as the thymus. However, no inhibition of production of antibodies has been observed.

25. The answer is D. *(Hamburg, Frontiers of Research, pp 64–71.)* The catecholamines (e.g., epinephrine, norepinephrine), which are found in the adrenal medulla and in the brain, as well as corticosteroids of the adrenal cortex, have been linked to stress for many years. The endorphins, which are morphinelike peptides found in the brain, pituitary gland, and adrenals, are also linked to stress and are involved in perception of and response to pain. Adrenocorticotropic hormone (ACTH) is the most responsive because it is related to stress through control of the adrenal cortex and is present in many neurons in various regions of the brain. A recently identified peptide that stimulates the secretion of ACTH is thought to be the key signal that mediates and integrates a person's endocrine, visceral, and behavioral responses to stress. ACTH is also linked to β-endorphin. ACTH and endorphins appear to be secreted together under stress conditions that are perceived by a person as being dangerous or threatening. Many other hormones are responsive to stress, e.g., prolactin, growth hormone, insulin testosterone, and luteinizing hormone.

26. The answer is C. *(Feuerstein, pp 433–437.)* The gate control theory of pain has demonstrated that pain is more than the single transmission from the pain source to the brain. Actually, pain is the net result of neurophysiologic and neurochemical processes that permit psychological factors such as motivation, emotion, and cognition (including memory) to modulate the pain experience. Cognitive factors are known to influence even spinal withdrawal reflexes; for example, a hot object that is valuable will be handled more carefully than another object that can be dropped safely. The spinal gate mechanism is in the substantia gelatinosa in the dorsal horn and is influenced by the relative amount of activity of the large-diameter rapidly conducting fibers (which inhibit transmission and close the gate) in comparison with the small-diameter low fibers (which facilitate and open the gate). The spinal gate mechanism can be influenced (inhibited) by cognitive factors that descend from the brain and by neuropeptide release. Even though the theory is not completely confirmed, it has resulted in the important clinical application of enabling physicians to diminish pain by stimulating the large-diameter dorsal column fibers to close the gate. The theory has also rejected the notion of pain as solely an afferent sensory experience.

27. The answer is B. *(Kaplan, 6/e. pp 466–469.)* Sleep is divided into two distinct states: D sleep (desynchronized EEG pattern sleep) and S sleep (synchronized EEG pattern sleep). D sleep is also known as REM (rapid eye movement) or dreaming sleep; S sleep as NREM (non–rapid eye movement), orthodox, or quiet sleep. S sleep (NREM) is divided into stages 1, 2, 3, and 4; stage 1 is the lightest and stage 4 the deepest. NREM sleep lasts from 60 to 100 min, followed by 10 to 40 min of REM sleep, and the cycle is continued throughout the night. Typically, about 80 percent of an adult's sleep time is spent in NREM sleep and 20 percent in REM sleep. REM sleep tends to increase during the second half of the night. The amount of REM sleep appears to determine the amount of rest. When REM sleep is interrupted, tiredness tends to develop. A newborn spends about 50 percent of sleep time in REM sleep. Deep sleep begins to be replaced by longer periods of lighter sleep after the age of 30.

28. The answer is A. *(Kandel, 3/e. pp 806–810.)* About 30 to 35 percent of the people who cannot sleep have a relatively simple organic cause for the problem. The two most frequent organic causes are disruption of normal circadian rhythms and the inevitable consequences of aging. The most common disruptions of normal circadian rhythms are related to travel, "jet lag," and behavioral changes in one's normal daily routine, such as napping, irregular sleep hours and conditions, alteration in meal times, and unusual work schedules. Normal aging is the next most common factor as it is more difficult to reset one's biologic clock the older one gets. It has been estimated that most people over age 60 sleep only about 5.5 h per day, and since stage 4 NREM sleep also declines with age, the lighter stages of NREM sleep allow the person to awaken more often, sometimes generating the worry that one cannot sleep or that one is not getting enough sleep. Accumulation of hepatic enzymes is a frequent side effect of prolonged use of sleeping pills. The most common psychosocial cause of insomnia is emotional disturbance.

29. The answer is B. *(Kandel, 3/e. pp 258–262.)* The cutting of a nerve tract within the brain or of a peripheral nerve results in the following sequence: Both ends of the cut axon immediately seal off the axoplasm, retract, and begin to swell; there is rapid degeneration of the axon and the myelin sheath; the macrophages from the general circulation enter the area and phagocytose axonal debris; there is also a proliferation of glial cells, which act as phagocytes; and fibrous astrocytes proliferate in the central nervous system, which leads to glial scar formation around the zone of trauma that often blocks the course taken by regenerating axons and causes a barrier against the reformation of central connections. Degeneration spreads along the axon in both directions from the zone of trauma. The retrograde reaction in the proximal segment usually progresses a short distance and appears in the cell body after 2 to 3 days. In the distal segment, degeneration appears in the axon terminal in about 1 day, and within 2 weeks the distal synapses degenerate completely.

30. The answer is B. *(Kandel, 3/e. pp 392–393.)* The gate control theory of pain was developing in the 1960s because of an interest in discovering mechanisms whereby other cutaneous stimuli and emotional states could alter the level of pain felt. It was postulated that the collateral input from large-fiber

(Aβ touch fibers) and small-fiber (Aδ and C fibers) interactions in the dorsal horn has an antagonistic effect on cells in the substantia gelatinosa. These were designated as gate cells that regulated the firing of cells deeper in the dorsal horn (probably lamina V) that give rise to the paleospinothalamic tract. Thus, a higher central decoding mechanism was hypothesized—one that monitored spinothalamic activity during which pain is felt. It was also postulated that the brain exerted descending control because cognitive factors could even influence spinal withdrawal reflexes. Subsequent experiments have found very little physiologic evidence for the gate control theory, although the negative results are probably not definitive. The gate control theory has persisted because some of its clinical predictions have proved empirically useful (e.g., stimulation of large-diameter dorsal column fibers can provide clinical pain relief for long periods). Furthermore, the emphasis of past research upon pain as solely an afferent sensory experience has been reversed so that the unique and motivational properties of pain (disruption of behavior, primary negative reinforcement) are now recognized. Attempts to use pharmacologic and surgical blocks exclusively have acted to prevent the exploration of other modalities of treatment and have delayed attempts to understand how the brain inhibits the perception of pain.

31. The answer is D. *(Feuerstein, pp 436–437.)* As a result of the research on the gate control theory of pain, further evidence was gained to conceptualize the pain experience as consisting of several components: sensory-discriminative, motivational-affective, and cognitive-evaluative. The sensory-discriminative component transmits information that tells us where we hurt and what it feels like (e.g., burning, aching, or piercing). The motivational-affective component influences what we do about the pain (e.g., motivation to escape, attack, or eradicate its source), and it includes our emotional reaction to the pain. The cognitive-evaluative component determines the meaning of the pain experience to the individual (e.g., the pain of childbirth will have a different meaning than the pain of terminal cancer, or the pain of a young mother with a terminal cancer and three young children will have a different meaning than that of an elderly grandmother). Operant conditioning with such reinforcers as attention, secondary gain, or financial compensation can act to exacerbate or maintain pain-related behavior. Imaging is not a major factor in the reflexes, even though cognitive factors can influence spinal withdrawal reflexes.

32. The answer is D. *(Kandel, 3/e. pp 808–810.)* Even though many sleeping pills are initially helpful, they lose their effectiveness within 2 weeks. The repeated administration of barbiturates (e.g., pentobarbital or phenobarbital) results in a gradual increase in hepatic enzymes, which normally are responsible for the degradation of the barbiturates. Not only is their pharmacologic action decreased, but since the liver enzymes are relatively nonspecific, the result is often a broad cross-tolerance to other hypnotics. Barbiturates are known to suppress REM sleep, so that when the drug is withdrawn, a marked REM rebound results, often aggravating insomnia. Even though the benzodiazepines are also addictive, flurazepam increases hepatic enzymes at a much slower rate; hence patients develop a tolerance much more slowly than for pentobarbital. However, an active metabolite of flurazepam remains in the body for a longer period of time (more than 24 h), which results in a gradual increase of these breakdown substances in the blood. Thus, the effects of the drug are often felt during the daytime as diminished alertness and hand-eye coordination. These symptoms are also aggravated by alcohol.

33. The answer is B. *(Kandel, 3/e. pp 795–799.)* The physiologic responses to dreaming listed in the question can easily be recorded in most people several times each night. If awakened at such times, people usually confirm that they were dreaming. This complex of physiologic signs (e.g., electroencephalographic desynchrony, rapid eye movements, loss of muscle tonus, and cardiorespiratory irregularities) is commonly referred to as *REM (rapid eye movement) sleep* or *paradoxical sleep*. The term *paradoxical sleep* was applied originally because the associated electroencephalographic pattern is characteristic of the alert waking state despite the fact that the dreaming person is, in fact, sound asleep. Dreams occurring during non-REM sleep are less easily recalled, less vivid, less visual, less emotional, and more pleasant.

34. The answer is B. *(Kandel, 3/e. pp 1027–1030.)* The relationship between social and biologic processes has historically been regarded by psychiatry and medicine as organic and functional. Organic mental illnesses have included the dementias and the toxic psychoses. The functional mental illnesses have included the various depressive syndromes, the schizophrenias, and the neuroses. When anatomic evidence of brain lesions was produced, the diseases were called *organic,* and those that lacked these features were labeled *functional.* This distinction should be considered artificial and historical since organic and functional diseases affect mentation and vice versa. In fact, all mental processes are biologic and any alteration of these processes is organic. The most significant questions to ask about disease or behavior concern the degree to which a biologic or behavioral process is determined by genetic and developmental factors versus toxic or infectious agents versus environmental, social, or behavioral determinants. Psychoanalytic (dynamic) approaches and an understanding of conditioning (learning) played important roles in the evolution and development of a more integrated biobehavioral understanding of human behavior and human biology.

35. The answer is D. *(Schneiderman, pp 379–399.)* It has been demonstrated that persons with a high degree of acquired tolerance are less apt to evidence impairments or exhibit overt signs of intoxication than those who drink "socially." Some tolerant persons can perform psychomotor skills and good mentation with blood alcohol levels between 200 and 300 mg percent. Also, estimates of intoxication based on observations of a drinker's behavior are apt to be invalid. Studies have shown that even trained clinical observers and law enforcement officers make frequent errors in estimating actual levels of intoxication of alcohol abusers. The rate of false positive errors (i.e., the identification of a sober person as intoxicated) ranged from 0 to 16.7 percent, while false negative errors (i.e., failure to identify persons with positive blood alcohol levels) ranged from 22.2 to 55 percent. Thus, the accuracy of estimates of blood alcohol is extremely variable, with most officers no more accurate than a similarly tested group of social drinkers. Women are more responsive than men to the same dose of alcohol, apparently as a function of hormonal level and stage in the menstrual cycle. Women attain higher blood levels, absorb alcohol faster, and reach peak blood alcohol levels sooner than men; women are even more responsive the day preceding the menstrual cycle and about the time of ovulation.

36. The answer is D. *(Feuerstein, pp 220–221.)* The use of relaxation techniques to reduce stress has proved very effective. Studies of diabetic patients who practiced progressive muscle relaxation showed significant improvement in glucose tolerance following relaxation training. Plasma cortisol levels were also reduced in patients trained in relaxation. Relaxation, however, did not affect insulin sensitivity or glucose-stimulated secretion of insulin. Stress reduction techniques, such as relaxation, are effective in reducing requirements for exogenous insulin and in the management of both insulin-dependent and non-insulin-dependent diabetes.

37. The answer is A. *(Gatchel, 2/e. pp 78–79.)* Stress without the sense of control has been found to influence the release of endogenous opioid peptides, such as β-endorphin. When one learns that one has no control over a stressful situation, an opiate-based analgesia occurs. Both uncontrollable and controllable stressors produce a brief poststressor analgesia, but only the opioid produced by inescapable stressors can be blocked by administering opiate antagonists. Both controllable and uncontrollable stress situations suppress the cytotoxicity of natural killer cells, but inescapable and uncontrollable stress results in greater suppression than does controllable and escapable stress. Corticosteroid release during uncontrollable or inescapable stress is somewhat greater than when the stress can be controlled or escaped. Corticosteroid levels also decline more slowly after uncontrollable stress.

38. The answer is B. *(Gatchel, 2/e. pp 77–79.)* Having some sense of control over a stressful situation is an important factor in coping with stress and reducing the physiologic reactions to stress. In situations that are uncontrollable, unpredictable, inescapable, or uncertain, the levels of corticosteroids and catecholamines are increased. Furthermore, corticosteroid levels decline more slowly after the termination of an uncontrollable or inescapable stress. Unpredictable shock with no control has also produced an increased incidence of gastric ulceration in animals. In stressful occupational situations, those workers whose jobs are self-paced show fewer symptoms of stress and less catecholamine excretion than those whose jobs are machine-paced. Thus, the potential danger of sustained higher levels of physiologic reactions to stress is reduced by the person's having some level of control. Situations involving uncertainty also involve an increase in the excretion of epinephrine, norepinephrine, and cortisol.

39. The answer is A. *(Kandel, 3/e. pp 653–654.)* *Paradoxical sleep* is a term given to REM sleep, which is considered paradoxical because its electroencephalographic pattern resembles that of the alert waking state. Dreaming occurs during REM sleep. When a person is repeatedly awakened during dreaming, a dream deprivation occurs and there is a rebound phenomenon of increased frequency and lengthening of dreaming when the person is permitted to sleep normally. Dream deprivation does not result in a major decrement in psychological or intellectual functions (as does sleep deprivation), but it does appear to retard the memory formation of emotionally toned words. While earlier studies suggested the presence of bizarre behavior, anxiety, irritability, and nightmares, more recent studies have found no such changes in humans even after 16 days of deprivation of dream sleep.

40. The answer is B. *(Rosen, pp 305–306.)* Of the immunologic components that interact with tumor cells, such as T lymphocytes, macrophages, and humoral antibodies, the natural killer cells show a decrease in activity after psychosocial stress; the most active mechanism is corticosteroid production through the hypothalamic-pituitary-adrenal axis. Natural killer cells play a role in the inhibition of tumor growth and in the surveillance against newly developing primary tumors, at distant sites as well as locally in the body. Recent studies by Glaser, Kiecolt-Glaser, Schleifer, Keller, and others have linked the activity of natural killer cells to examination stress, vulnerability to viruses, depression, infectious illness, and bereavement.

41. The answer is B. *(Rosen, pp 116–117.)* It has been recognized that exercise decreases the symptoms of hyperglycemia. Under conditions of oral glucose challenge or glucose infusion into the blood stream, physically active persons have an increased rate of glucose removal and a decreased amount of insulin required. Also, the insulin receptors in skeletal muscle and adipose tissue show an increase in sensitivity. Thus, carbohydrate metabolism improves with exercise and physical activity and, within limits, appears to improve with the intensity and duration of the exercise. In addition, the metabolic rate will remain elevated for some hours after moderate-to-vigorous exercise.

42–46. The answers are: 42-E, 43-B, 44-C, 45-D, 46-A. *(Carlson, 4/e. pp 47–72.)* Acetylcholine is the transmitter agent at the neuromuscular junction. It is released from presynaptic neuron terminals in quantal amounts and excites contractile mechanisms in postsynaptic muscle fibers. Since muscular contractions are the substrate of all behavior patterns, it may be said that acetylcholine is the ultimate mediator of all behavior.

The enzyme dopamine-β-hydroxylase catalyzes the conversion of dopamine to norepinephrine. Evidence suggests that the brains of schizophrenic persons may be deficient in this important enzyme. It is unclear whether this psychopathology results from an accumulation of dopamine or from a relative lack of norepinephrine.

Schizophrenia may result in part from the presence of 6-hydroxydopamine in the brain. This substance destroys noradrenergic terminals because of its tendency to form toxic peroxides. In theory, an inborn error of metabolism could produce a high cerebral concentration of 6-hydroxydopamine. Schizophrenia would then occur because of disturbed function in the noradrenergic terminal fields of the brain.

The brain structure most effective in producing positive reinforcement of operant behavior from electric stimulation is the median forebrain bundle. This structure is closely related anatomically and physiologically to the lateral hypothalamic nucleus. The median forebrain bundle contains very high levels of norepinephrine. Apparently, as a neurotransmitter norepinephrine is involved in mediating behavioral reward and motivational processes.

Both dopamine and norepinephrine are capable of functioning as neurotransmitters. Norepinephrine is formed from dopamine in the presence of dopamine-β-hydroxylase. Insofar as norepinephrine may be involved in behavioral reward, its precursor, dopamine, also would be involved.

47–52. The answers are: 47-C, 48-D, 49-A, 50-A, 51-D, 52-D. *(Kandel, 3/e. pp 792–803.)* Sleep is a rhythmic and active neural and behavioral process. The sleep-wake cycle is an endogenous rhythm of the body (as are such rhythms as body temperature, urine formation, and cortisol secretion). Human sleep varies from five to seven orderly cycles each night and is characterized by stages 1 through 4 (with increasing slow wave NREM sleep) occurring in the first 30 to 45 min, stage 4 being the deepest sleep; the EEG shows that the same stages are then retraced in reverse order. As the stages or depths of sleep increase, the autonomic indicators demonstrate a parasympathetic dominance, with heart rate, blood pressure, and respiration declining and becoming more even, and gastrointestinal mobility increasing. The sleeper is more apt to be awakened spontaneously in stage 1 REM sleep than in stage 4 REM sleep.

Stage 1 REM (rapid eye movement) sleep is distinguishable from stage 1 NREM (non–rapid eye movement) sleep by additional electrooculographic and electromyographic criteria. Stage 1 REM sleep is considered to be the dream phase. The first REM sleep period is usually short (5 to 10 min) but tends to increase with each successive sleep cycle. Stages 3 and 4 NREM sleep dominate during the first third or half of the night and are less frequent during the later or early morning cycles. Dreams are recalled best when one is awakened from stage 1 REM sleep and less well during subsequent deeper NREM stages of sleep.

Stage 4 NREM sleep decreases with age and sometimes disappears in persons over 60 years of age. This continuous decline in the elderly is correlated with an increase in the number of spontaneous awakenings. REM sleep and stage 4 NREM sleep are differentially affected by certain psychoactive drugs, especially alcohol and barbiturates, which suppress REM sleep, while stage 4 NREM sleep is especially decreased by the benzodiazepines diazepam (Valium) and chlordiazepoxide (Librium).

Stage 2 NREM sleep increases toward the end of the sleep period and occupies about half of the total sleep time. Dream recall is less if one is awakened during stage 2 NREM sleep than if awakened during stage 1 NREM or stage 1 REM sleep.

53–58.   The answers are: 53-E, 54-C, 55-C, 56-A, 57-B, 58-B. *(Tryon, pp 85–100.)* Carbon monoxide produced by smoking behavior is a major health hazard for smokers and nonsmokers. Elevated levels play a role in the etiology of most cardiovascular diseases, including coronary heart disease. It has been associated with peripheral vascular disease, reduced cardiac output, and reduced duration of exercise prior to angina. It also results in decreased oxygen content of fetal blood in a pregnancy as well as subsequent complications in pregnancy. The combination of carbon monoxide and nicotine in smokers contributes to the increased prevalence of fatal and nonfatal cardiovascular disease.

Even though cigarette smoking is by far the major source of exposure to carbon monoxide, occupational exposure (e.g., in blast furnace workers, automobile mechanics, traffic control officers, taxi drivers, truck drivers) as well as urban living and exposure to other people's cigarette smoke can lead to elevated carbon monoxide levels, often with concentrations as high as those of smokers. Other factors affecting one's carbon monoxide level include individual response variability, the way a cigarette is smoked, rate of consumption, the smoker's activity levels, and the variety of tobacco product being smoked. Alcohol consumption will also affect carbon monoxide levels.

Hydrogen cyanide gas is a constituent of cigarette smoke and a primary ciliatoxic agent in cigarette smoking. It is implicated in the development of chronic obstructive pulmonary disease, emphysema, and chronic bronchitis. The combination of hydrogen cyanide gas and carbon monoxide is also implicated in the development of atherosclerosis. Measurement of thiocyanate, the primary metabolite of hydrogen cyanide, serves as an excellent index of smoking behavior and it is also valuable in the discrimination of smokers from nonsmokers. Thiocyanate is also associated with stomach cancer.

Nicotine is inhaled with each puff of cigarette smoke and is now regarded as the major pharmacologic addicting agent in smoking. It is absorbed from the lungs so quickly that in only 5 min it can be found in the brain, adrenal medulla, and sympathetic ganglia. Most persons smoke to obtain pharmacologically satisfying doses of nicotine, and they become so accustomed to certain levels of nicotine that they maintain these levels by titrating nicotine intake by adjusting their smoking behavior accordingly. Even though it has central nervous system and cocarcinogenic effects, it primarily acts upon the cardiovascular and respiratory systems. Its deleterious actions on the cardiovascular system include a hemodynamic response of increased work for the heart, increased circulation of fatty acids, and an increase in platelet adhesion and aggregation. While nicotine increases the amount of work of the heart, carbon monoxide reduces the amount of oxygen available to the heart muscle; thus, the combination of carbon monoxide and nicotine links smoking behavior with an increased incidence of atherosclerosis and thrombosis.

59–64.   The answers are: 59-E, 60-B, 61-B, 62-D, 63-C, 64-A. *(Williams, RB, pp 3–9, 25–29.)* One of the major advances of recent research has been the revelation of the brain's strong regulatory influence on the endocrine and autonomic nervous systems. This is most relevant when the organism is exposed to changes in its environmental conditions. The more severe the changes, the more severe the stress. The transmission of information in the brain and between the brain and other tissues and systems involves about a dozen amino acids and monoamines. These neurotransmitters function either at the level of the synapse, or as modulators of information flow between neurons. The best-documented neurotransmitters are dopamine, norepinephrine, serotonin, and gamma-aminobutyric acid.

Each neurotransmitter is differentially distributed in the brain for transmission of information from cell to cell. One such system is the dopaminergic circuit or system. Parkinson's disease is strongly related to the dopaminergic system. The dopaminergic system is also related to schizophrenia. The hypothalamic-limbic-midbrain circuits exert a strong regulatory influence on both the endocrine system and the autonomic nervous system. As such, these circuits have a major influence on the cardiovascular and gastrointestinal systems. They also play a major role in mediating the adaptive functions of memory, appraisal, and motivational-emotional responses. Thus, the human neocortex is able to mobilize a metabolic and cardiovascular adaptive response for action by first using these circuits to appraise the functional significance of the environment or of ongoing events. By the brain's maintaining a constant reappraisal from ongoing feedback, these hypothalamic-limbic-midbrain circuits are able to mediate the integrative processes relevant to action or survival.

These circuits are also influenced by neuropeptides (e.g., endorphins, enkephalins, vasopressin). Neuropeptides exist as neurotransmitters and as hormones. By clinging to the nerve cell membrane for varying periods of time, they can modulate the flow of information. Thus, it is believed that the neuropeptides may be able to "fine tune" one's mood.

Psychological stress influences the adrenal cortex and the thyroid. These functional changes occur when one is very upset, anxious, angry, or depressed for a long period of time. In effect, all glands controlled by the anterior pituitary are influenced by a stressful experience.

The hypothalamic hormones influence and coordinate the endocrine system and the autonomic nervous system. They are known as the coordinators of coordinators, since the endocrine system and autonomic nervous system each has major coordinating functions.

65–72.   The answers are: 65-C, 66-A, 67-B, 68-D, 69-B, 70-A, 71-C, 72-E. *(Feuerstein, pp 114–117, 188–189.)* The sympatho-adrenomedullary system increases metabolic activity in response to stressful situations. It generally involves physical exertion. The activity of the sympatho-adrenomedullary system is typically measured by norepinephrine and epinephrine. The system is implicated in such physical disorders as hypertension, atherosclerosis, angina pectoris, cardiac arrhythmias, and myocardial ischemia.

The hypothalamic-pituitary-adrenocortical (HPAC) system responds to emotionally stressful situations in which active coping may not be possible. It also responds to heat, cold, infection, sympathomimetic drugs, and surgery. The system is associated with a "conservation-withdrawal" pattern, characterized by such activities as vigilance, sympathetic nervous system activation, inhibition of movement, and bradycardia associated with the parasympathetic nervous system. Less associated with the "conservation-withdrawal" pattern are various cardiovascular diseases, peptic ulceration, suppression of the immune system, and clinical depression.

The immune system is one of several physiologic systems affected by active and passive attempts to cope with stress. Acute stress increases the steroid hormones that are known to be lympholytic, and this response suppresses the immune system. A suppressed immune system increases susceptibility to infection and tumor growth. The immune system is affected by the hypothalamic-pituitary-adrenocortical and central nervous systems.

The endorphin-enkephalin system is involved in aversive situations requiring active coping. It helps reduce fear, inhibit pain-related withdrawal behaviors, and reduce pain during coping responses. These endogenous opiates provide another way for measuring the physiologic components of stress.

When stimulated the anterior hypothalamus elicits the relaxation response. Its counterpart, the posterior area of the hypothalamus, stimulates the fight-or-flight reaction. The relaxation response results in hypo- or adynamia of skeletal musculature, decreased blood pressure, decreased respiratory rate, and constricted pupils. These physiologic changes are consistent with a generalized decrease in sympathetic activity and are different from changes recorded during quiet sitting or sleep.

Behavioral Genetics

DIRECTIONS: Each question below contains five suggested responses. Select the **one best** response to each question.

73. Siblings of schizophrenics are more likely to become schizophrenic than are persons chosen randomly from the population by a factor of about

(A) 2
(B) 4
(C) 6
(D) 8
(E) 10

74. The prominence of genetic factors in alcoholism is illustrated by all the following findings EXCEPT that

(A) close relatives of alcoholics have a fourfold increased risk
(B) an alcoholic's children who are given up for adoption at birth are at fourfold increased risk
(C) the risk for the identical twin of an alcoholic is much higher than for a fraternal twin
(D) close relatives of alcoholics are significantly more vulnerable for other psychiatric illnesses
(E) children of an alcoholic become less intoxicated at a given alcohol level than do controls

75. The most important (frequent) genetic cause of mental retardation is

(A) Bartholin-Patau syndrome
(B) Edwards' syndrome
(C) Down's syndrome
(D) Turner's syndrome
(E) Klinefelter's syndrome

76. Genetic factors are most likely to predispose a person to alcoholism by increasing any of the following EXCEPT

(A) positive reinforcement of alcohol consumption
(B) functional tolerance of alcohol
(C) level of alcohol dependence
(D) rate of alcohol metabolism
(E) level of acetylaldehyde

77. A person with Klinefelter's syndrome has the genotype

(A) XY
(B) YY
(C) XXY
(D) XYY
(E) XXX

78. Factors that influence a person's gender identity include all the following EXCEPT

(A) chromosomal configuration (XX or XY)
(B) gender assigned at birth
(C) internal reproductive structures
(D) role model of parent
(E) response of parent to child's assigned gender

79. Heredity accounts for approximately what percentage of total variation in IQ scores within a family?

(A) 5 percent
(B) 25 percent
(C) 50 percent
(D) 75 percent
(E) 100 percent

80. Ethology is characterized by all the following concepts EXCEPT

(A) behavior is best studied under controlled conditions
(B) behavior is best studied comparatively
(C) behavior is the result of interaction between genetic endowment and environment
(D) innate behavior is triggered by a sign stimulus or releaser
(E) previous learning is unnecessary for the successful expression of a fixed action pattern

81. The complex of severe psychologic disorders known as schizophrenia has a demonstrable basis that is characterized as

(A) environmentally determined
(B) polygenic
(C) a chromosomal aberration
(D) a simple recessive trait
(E) an inborn error of metabolism

82. Ethology has made major contributions to understanding human behavior through all the following concepts EXCEPT

(A) fixed action pattern
(B) critical period
(C) imprinting
(D) ethnic bonds
(E) sign stimulus

83. A disorder resulting from a single gene defect that may produce severe mental problems is

(A) manic-depressive psychosis
(B) dyslexia
(C) phenylketonuria
(D) Porter's syndrome
(E) Down's syndrome

84. Emotional expressions involving a stereotyped sequence of fixed action patterns include all the following EXCEPT

(A) smiling
(B) brow flash response
(C) startle response
(D) apprehension
(E) joy

85. Which of the following is
LEAST likely to be considered an
ontogenetic stage of synaptic development and modification?

(A) Synapse formation under genetic and developmental control
(B) Maintenance of newly developed synapses occurring during
critical periods
(C) Regulation of transient and
long-term effectiveness of synapses
(D) Integration of cellular structure
for human mentation
(E) Alteration of preexisting pathways and development of new
patterns

86. Human behavioral patterns that
have the potential of containing major innate (i.e., genetic, or not
learned) components include all the
following EXCEPT

(A) intelligence
(B) brow flash response
(C) facial expressions of anger, fear,
disgust, and joy
(D) smiling
(E) handshake greeting

Behavioral Genetics
Answers

73. The answer is D. *(Plomin, 2/e. pp 303–307.)* The risk of schizophrenia in the general population is about 1 percent. Studies of the risks for relatives of schizophrenics reveal that schizophrenia runs in families. Siblings of schizophrenics are approximately eight times more likely to become schizophrenic than are persons chosen randomly from the population; this rate almost doubles when those siblings have an affected parent as well as an affected sibling. The risk is no greater when the mother is schizophrenic than when the father is schizophrenic. If both parents are schizophrenic, the risk becomes four times as great as when only one parent is schizophrenic. Grandchildren of schizophrenics have about twice the risk as the general population since grandchildren share about one-fourth of the grandparent's segregating genes; great-grandchildren (sharing about one-eighth of the genes) have a slightly more than average chance of becoming schizophrenic.

74. The answer is D. *(Wilson, 12/e. pp 2148–2149.)* Family, twin, and adoption studies support the importance of genetic factors in alcoholism. Close relatives of alcoholics have a fourfold increased risk, which is still true even if the children of alcoholics are given up for adoption at birth without the alcohol problems of their parents being known. The fourfold increased risk of close relatives for alcoholism does not make them significantly more vulnerable for other psychiatric illnesses. Twin research has shown that the risk for the identical twin of an alcoholic is much higher than for a fraternal twin. Other studies suggest that the children of an alcoholic become less intoxicated at the same blood alcohol level than do controls. This occurs even before alcoholism develops.

75. The answer is C. *(Plomin, 2/e. pp 130–136.)* Almost all chromosomal abnormalities influence general cognitive ability and growth. Down's syndrome is the most frequent genetic cause of mental retardation. It often bears a strong relationship to maternal age. Persons with Down's syndrome have 47 chromosomes instead of the normal 46. The syndrome was originally named trisomy 21 because, at the time, the trisomy was thought to involve the next to the smallest autosome (number 21 by the Denver system of enumeration). It is now known that the smallest autosome is the one in triplicate. Even though Down's syndrome should really be called trisomy 22, the error is so firmly entrenched in the literature that it is still referred to as involving chromosome 21. Turner's syndrome (XO) occurs in females with the absence of one of the two X chromosomes. Although most sufferers have a normal IQ, Turner's syndrome nearly always involves sterility, with some limited secondary sexual development. Persons with Klinefelter's syndrome (XXY) are phenotypic males with an extra X chromosome. About 1 percent of males institutionalized for retardation have Klinefelter's syndrome. Bartholin-Patau syndrome (trisomy 13) and Edwards' syndrome (trisomy 18) are caused by trisomy of chromosomes 13 and 18, respectively. Sufferers are characterized as severely retarded, and most die in the first few months of life.

76. The answer is E. *(Linden, pp 22–24.)* Studies have demonstrated that animals can be selectively bred for their preference for and consumption of alcohol and for their susceptibility to the effects of alcohol upon the central nervous system. Individual differences also occur in the amount of acquired functional tolerance and positive reinforcement. The rate of metabolism is more concordant in monozygotic twins than in dizygotic twins. Alcohol dehydrogenase (ADH) metabolizes alcohol and results in an increased level of toxic acetylaldehyde. This acts to suppress alcohol consumption, presumably through aversion control. Studies have also shown that some aspects of dependence are heritable, especially severity of dependence and craving for alcohol.

77. The answer is C. *(Plomin, 2/e. pp 141–143.)* Persons with Klinefelter's syndrome, a genetic disorder of men, exhibit a variety of male morphologic and behavioral characteristics. This phenomenon is attributed to the extra X (male) chromosome in such a person's genotype (XXY). These persons represent nearly 1 percent of males institutionalized for retardation, epilepsy, or mental illness; the incidence in the general population is 2 per 1000 newborn males. They generally have abnormally small testes, low levels of male hormone (testosterone), and sterility. In spite of a high incidence of mental retardation, about 75 percent have IQs within the normal range.

78. The answer is B. *(Schuster, 2/e. p 329.)* Seven significant variables potentially influence one's gender identity. They are (1) chromosomal configuration (XX or XY), (2) gonad endowment (ovaries or testes), (3) internal reproductive structures (uterus or prostate), (4) external genitalia (vagina or penis), (5) hormonal balance (estrogen or androgen), (6) gender assigned at birth, and (7) response of the parents to the child's assigned gender. The role model of either parent is an important influence on a person's gender behavior but not on gender identity, which occurs earlier than the learning of gender behavior.

79. The answer is C. *(Plomin, 2/e. pp 297–303.)* Studies of several decades ago calculated that heritability accounted for about 70 to 75 percent of the total variation in IQ scores within a family. More recent studies involving much larger samples show that the individual differences in general cognitive ability within families are actually closer to 50 percent. Inheritance is still a major factor in the development of individual differences in IQ, since no specific environmental influence has been found to account for even as much as 10 percent of the variance in IQ scores within families.

80. The answer is A. *(Kandel, 3/e. pp 987–995.)* Ethology was developed by Konrad Lorenz and Nicholaas Tinbergen during the period from 1920 to 1950 by conducting comparative studies of unlearned behavior with special emphasis on its mechanisms, ontogeny, and evolution. They emphasized the observation of behavior under natural conditions and recognized that all behavior is the result of the interaction between the animal's genetic endowment and the animal's internal and external environment. Innate behavior is a relatively complex sequence of responses, called a *fixed action pattern,* which is triggered by a sign stimulus or releaser. Thus behavior patterns (e.g., mating) in lower animals can be activated by a specific stimulus (e.g., the male stickleback fish develops a bright red abdomen [the sign stimulus] that triggers mating behavior [fixed action patterns] of the female). A fixed action pattern, somewhat like a reflex, does not require previous learning for its expression.

81. The answer is B. *(Plomin, 2/e. pp 303–307.)* Complex behavioral traits such as schizophrenia, which may vary widely in nature from person to person, are considered to involve anomalies at more than one gene locus. The science of behavior genetics deals with the quantitative analysis of these polygenic traits. The results of a great variety of investigations now favor the view that schizophrenia is a genetically determined disorder, but it also may be substantially affected by environmental influences.

82. The answer is D. *(Kandel, 3/e. pp 987–991.)* Ethology in psychology and biology has made a number of conceptual contributions to understanding human behavior through the comparative study of animal behavior in relation to natural habitat. Ethologists have found evidence to suggest that some aspects of human behavior may be a function of species membership in the form of predispositions to learn and respond in certain ways rather than the fixed sequences of motor activity found in lower animals. The fixed action pattern is a genetically established sequence of motor activity that is triggered by a sign stimulus that is sufficient to release the fixed action pattern of behavior. These links between sign stimulus and fixed action pattern are weaker and more variable in humans because of the overriding effects of experience and learning. However, certain predispositions to respond to certain stimuli in certain ways are presently being explored. Imprinting is the tendency of very young animals to become fixed on and follow a member of their own species (usually their mother, but another animal or even an object can be substituted). The period of development when there is maximum receptivity to these crucial cues is known as the critical period. Bond formation between infants and adults does occur in both humans and lower animals, but ethnic bonds appear to be almost totally learned rather than biologically established.

83. The answer is C. *(Plomin, 2/e. pp 8–9, 66–67.)* Phenylketonuria (PKU) results from the inheritance of a double recessive gene. Affected persons suffer an inability to metabolize phenylalanine, a common amino acid in food. If the condition is undetected in time for treatment with special diets, serious mental deficiency results, presumably as a consequence of the toxic effect of abnormal blood levels of phenylpyruvic acid on the developing brain. About 1 percent of institutionalized retarded persons are retarded because of PKU. Most persons with PKU do not become mentally retarded if they are given a diet low in phenylalanine during the developing years. Early identification of affected infants combined with replacement of milk with galactose-free substances has been quite successful in reducing the subsequent mental retardation. PKU is a good example of genes affecting behavior in the same way genes affect phenotypes. Its treatment also provides an example of an environmental intervention successfully bypassing a genetic problem.

84. The answer is D. *(Kandel, 3/e. pp 990–995.)* Humans have a number of simple behaviors that resemble the fixed action patterns of lower animals. Such emotional expressions as the startle response and smiling are stereotyped sequences of movements. In human infants smiling appears to be under the control of a specific sign stimulus. Studies show that the smiling response is not triggered by the face as a whole, but rather by certain specific features. For example, the eyes are of particular importance as a sign stimulus, and as the child matures, other features of the face become important. The brow flash response (rapid raising and dropping of eyebrows) is a stereotyped response present in widely different cultures and is used as part of a greeting response. A complex set of human behaviors that is universal in emotional expression across cultures and that involves a stereotyped sequence of fixed action patterns includes the facial expressions of anger, fear, disgust, and joy. As an example, babies who are born blind can have emotional facial expressions that appear normal. While apprehension may include some of the responses also found in fear, it does not include as many as found in fear, nor are the responses as severe.

85. The answer is D. *(Kandel, 3/e. pp 945–957.)* In general, there are at least three ontogenetic stages of synaptic modification. The first is the stage of synapse formation, which occurs under genetic and developmental control. The next stage is that of maintaining and "fine tuning" of the newly developed synapses during early critical periods of development. This requires an appropriate pattern of environmental stimulation. The third stage is the regulation of the transient and long-term effectiveness of the synapses, which takes place throughout life as one initiates and accumulates day-to-day behavioral experience. An overall stage involving environmental and learning factors brings out the latent and potential capabilities for all behaviors by altering the effectiveness of preexisting neural pathways and effecting the expression of new patterns of behavior.

86. The answer is E. *(Kandel, 3/e. pp 993–995.)* Even though most research on innate behavior has been done on nonmammalian species, nonhuman primates also exhibit innate behavior with innate releasing mechanisms. Some studies with humans demonstrated innate (i.e., genetic, or not learned) determinants of human behavior (e.g., hormonal determinants of gender identity). Since genes control so much of the formation and organization of the basic components of all behavior, including human behavior, behavior must to some extent be under genetic control. Inherited factors nearly always depend on the interaction of genetic and environmental factors in order to be expressed. Some severe mental illnesses, such as schizophrenia, Down's syndrome, and bipolar depression, have known hereditary factors. Intelligence also has a strong genetic component. Certain human behaviors are universal across cultures—for example, deep tendon reflexes, the eyeblink, and startle reflexes. There are also common drives and needs—for example, hunger, thirst, and sex, and probably the need for social contact and a number of sensory experiences. Certain emotional expressions and facial motor patterns are also universal—for example, facial expressions of anger, fear, disgust, and joy. Infant smiling is a stereotyped behavior that appears to be controlled by a specific sign stimulus, not always in response to another smiling human face. The brow flash response is also stereotyped and consists of a rapid raising and dropping of the eyebrows as a part of the greeting response between persons who know each other, while a handshake is a learned cultural behavior.

Individual Behavior and Personality

DIRECTIONS: Each question below contains five suggested responses. Select the **one best** response to each question.

87. Intelligence quotient (IQ) is given by the relationship between chronologic age (CA) and mental age (MA) expressed as a percentage. The quantitative representation of this relationship is given by which of the following expressions?

(A) $\dfrac{CA}{MA} \times 100$

(B) $\dfrac{CA}{MA} - 100$

(C) $\dfrac{MA}{CA} \times 100$

(D) $\dfrac{MA}{CA} - 100$

(E) $\dfrac{CA}{100} \times MA$

88. Illness tends to activate all the following EXCEPT

(A) dependence on other people
(B) recall of relationships of early childhood
(C) sense of vulnerability
(D) sense of control
(E) helplessness

89. Which of the following negative emotional states or conditions most commonly precedes relapse in the treatment of addictive behaviors?

(A) Stress
(B) Depression
(C) Anxiety
(D) Anger
(E) Frustration

90. True statements about personality traits and aging include all the following EXCEPT

(A) a person's personality traits after age 30 tend to be less variable
(B) the personalities of adolescents show lower levels of stability than those of adults
(C) most people redefine and make alterations in their personalities during the period of midlife crisis
(D) the neuroticism trait in personality has a high correlation with lower levels of stability
(E) personality traits are relatively stable over one's life span

91. Although there is no uniform asthmatic personality type, the most frequent psychological characteristic of boys with bronchial asthma is

(A) hostility
(B) general anxiety
(C) frustrated oral needs
(D) dependency
(E) latent homosexuality

92. Hypochondriacal patients tend to exhibit each of the following EXCEPT

(A) quick improvement with treatment
(B) dependent personalities
(C) depression
(D) anxiety
(E) chronic reaction to stress as a "way of life"

93. The obese person is overresponsive to all the following cues EXCEPT

(A) gastric contraction
(B) taste
(C) smell
(D) attractiveness of food
(E) abundance of food

94. According to psychoanalytic theory, which of the following statements about the development of the superego is true?

(A) It is present at birth
(B) It begins to develop during the first 2 years of life
(C) It begins to develop during the fifth or sixth year of life
(D) It begins to develop during puberty
(E) It begins to develop in late adolescence

95. All the following will remain fairly constant from middle to old age EXCEPT

(A) emotional stability
(B) sociability
(C) assertiveness
(D) selfishness
(E) wisdom

96. Freud maintained that neuroses were primarily a result of

(A) overly severe toilet training
(B) inappropriate identification
(C) primary processes
(D) inadequate superego development
(E) sexual disturbances

97. In the health belief model, the patient's compliance is significantly affected by all the following factors EXCEPT

(A) patient's analysis of costs and benefits
(B) patient's perception of severity of the illness
(C) patient's readiness to act
(D) cue to action
(E) objective characteristics of the illness

98. Freud maintained that interruptions in the flow of free association were indicative of which of the following?

(A) Reaction formation
(B) Resistance
(C) Repression
(D) Parapraxis
(E) The pleasure principle

99. Factors associated with a favorable prognosis in patients who have schizophrenia include each of the following EXCEPT

(A) onset during adulthood
(B) presence of depression or familial history of depression
(C) good premorbid adjustment
(D) a clear precipitating event
(E) an acute onset of symptoms

100. In traditional psychoanalysis, transference is the process wherein

(A) psychic energy, or libido, is transferred from the id to the ego and superego
(B) a patient invests the analyst with attitudes and feelings derived from vital earlier associations
(C) certain psychological symptoms seemingly defer to new symptoms that frequently are more accessible to analysis
(D) early object choices are gradually decathected
(E) latent dream content is transformed into manifest content

101. In Carl Rogers's personality theory, the essential components of a psychotherapeutic process involve all the following EXCEPT

(A) a therapist's empathy
(B) a therapist's unconditional positive regard
(C) interpretation of unconscious wishes and feelings
(D) reflection of a client's feelings
(E) clarification of conflictive feelings and attitudes

102. The thematic apperception test (TAT) would be most useful for which of the following purposes?

(A) As an aid in differential diagnosis
(B) In prediction of suitability for psychotherapy
(C) In assessment of suicidal risk
(D) In assessment of intellectual level
(E) In assessment of motivational variables

103. All the following are examples of projective tests EXCEPT

(A) thematic apperception test (TAT)
(B) draw-a-person test
(C) sentence completion test
(D) Rorschach test
(E) Minnesota multiphasic personality inventory (MMPI)

104. In the assessment of personality, the normative and objective method refers to

(A) the use of "inkblot" techniques
(B) sophisticated techniques for measuring the accuracy of a person's perception of reality
(C) predictions of behavior on the basis of intensive interviewing
(D) predictions of behavior on the basis of data from personality tests
(E) a way of really evaluating personality rather than of simply assessing how a person behaves

105. Posttraumatic stress disorder is characterized by all the following EXCEPT

(A) reexperience of the event through dreams and nightmares
(B) impulsive or aggressive outbursts of behavior
(C) apathy, depression, and loss of initiative
(D) clear and vivid memory of details
(E) intrusive thoughts

106. In Freudian theory, patients suffering from obsessive-compulsive neurosis customarily display which of the following behavior patterns?

(A) Explosive outbursts of temper
(B) Isolation, undoing, and reaction formation
(C) Conversion of psychological conflicts to somatic symptoms
(D) Willingness to engage in antisocial activities and in deviant sexual activity
(E) None of the above

107. All the following statements about schizophrenia are true EXCEPT that

(A) twin, family, and adoption studies have demonstrated that schizophrenia has a significant genetic basis
(B) higher socioeconomic status correlates positively with the incidence of schizophrenia
(C) auditory hallucinations are frequently present
(D) chlorpromazine is an effective form of treatment
(E) communication conflicts in families of schizophrenics play an etiologic role

108. Anterograde amnesia is associated with which of the following disorders?

(A) Mild retardation
(B) Hypochondriasis
(C) Sociopathy
(D) Korsakoff's psychosis
(E) Manic-depressive psychosis

109. All the following statements about manic-depressive disorders are true EXCEPT that

(A) the depressive phase is not noticeably different from the disorder of unipolar depression
(B) the manic episodes are of longer duration than are the depressive phases
(C) the suicide risk among manic-depressive patients is greater than that for patients suffering from schizophrenia
(D) the disorder is basically affective and does not involve permanent cognitive deterioration
(E) flight of ideas and euphoria or delusions of grandeur are common symptoms during the manic phase

110. All the following statements about paranoid disorders are true EXCEPT that

(A) denial and projection are the most common defense mechanisms
(B) affected patients characteristically experience high levels of anxiety
(C) hallucinations are frequent, although thinking is rarely delusional
(D) repression of homosexual wishes may be a frequent psychodynamic determinant of the disorder
(E) the prognosis for patients who have classic paranoia is poor

111. According to Freud, the superego contains the

(A) conscience
(B) pleasure principle
(C) ego instincts
(D) reality principle
(E) internalized ego

112. All the following are tenets of psychoanalytic theory EXCEPT that

(A) all mental events and attitudes have unconscious antecedent causes
(B) a significant portion of the contents of the mind is unconscious
(C) normal and pathologic mental functioning are qualitatively different
(D) people strive to maximize pleasure and minimize tension
(E) early experience is important in the formation of individual personality

113. Which of the following type A, or coronary-prone, behavioral factors appears to be the most important?

(A) Hostility
(B) Competitiveness
(C) Time urgency
(D) Explosive speech
(E) Hyperactivity

114. All the following statements about anxiety are true EXCEPT that

(A) intense, manifest anxiety reactions usually involve cardiovascular, respiratory, and gastrointestinal changes
(B) anxiety as subjectively experienced bears no consistent relationship to physiologic responses commonly associated with it
(C) anticipation of a stressful event usually reduces the actual level of anxiety the event evokes
(D) performance levels rise and fall with anxiety levels in a linear fashion
(E) avoidance behavior is reinforced when it reduces an anxiety state

115. Which of the following defense mechanisms is most frequently observed on the medical and surgical wards?

(A) Rationalization
(B) Projection
(C) Displacement
(D) Sublimation
(E) Denial

116. Prominent symptoms associated with the psychiatric diagnosis of "adjustment disorder" in adults include all the following EXCEPT

(A) substance abuse
(B) anxiety
(C) irritability
(D) depression
(E) physical complaints

117. The importance of unconscious determinants was most strongly emphasized by which one of the following personality theorists?

(A) B. F. Skinner
(B) Carl Jung
(C) Kurt Lewin
(D) Henry Murray
(E) Margaret Mead

118. Which of the following methods of assessment would be most useful in the detection of brain damage?

(A) Thematic apperception test
(B) Bender-Gestalt test
(C) California personality inventory
(D) Minnesota multiphasic personality inventory (MMPI)
(E) Millon behavioral health inventory (MBHI)

119. The highest compliance with medication treatment is found in which of the following illnesses?

(A) Diabetes
(B) Cancer
(C) Hypertension
(D) Coronary heart disease
(E) Glaucoma

120. Contrary to coping mechanisms, defense mechanisms

(A) confront a problem directly and
continue to generate possible
solutions
(B) get help when one is unable to
handle the problem
(C) work to remove awareness of
the conflict
(D) consciously drop certain habits
or form new ones
(E) gather information

DIRECTIONS: Each group of questions below consists of lettered headings followed by a set of numbered items. For each numbered item select the **one** lettered heading with which it is **most** closely associated. Each lettered heading may be used **once, more than once, or not at all.**

Questions 121–125

For each of the descriptions below, select the psychological test with which it is most closely associated.

(A) Halstead-Reitan battery (HRB)
(B) Wechsler adult intelligence scale (WAIS)
(C) Minnesota multiphasic personality inventory (MMPI)
(D) Thematic apperception test (TAT)
(E) Bender-Gestalt test

121. Assesses visual motor coordination

122. Provides scores on ten standardized clinical scales so as to separate medical or psychiatric patients from normal controls

123. Determines the location and effects of specific brain lesions

124. Consists of six verbal subtests and five performance subtests

125. Infers wishes, motivation, and conflictual aspects of behavior

Questions 126–128

For each pairing of unconscious attitude and conscious attitude that "conceals" it, choose the defense mechanism to which it most closely corresponds.

(A) Reaction formation
(B) Undoing
(C) Denial
(D) Projection
(E) Isolation

126. I hate him (unconscious)—I love him (conscious)

127. I hate him (unconscious)—he hates me (conscious)

128. I hate him (unconscious)—I don't hate him (conscious)

Questions 129–131

For each of the following concepts or theoretical constructs, select the worker with whom it is most closely associated

(A) Harry Stack Sullivan
(B) Sigmund Freud
(C) Erik Erikson
(D) Alfred Adler
(E) C. G. Jung

129. Collective unconscious

130. Self-system

131. Postponement of lifetime commitment

Questions 132–136

For each combination of sibling relatedness and rearing, select the IQ correlation coefficient with which it is most closely associated.

(A) 0.86
(B) 0.72
(C) 0.60
(D) 0.47
(E) 0.24

132. Fraternal twins reared together

133. Identical twins reared together

134. Identical twins reared apart

135. Siblings reared together

136. Siblings reared apart

Questions 137–141

For each concept relating to stress, select the investigator or team of investigators with whom it is most closely associated.

(A) Hans Selye
(B) Walter Cannon
(C) Hippocrates
(D) John Mason and Marianne Frankenhauser
(E) Richard Lazarus

137. Toil and wear of resisting and fighting disease

138. Emotional and physiologic response to danger

139. General adaptation syndrome

140. Psychological appraisal of a potentially stressful event or stimulus followed by coping strategies and/or reappraisal

141. Linkage of psychological factors to physiologic secretions and physiologic responses to psychological reactions

Questions 142–146

Match each of the statements linking heart disease to stress and type A behavior with the correct researcher or team of researchers.

(A) Karen Mathews
(B) Richard Rosenman and Milton Friedman
(C) D. R. Ragland and R. J. Brand
(D) David Glass
(E) David Jenkins

142. Developed a reliable technique for the assessment of type A patterns of behavior

143. Developed a self-report survey of activity to assess type A behavior

144. Emphasized type A pattern as a coping style used to establish and maintain control over stressful situations

145. Found that in patients who had experienced a first coronary event, those with type B patterns of behavior were more apt to develop a subsequent coronary event

146. Developed a measure of type A behavior in children and adolescents

Individual Behavior and Personality

Answers

87. The answer is C. *(Lerner, Human Development, pp 176–177.)* In standard IQ tests such as the Stanford-Binet, mental age is calculated from a test score. A mental age of 9 indicates that test performance was equivalent to that of the average 9-year-old child. If the mental age is disproportional to the chronologic age, the intelligence quotient correspondingly will be above or below 100. The use of this formula assures that the average score (IQ) will be 100.

88. The answer is D. *(Simons, 3/e. pp 6–7.)* When people become ill, they become anxious and feel vulnerable to the disease process. They lose a part of their sense of control and autonomy and often become dependent on others, especially if they seek help. The anxiety, dependence, helplessness, and vulnerability will reawaken feelings and recollections of relationships of early childhood and previous life experiences. Their reactions to the illness and to those who are caring for them will be influenced by the way in which they were cared for previously, especially when they were young.

89. The answer is C. *(Linden, pp 292–294.)* Negative emotional states of anxiety, anger, frustration, depression, and stress are related to relapse in the treatment of addictive behaviors involved in such disorders as alcoholism, smoking, obesity, and drug addiction. Most patients (about 70 percent) have negative affects preceding the relapse. The most common negative affect or mood state is anxiety, followed by anger or frustration, and depression. Furthermore, patients are at increased risk for relapse if they smoke, drink, eat, and so on in an attempt to reduce negative affect.

90. The answer is C. *(Hazzard, 2/e. pp 103–106.)* There is much conventional wisdom about how personality changes over the life span, especially during midlife crises and retirement, and how dormant aspects of personality emerge in late life, but the data show otherwise. Studies of adolescents who are followed into adulthood do show somewhat lower levels of stability during adolescence, but there is still considerable continuity in personality from childhood on throughout life. By age 30, both men and women have attained their adult personality, which remains stable with little or no change. While some people experience the legendary midlife crisis, most often this phenomenon takes the form of concern over career choice, physical decline, or discontent with marriage; it is a crisis for only a relatively small portion of middle-aged persons and does not usually result in a personality change. The personality traits of neuroticism, extraversion, openness, agreeableness, and conscientiousness are remarkably stable over time, with the exception that persons with high levels of neuroticism seem to be predisposed to having crises at all ages. Since personality affects health perceptions and health behaviors, it is important that physicians be able to assess and predict the interaction of personality and the patient's reactions to health, illness, and treatment.

91. The answer is D. *(Kaplan, 6/e. p 505.)* Clinical research has determined that the historical formulation of the so-called asthmatic personality is not valid. Psychological factors are important, however, and it has been determined that about one-half of the patients with asthma have strong unconscious wishes for protection centering on persons on whom they are dependent. Threat of loss or separation from the mother can produce attacks of bronchial asthma in some persons, whereas in others the wish for protection produces an intense conflict, so that separation can actually produce a remission from an attack. Asthmatic boys, rather than girls, tend to be more dependent on their mothers, whereas asthmatic girls tend to be more dependent on their fathers. Although girls may try to be self-sufficient, they are frequently chronically depressed. Boys are also apt to be passively dependent, timid, and immature. Both, however, appear to be dominated by a fear of losing parental support. Studies have found that about 50 percent of all asthmatic attacks, regardless of a patient's age at the time of occurrence, are initiated or precipitated by actual or anticipated separation from or loss of the person on whom he or she is dependent.

92. The answer is A. *(Simons, 3/e. pp 73–78.)* Hypochondriasis is usually characterized as a generalized chronic expression of emotional conflicts through physical symptoms. Such patients are often depressed and may have dependent personalities rather than the histrionic or hysterical personalities seen in patients with conversion disorder. They have a long history of multiple complaints rather than a specific anesthesia or paralysis, and they are usually anxious and worried rather than indifferent. Hypochondriacal patients have a chronic reaction to stress as a "way of life" rather than an acute reaction, and they rarely improve quickly, while a patient with conversion disorder may respond suddenly to treatment.

93. The answer is A. *(Wilson, 12/e. pp 411–417.)* Many studies have shown that obese persons respond less well than do normal persons to internal cues, such as gastric contraction. They also overrespond to external cues such as the taste, smell, attractiveness, abundance, and accessibility of food. This is significant because behavior modification can be used to influence eating behaviors by changing the exposure to and pattern and nature of the external cues. Since behavior patterns are learned, they can be changed or unlearned.

94. The answer is C. *(Kaplan, 6/e. pp 180–181.)* Freud maintained that the superego begins to develop around the age of 5 or 6 as part of the resolution of the Oedipus complex. At the end of the phallic stage of psychosexual development (which lasts from around 2½ to 6 years of age), children must abandon the sexual and aggressive impulses that were directed toward their parents in order to avoid the parents' strong disapproval. In abandoning these impulses, children identify with their parents. Part of this identification involves the internalization of parental standards of morality; this internalization marks the beginning of the superego.

95. The answer is E. *(Hazzard, 2/e. pp 101–106.)* Theorists have postulated that the universal processes of aging include the decline of emotionality, the reversal of sex-role–linked characteristics, and the development of wisdom. Longitudinal studies, however, have shown that a person's personality shows little or no change with age. There is little or no change in traits such as emotional stability, sociability, assertiveness, and other characteristics of the individual personality. In other words, a 40 year old who is well adjusted, assertive, and liberal is apt to be a well-adjusted, assertive, liberal 80 year old; likewise, a 40-year-old person who is neurotic and selfish is apt to be a neurotic and selfish 80 year old. Wisdom does appear to increase with age because of experience and education. This is consistent with Erik Erikson's final stage of human development—one attains either integrity or despair.

96. The answer is E. *(Lerner, Human Development, pp 64–70.)* Although Freud modified many aspects of his theory of neuroses, he never wavered in his conviction that sexual disturbances were the most important causal factor in neurotic development. One of the first to recognize the existence of sexual feelings and curiosity in children, Freud maintained that in the course of socialization some of a child's sexual feelings become repressed. Occasionally, the act of repression reaches extreme proportions, consuming enormous amounts of psychic energy. Freud believed that under stress, this repression often would fail, allowing the sexual impulses, partially freed, to appear in the form of neurotic symptoms.

97. The answer is E. *(Gatchel, 2/e. pp 190–192.)* The health belief model is based on three components of predicting one's compliance behavior: the patient's perceived readiness to act or perception that action is necessary, an estimation of costs and benefits of compliance, and the need for a cue to action, i.e., for an indication that something is wrong. The health belief model takes into account the patient's subjective state or belief regarding his or her health, rather than the objective characteristics of it. The costs and benefits are emphasized, as the patient must believe that the treatment will be effective; i.e., the benefits must outweigh the costs in terms of side effects, disruptiveness, and unpleasantness. The patient's readiness to comply is important, either in terms of internal signals such as pain or discomfort, or external stimuli such as screening programs, costs, and benefits. The health belief model also considers that the patient's perception of the severity of an illness is much more predictive of compliance than is the actual severity of the illness as defined by the doctor or other data.

98. The answer is B. *(Lerner, Psychology, pp 511–513.)* One of the most important techniques in psychoanalysis is free association, in which a patient is encouraged to say whatever comes to mind, however absurd or objectionable it might seem. This can be a difficult undertaking. Frequently, the flow of associations is interrupted and a patient's train of thought is blocked or lost because of resistance, which is a defensive maneuver that prevents repressed material from emerging into consciousness.

99. The answer is A. *(Suinn, pp 400–401.)* Considerable attention has been directed toward identifying favorable prognostic indicators in schizophrenia. Those factors most frequently associated with favorable prognosis for recovery are the acute onset of symptoms, a clear precipitating event, good premorbid adjustment, presence of confusion and disorientation, early age of onset (in adolescence or young adulthood), and the presence of depression or familial history of depression. The presence of these factors is associated with briefer hospitalization and with a lower relapse rate.

100. The answer is B. *(Kaplan, 6/e. p 573.)* In traditional psychoanalytic treatment, analysts purposely reveal very little about themselves to their patients. That is intended to help promote transference—to create an ambiance that facilitates a patient's ability to transfer his or her past emotional attachments to the psychoanalyst. The analyst becomes a substitute for the parental figure. In positive transference, the patient becomes attached to the analyst in order to obtain love and emotional satisfaction, whereas in negative transference the analyst is seen as an unfair, unloving, and rejecting parental figure. Interpretations of transference may help the patient see the positive or negative feelings as a reflection of previous emotional entanglements.

101. The answer is C. *(Lerner, Psychology, pp 418–419, 514–516.)* Carl Rogers's formulation of client-centered therapy requires that therapists establish an atmosphere of empathic understanding and of unconditional positive regard for their clients by communicating to them that they are liked and respected whatever they may say or do. Once this atmosphere is established, Rogers's main therapeutic technique is to reflect clients' feelings back to the clients. Rogers feels that this helps them to clarify feelings and attitudes that are conflictive or otherwise difficult. He further argues that a client-centered therapist should not offer interpretations of behavior, attitudes, or unconscious wishes and feelings.

102. The answer is E. *(Kaplan, 6/e. pp 159–163.)* The thematic apperception test (TAT), which consists of a series of 30 ambiguous pictures about which subjects are asked to construct a story, is most useful in assessing motivational variables. It provides a case-study exploration of a person's personality. Although it also has been employed to assess variables such as intellectual level, other tests are more suitable for such purposes (e.g., IQ tests). The TAT is not particularly helpful in differential diagnosis.

103. The answer is E. *(Kaplan, 6/e. pp 157–163.)* Projective methods of personality assessment comprise those measures that are relatively unstructured and have no correct answers. Subjects' responses to such measures are presumed to be more indicative of individual characteristics than is the case with more structured tests, responses to which are inclined to be determined more by the nature of the test than of the subject taking it. The thematic apperception test, draw-a-person test, sentence completion test, and Rorschach test are all considered to be projective methods of measurement. The Minnesota multiphasic personality inventory (MMPI) is a structured personality inventory of 550 items that must be answered "True," "False," or "Cannot Say."

104. The answer is D. *(Kaplan, 6/e. pp 155–163.)* Normative and objective methods involve statistical prediction based on quantified data. Applied to the assessment of personality, such methods are independent of any particular theory of personality, relying on the use of a mathematical relationship between relevant test scores and a particular behavioral outcome that is to be predicted. The 1950s and 1960s witnessed a controversy over the relative merits of personality assessment and prediction on the basis of clinical interviewing techniques versus those of actuarial and statistical data. Today, researchers and clinicians usually view these procedures as complementary, and both methods currently are employed for different types of research or personality assessment.

105. The answer is D. *(Suinn, pp 143–149.)* Posttraumatic stress disorder is clearly linked to a traumatic event, such as a natural disaster, accidental disaster, or warfare. Physicians should be alert to anxiety symptoms that can follow such catastrophes. They may include reexperiencing the trauma through nightmares or reliving the event. These symptoms may also include emotional numbness, exaggerated startle response, inability to fall asleep, apathy or depression, apprehension, tremors, poor concentration, intrusive thoughts, poor memory following the event, and impulsive or aggressive outbursts of behavior. The person is so overwhelmed that there is a breakdown of normal coping patterns and a physiologic strain imposed on the person. Early treatment is crucial and consists of the prevention of the patient's refuge in escape, the reassurance that complete breakdown has not occurred, and the physician's acceptance of the patient's fear and exhaustion. Prevention includes emphasizing to physicians the reactions to expect of victims of various ages.

106. The answer is B. *(Kaplan, 6/e. pp 404–406.)* The rigid defensive style characteristic of persons who have obsessive-compulsive neurosis is accomplished by the mechanisms of isolation, undoing, and reaction formation. Isolation is the exclusion of an event from the continuum of meaningful experience; for example, an idea or action may be separated from its original emotional content. Undoing connotes the repetitious patterns of ideation and behavior that are typical of obsessive rituals; an affected patient may feel compelled to undertake an action that counteracts an idea that has recently been expressed or an event that has just occurred. Reaction formation refers to the way in which obsessive-compulsive patients attempt to control an unacceptable wish by undertaking an exaggerated opposing action; kindly actions, for example, may be a reaction against sadistic wishes. In learning theory, obsessions can represent a conditioned stimulus to anxiety so that formerly neutral objects or thoughts become conditioned stimuli that are able to trigger anxiety or discomfort. In compulsion, a certain action is found to reduce anxiety; thus, avoidance strategies (compulsions or rituals) are developed to control the anxieties.

107. The answer is B. *(Wilson, 12/e. pp 2128–2131.)* Schizophrenia is a serious mental disorder with about 1 percent prevalence across all cultures. It has a 6-month or longer duration and causes significant social, occupational, and personal disability and suffering. Diagnosis includes at least 6 months of bizarre delusions often with persecutory or jealous content, auditory hallucinations, and grossly disorganized behavior. The most significant etiologic factor is genetic as confirmed by twin, family, and adoption studies. There is a higher incidence in persons of lower socioeconomic status, but it is difficult to determine whether this is because of a "social drift" of more vulnerable persons or the stresses of lower socioeconomic status, especially in genetically vulnerable persons. A major psychosocial factor is a frequent pattern of communication conflicts between parents and between parents and the child or developing adult. There is also a stress-diathesis model whereby predisposed persons are vulnerable to certain stressful circumstances. The phenothiazines are the most effective form of chemical treatment.

108. The answer is D. *(Suinn, p 275.)* The characteristic symptoms of Korsakoff's psychosis are disorientation in time and place, confabulation, and anterograde amnesia. Anterograde amnesia is a specific cognitive deficit in which events that have just occurred are not recalled. Affected patients typically fabricate responses to questions about the forgotten occurrences. Inadequate nutritional habits (specifically, deficiency in intake of vitamin B) are the probable cause of Korsakoff's psychosis; hence the disorder frequently is associated with a history of chronic alcoholism.

109. The answer is B. *(Suinn, pp 354–363.)* Manic-depressive disorders involve recurrent affective disturbances alternating between manic and depressive periods. Characteristically, the manic phase is much shorter than the depressive phase; whereas the mania may last from a matter of days or weeks to 3 or 4 months, the depression lasts 9 months or more. Many clinicians now believe that such mood swings can be controlled effectively by lithium carbonate. Chromosome 11 has recently been demonstrated to be involved, but other investigators believe that it is a polygenic disorder.

110. The answer is C. *(Suinn, pp 400–405.)* Although hallucinations are not unknown in paranoid disorders, they are very infrequent. Such disorders usually are identified by markedly delusional thinking of a persecutory, grandiose, or jealous character. Cognitive functioning in paranoid disorders generally is not grossly impaired except in relation to the subject matter of the delusional symptoms.

111. The answer is A. *(Kaplan, 6/e. pp 180–181.)* According to Freud, the superego is the conscience and develops in the ego with the resolution of the Oedipus complex. The conscience refers to the set of internalized moral prohibitions that guides personal behavior. Children build identifications with heroes, teachers, and admired persons in order to form their moral standards, values, aspirations, and ideals. The ego maintains a relationship to the outside world through a sense of reality, reality testing, and adaptation to the reality.

112. The answer is C. *(Kaplan, 6/e. pp 171–186.)* Before the development of psychoanalytic theory, psychopathologic manifestations were considered to be evidence of mental disorders having nothing in common with normal mental functioning. One of Freud's greatest contributions lay in his recognition that the same psychological processes operate in both normal and abnormal mental functioning, i.e., that any differences between normality and abnormality are quantitative, not qualitative. The necessary implication of Freud's perception is that any judgments as to a person's "normality" are relative and that there are no absolute criteria by which a person can be classified as psychologically ill.

113. The answer is A. *(Weiss, Stress, pp 44–45.)* Among the psychosocial variables considered to be risk factors for coronary heart disease, the type A, or coronary-prone, behavior pattern is most prominent. The type A behavior pattern consists of extremes of competitiveness, a chronic sense of time urgency, easily evoked hostility, aggressiveness, explosive speech, and increased rate of activity. More recent studies have shown that aggressiveness and hostility (especially unexpressed hostility) are the most consistent and important factors.

114. The answer is D. *(Kaplan, 6/e. pp 389–394.)* There is no simple linear relationship between task performance and level of arousal or anxiety. The Yerkes-Dodson theory posits a curvilinear relationship between these variables in which performance is enhanced at a certain optimal level of arousal; anxiety levels lower or higher than this optimum have a detrimental effect on performance. There is evidence in support of the Yerkes-Dodson formulation. It also has been demonstrated that such factors as task complexity, instructional set, and intelligence alter the quantitative features of the curvilinear relationship between performance and anxiety.

115. The answer is E. *(Simons, 3/e. pp 48–52.)* Of the psychological defense mechanisms listed, denial is the most common. Most defense mechanisms involve an unconscious mental process and are protective measures for the relief of anxiety or guilt. In denial, the patient attempts to reject the threat of the perception of illness and the developing anxiety. While failure to face one's illness can be harmful, denial can also be a useful defense mechanism, especially during recovery or rehabilitation. In rationalization, a patient attempts to justify an irrational feeling, behavior, or thought. Projection involves attributing one's own problem or conflict to another person or situation. In displacement, a feeling, thought, wish, or fear that is unacceptable is transferred to another person or situation. Sublimation is a defense mechanism whereby wishes that are unacceptable are diverted into acceptable channels; thus partial gratification is achieved. Of the many defense mechanisms, denial is exceeded in frequency only by regression, whereby an illness causes a person to return, in part, to earlier patterns of adapting and behaving.

116. The answer is A. *(Kaplan, 6/e. pp 494–497.)* The most prominent symptoms associated with the psychiatric diagnosis of "adjustment disorder" are anxiety and depression. The American Psychiatric Association's *Diagnostic and Statistical Manual of Mental Disorders,* revised third edition (*DSM III-R*), defines an adjustment disorder as a maladaptive reaction to a clearly identifiable psychosocial stressor or stressors that occurs within 3 months of the stressor's onset. In general, it is a pathologic or maladaptive response to the stress of a life event or circumstance, such as loss of parent, divorce, business difficulties, loss of job, intrafamily disorders, or retiring. The basis of the disorder can be viewed as the person's experiencing of trauma as psychic overload with the response being disproportionately intense. The ability of the person to participate in the ordinary activities of everyday life is impaired. The most common symptoms are anxiety, depression, irritability, and physical complaints. Assault, reckless driving, defaulting of legal responsibilities, excessive drinking, and withdrawal can also occur. A concurrent physical disorder or chronic disease may make a person more vulnerable to an adjustment disorder.

117. The answer is D. *(Kaplan, 6/e. pp 171–191.)* Although Sigmund Freud is best known for the development of the theory of the unconscious, Henry Murray also strongly emphasized the unconscious in the development of his theory of personality. Both Freud and Murray constructed a system of human needs and wishes that existed in the unconscious part of the mind. According to the theory, these unconscious needs and wishes express themselves through the personality and exert considerable influence on individual behavior. Freud arrived at his discovery through the observation of his patients and the analysis of his own dreams, from which he developed his technique of dream analysis. Murray applied the concept of the unconscious in his theory of personality. He is best known for his development of the thematic apperception test, which uses a projective technique to elicit personal and interpersonal conflicts, needs, and attitudes. Carl Jung also placed a strong emphasis on unconscious factors in personality. B. F. Skinner and Kurt Lewin deemphasized the unconscious in the normal personality. Skinner provided experimental analyses of operant behavior to demonstrate that personality is the result of reinforcement and conditioning. Lewin constructed a field theory of action and emotion modeled on physical theory and topology. Margaret Mead had confidence in the psychodynamic unconscious as developed by Freud, but she is best known for her studies demonstrating the importance of cultural mores in molding personality.

118. The answer is B. *(Kaplan, 6/e. pp 166–167.)* The Bender-Gestalt test can be useful in the assessment of maturation and of brain damage. Various atypical responses to the Rorschach cards (e.g., poor form responses) have been found also to be related to brain damage. The Bender-Gestalt test consists of nine test figures that a subject is asked to copy; difficulties in this easy task often are indicative of brain dysfunction. Neither the thematic apperception test nor the California personality inventory has been found to be a sensitive indicator of cerebral damage. The MMPI tests a wide range of personality factors and the MBHI is a psychodiagnostic inventory of personality, coping style, and symptoms for the physically ill. Other than a few cognitive factors, neither is adequate for the detection of brain damage. A frequently used test for brain damage is the Halstead-Reitan battery of neuropsychological tests.

119. The answer is B. *(Gatchel, 2/e. pp 186–187.)* The most usual kinds of compliances are prevention, taking of medication, and alteration in life-style. Medication treatment has an alarmingly low level of compliance and prevention has the lowest. Compliance with chemotherapy for cancer is very high— better than 90 percent. Medication treatment for hypertension, glaucoma, coronary heart disease, and diabetes achieves from 40 to 70 percent compliance from the patient.

120. The answer is C. *(Kaplan, 6/e. pp 390–391.)* Coping mechanisms are actions that resolve conflicts in socially or personally desirable and effective ways. Conflicts are often the results of inconsistencies that exist in our behaviors, our cognitions, or between conflicting cognitions and behaviors. If we are capable of coping, we take action to resolve the problem as well as we can and see that it does not occur again. For example, if there is a conflict between two behaviors, resolution may require considering the behaviors in relationship to our ideals and then changing one or both of them. Or, if the conflict is between two cognitions, we may need to seek information, then pursue changing one or both of the cognitions. If the conflict is between cognition and behavior, then we generally attempt to change either or both to make one conform with the other. Thus coping involves a resolution of the conflict achieved by changing one or both of the conflicting elements. This is not to be confused with the use of defense mechanisms to resolve conflicts. Although defense mechanisms can be appropriate or at least preferable to other available alternatives, they generally "defend" us and do not generally change behavior or resolve the conflict itself. Coping mechanisms confront the problem directly, continue to generate possible solutions, generate more information, get help when needed, and allow us consciously to drop certain habits or form new ones. They allow us to take action to eliminate the undesirable cognition or behavior causing the conflict. Defense mechanisms are most often driven by unconscious forces, such as repression of threatening impulses or ideas, and tend to remove awareness of the conflict. They allow the conflicting elements to continue and provide an illusion of solution, but the problem continues.

121–125. The answers are: 121-E, 122-C, 123-A, 124-B, 125-D. *(Kaplan, 6/e. pp 155–170.)* The Bender-Gestalt test is a test of visual motor coordination and is useful in both children and adults. Initially it was used as a measure of a child's maturational level, according to how many of the nine designs a child could reproduce at various levels of accuracy. It is now used most frequently with adults as a screening device for signs of organic brain dysfunction. It can also be used in assessing mental retardation, aphasias, psychoses, neuroses, and malingering.

The Minnesota multiphasic personality inventory, an objective self-report test to assess personality, is one of the most widely used tests for clinical and research purposes. It provides scores on ten clinical scales: hypochondriasis (Hs), depression (D), hysteria (Hy), psychopathic deviation (Pd), masculinity-femininity (Mf), paranoia (Pa), psychasthenia (Pt), schizophrenia (Sc), hypomania (Ma), and social distance (Si); plus three additional scales: a lie scale (L) to detect attempts to present oneself in a good light, a frequency scale (F) of unconventional beliefs and attitudes, and a correction scale (K) for guardedness or defensiveness in test-taking. The MMPI, like all tests, is most effectively used in conjunction with other information about the patient. It is currently being restandardized based on a contemporary sample of normal people.

The Halstead-Reitan battery of neurologic tests was developed in the early 1940s to determine the location and effects of specific brain lesions. It is composed of ten tests: category test (to identify common elements in a set of pictures for concept function, abstraction, and visual acuity), tactual performance test, rhythm test, finger-oscillation test, speech-sounds perception test, trial-making test, critical flicker frequency, time sense test, aphasia screening test, and sensory-perception test. The usefulness of the Halstead-Reitan battery can be enhanced by using it in conjunction with the MMPI and the Wechsler adult intelligence scale.

The Wechsler adult intelligence scale (WAIS) is the best standardized test of intelligence in use today. There are six verbal subtests and five performance subtests and it yields a verbal IQ, a performance IQ, and a combined IQ. The eleven subtests are general information, comprehension (proverbs), arithmetic, similarities (between two things), digit-span (recall of two to nine digits), vocabulary (definitions), picture completion (with a missing part), block design (matched color and designs), picture arrangements (arrange series to tell a story), object assembly (organize objects in order), and digit symbol (pair symbols with digits). There is also a scale for children ages 5 through 15, and a preschool version for ages 4 to 6½ years.

The thematic apperception test (TAT), designed by Henry Murray and Christiana Morgan in 1943, has 30 pictures with ambiguity in each picture. The subject creates a story about each picture that reveals approach to organization, sequence, vocabulary, style, preconceptions, assumptions, and outcome. It is especially useful for inferring motivational aspects of behavior rather than as a diagnostic test.

126–128. The answers are: 126-A, 127-D, 128-C. *(Kaplan, 6/e. pp 181–185.)* Reaction formation is the defensive process whereby an unacceptable feeling or impulse is converted into, and consciously experienced as, its opposite. Thus, in reaction formation, "I hate him" becomes "I love him."

Projection is the process through which unacceptable impulses are at once denied and attributed to someone else or to something in the environment. Thus, in projection, "I hate him" is converted into "he hates me."

Denial is the defense mechanism by means of which any aspect of reality, e.g., forbidden thoughts, is actively denied. With this defense mechanism, "I hate him" becomes "I don't hate him."

The defense mechanism of undoing refers to an action that is meant somehow to reverse or "undo" the damage that is felt to have been caused by an unacceptable wish.

Isolation is the conscious experience of an unacceptable wish or thought without the painful effect associated with it. Isolation and undoing both are defenses characteristic of people who have obsessive-compulsive personality styles.

129–131. The answers are: 129-E, 130-A, 131-C. *(Kaplan, 6/e. pp 186–191.)* C. G. Jung believed that every person inherits the potential to experience and recall memories and images from humanity's evolutionary past. Referring to these predispositions as the collective unconscious, Jung considered this to be one of the most powerful components of the mind, especially in persons who suffer psychological illness.

Harry Stack Sullivan coined the term self-system to describe the series of behavioral controls and defensive operations that a person adopts in order to avoid the disruptive effects of anxiety. Sullivan felt that the more anxiety a person has experienced, the more active role the self-system plays in that person's personality. Indeed, the self-system can assume such dominance that, in attempting to ward off anxiety, it interferes with an affected person's perception of reality and hence with the ability to function adaptively.

Erik Erikson's idea of the psychosocial moratorium describes the prolonged adolescence characterizing modern American culture, an adolescence that allows persons in their late teens or twenties to postpone lifetime commitments such as marriage and definite careers. During this moratorium, people can experiment with various life-styles and career possibilities. Erikson believes that this moratorium serves a very positive function in society.

132–136. The answers are: 132-C, 133-A, 134-B, 135-D, 136-E. *(Plomin, 2/e. pp 349–354.)* Dizygotic (fraternal) twins have similar but not identical genes. The similarity of their genes, however, is not significantly greater than that of other siblings. The fact that the IQs of fraternal twins reared in the same environment are more alike (correlation coefficient: 0.60) than those of other siblings reared in similar circumstances (0.47) must reflect experiential influences on IQ.

The highest correlation between IQ scores is obtained from monozygotic (identical) twins. Identical twins reared together have a correlation coefficient of 0.86; those reared apart, 0.72. This high correlation may be assumed to be a result of both hereditary and environmental factors. In fact, since monozygotic twins have identical genomes, it may be argued that an even higher correlation would exist were it not for the unavoidable factor of slight differences in experience.

The correlation between IQs of siblings reared together (0.47) is higher than that for siblings reared apart (0.24). This observation seems to suggest that environmental factors affect IQ scores considerably. The fact that there is a significant correlation between IQs of siblings reared apart demonstrates the contribution of hereditary factors to intelligence.

A relatively high correlation appears between the IQ scores of siblings reared together. It is much lower, however, than the correlation between dizygotic twins, although their genomes are about equally heterogeneous. This difference is probably attributable to the fact that both society and families tend to treat twins more alike than they do other siblings.

The lowest observed correlation between IQs of offspring occurs for siblings reared apart. However, the correlation is significantly higher than that for unrelated persons who are reared together. Thus it seems that hereditary factors are somewhat more potent determinants of IQ than either environmental or experiential factors.

137–141. The answers are: 137-C, 138-B, 139-A, 140-E, 141-D. *(Gatchel, 2/e. pp 39–49.)* The medical profession has been concerned with stress for centuries. Hippocrates spoke of suffering caused by disease *(pathos)*, but separated it from the toil involved in resisting and fighting disease *(ponos)*. He thus suggested a stresslike aspect of illness.

Walter Cannon suggested that stress had both physiologic and psychological components in response to danger. He is most famous for his description of the sympathetic nervous system acting to ready a threatened organism for "fight or flight" by producing a heightened state of arousal. Stress can aid in survival, but it can also disrupt emotional and physiologic stability (homeostasis). Thus, emotional stress could cause physiologic disturbances that lead to medical problems.

Hans Selye developed the general adaptation syndrome (GAS), which consisted of three stages: the alarm reaction, the stage of resistance, and the stage of exhaustion. The presence of a noxious stimulus or stressor causes an alarm reaction in preparation for resisting the stressor. When the body reserves are mobilized, the stage of resistance applies various physiologic and psychological coping mechanisms to adapt or fend off the stressor, but usually with a decrease in resistance to other stimuli or threats. When these reactions are repeated many times or over a prolonged time, the stage of exhaustion is reached and the organism is at risk for irreversible physiologic damage. With reserves depleted and resistance no longer possible, the wear and tear and exhaustion then lead to the onset of diseases of adaptation, such as kidney disease, arthritis, and cardiovascular disease.

John Mason and Marianne Frankenhauser extended Selye's GAS into the psychosocial realm. They postulated that stress is more than a reaction to nonspecific stimuli and that some kind of psychological awareness of noxious or stressful events may be necessary for stress to occur. More importantly, they demonstrated that psychological factors can actually alter bodily functioning and lead to illness. These and other findings have established an important link between psychosocial factors and health.

Richard Lazarus recognized the significance of psychological stress. In order for an event to evoke a stressful reaction, it must be appraised by the individual as threatening. This allows one to evaluate the dangers and benefits of the stressful event, select a coping option, and even reappraise the event as it evolves. Personality, experience, and goals can also affect the interpretation. Thus, the same event can be interpreted by one person as a threat and by another as a challenge. Lazarus also postulated that daily problems can be just as important in causing stress as less frequent but more severe threats.

142–146. The answers are: 142-B, 143-E, 144-D, 145-C, 146-A. *(Gatchel, 2/e. pp 105–112. Ragland, N Engl J Med 318: 65–69, 1988.)* Sir William Osler (1892) observed that the typical coronary patient was robust, keen and ambitous, vigorous in mind and body, and one "whose engine is always at full speed ahead." In the late 1950s Richard Rosenman and Milton Friedman described the type A behavior pattern and developed a reliable technique for its assessment. They characterized the type A behaviors as excessive competitive drive, impatience, hostility, and vigorous speech. The type B person was considered to possess a relative lack of these characteristics and have a more easy-going style of coping. Rosenman and Friedman developed a structured interview focused on observable behavior based on speech characteristics and how persons responded to questions rather than how they described themselves.

David Jenkins in the early 1970s developed the Jenkins Activity Survey (JAS). The JAS is a questionnaire relying on a person's report of his or her own behavior. It is still frequently used as a clinical screening measure as well as a research tool.

David Glass emphasized that the type A pattern should be considered more as a coping style used to establish and maintain control over stressful situations. Type A persons respond to stress or to a challenge by accelerating the pace of their work and by becoming more competitive, aggressive, or hostile. He found that type A persons respond to uncontrollable stress or situations by working harder or faster than do type B persons. Also, they perceive challenges as more threatening, which arouses a sense of time-urgency, competitiveness, hostility, and a greater physiologic response with increased sympathetic arousal and secretion of epinephrine and norepinephrine.

Karen Mathews explored the genesis of type A behavior in one's early years, as early as age 5. She developed the Mathews Youth Test for Health, which is completed by an observer of a child's behavior. Mathews has demonstrated type A and type B patterns of behavior in children as young as age 9 and has recently developed a scale for adolescents. She has found that the behaviors of achievement, anger-arousal, and impulsiveness are stable from about 6 to 10 years of age to adulthood and that these type A children experience the same elevations in heart rate and blood pressure in response to psychological challenges as do their adult counterparts.

D. R. Ragland and R. J. Brand in a recent study (1988) found that if one studies persons who have already survived a coronary event, the type B patients are more apt to suffer a subsequent coronary event than are their type A counterparts. While this does not negate the increased risk of type A persons for the initial coronary event, it does raise the question of other interactive factors; for example, type A patients may respond differently than type B patients to a coronary event. Type A patients may be better able to cope, comply with treatment, change life-style, and so on, and thus improve their prognosis.

Learning and Behavioral Change

DIRECTIONS: Each question below contains five suggested responses. Select the **one best** response to each question.

147. All the following are basic principles of the neural basis of learning and memory EXCEPT

(A) memory has stages and is continually changing
(B) long-term memory results in physical changes in the brain
(C) memory traces are widely distributed throughout the nervous system
(D) the hippocampus and temporal lobes are most actively involved in the human memory process
(E) localized trauma can completely destroy stored memory

148. A behavior pattern that increases in frequency when followed by a reward is an example of

(A) classical conditioning
(B) shaping
(C) respondent conditioning
(D) operant conditioning
(E) generalization

149. In order for operant conditioning to be effectively applied to a psychiatric disorder (e.g., shouting obscenities), one can increase positive, constructive behavior by all the following EXCEPT

(A) precisely defining desired behavior
(B) identifying an effective reinforcer
(C) providing reinforcement when desired behavior is emitted
(D) punishing undesired behavior
(E) exchanging a preferred food for desired behavior

150. In operant conditioning, the rate of extinction is most effectively slowed when the response or learning has been maintained on a reinforcement schedule of

(A) fixed ratio
(B) variable ratio
(C) fixed interval reinforcement
(D) continuous reinforcement
(E) piecework reinforcement

151. Learned helplessness is associated with depression in that both are characterized by each of the following EXCEPT

(A) continued failure from lack of ability
(B) passive behavior
(C) negative expectations
(D) hopelessness
(E) feelings of no control over events

152. The idea that experimental extinction, which is produced by nonreinforcement after classical conditioning, is an active inhibitory process finds support in the phenomenon of

(A) generalization
(B) spontaneous recovery
(C) experimental neurosis
(D) passive avoidance
(E) active avoidance

153. Significant decreases in blood pressure can be achieved by each of the following methods of behavioral treatment EXCEPT

(A) biofeedback
(B) meditation
(C) contingency conditioning
(D) relaxation
(E) weight loss

154. Which of the following behavioral methods of treating asthma has proved to be most effective when combined with medical treatment?

(A) Psychotherapy
(B) Behavioral self-management
(C) Psychoanalysis
(D) Employment of suggestion strategies
(E) Diminishment of emotional reactions

155. All the following factors are critical in both classical and operant conditioning EXCEPT

(A) timing
(B) stimulus discrimination
(C) specific reflex responses
(D) extinction
(E) learning of predictive relationships

156. In classical conditioning, the "partial reinforcement effect" is the

(A) inability to learn with fractional reward
(B) increased response retention following partial reinforcement
(C) increased conditioned response amplitudes after nonreinforced trials
(D) reduced response latencies on nonreinforced trials
(E) contrast effects for partial reinforcement schedules

157. A social learning approach to attitude change includes all the following methods EXCEPT

(A) modeling
(B) desensitization
(C) extinction
(D) direct reinforcement
(E) integration of nature (vs. nurture)

158. A major distinction between the methods for producing classical and instrumental conditioning is that in instrumental conditioning the reinforcing stimulus is

(A) always appetitive in nature
(B) contingent on the behavior to be learned
(C) invariant
(D) solely under the control of the experimenter
(E) unnecessary to produce learning

159. Correct statements regarding systematic desensitization include all the following EXCEPT

(A) it was developed by Joseph Wolpe
(B) it is used to decrease neurotic anxiety or phobia
(C) anxiety-provoking situations are brought to mind to be resolved through reality therapy
(D) anxiety-provoking situations are paired with anxiety-reducing relaxation
(E) the patient is taught a technique of muscular relaxation

160. The term *learning disabilities* most often refers to problems in learning

(A) to do arithmetic
(B) to read
(C) to write compositions
(D) eye-hand coordination
(E) achievement orientation

161. When achievement motivation is emphasized and rewarded in early childhood, it is apt to produce all the following EXCEPT

(A) feelings of personal worth
(B) tolerance for frustration
(C) higher levels of persistence
(D) lower goals than could be achieved
(E) expectations of success

162. The most important component of biofeedback is

(A) feelings
(B) information
(C) motivation
(D) attitude
(E) interpersonal relations

163. Migraine headaches can be effectively relieved by all the following behavioral techniques EXCEPT

(A) psychotherapy
(B) relaxation training
(C) biofeedback of finger temperature
(D) systematic desensitization
(E) constriction of extracranial arteries

164. In patients with cancer who are to receive chemotherapy, behavioral conditioning results in anticipatory nausea in

(A) two-thirds of these patients
(B) the more hopeful and optimistic patients
(C) patients high in chronic anxiety
(D) the more gregarious patients
(E) the less inhibited patients

165. In attempting to understand how adolescents develop the habit of smoking, social learning theory cites all the following reasons EXCEPT

(A) lack of learned negative expectations
(B) acquired positive expectations
(C) inhibition
(D) learned behaviors
(E) powers of observation

166. In treatment programs for alcohol dependence, the risk of relapse is increased if the patient is

(A) maintained in an environment free of alcohol-associated stimuli
(B) provided therapeutic strategies to extinguish alcohol-compensatory conditioned responses
(C) returned to an environment different from the one in which the dependence was acquired
(D) provided procedures to extinguish conditioned associations between aversive affective states and alcohol
(E) allowed to substitute the use of other non-alcoholic drugs when negative affective states occur

167. Accurate statements regarding our knowledge of intervention and skills in changing health behavior include all the following EXCEPT

(A) we know a lot about how to help people change initially, but are not as successful at helping them sustain the new behavior
(B) we are not well informed about preparing and motivating people to undertake change
(C) we know more about health promotion than about risk reduction
(D) we know very little about how people successfully change their own behavior without assistance
(E) we know very little about how to assure patient compliance

168. Which of the following strategies of intervention would be LEAST effective in changing a person's type A pattern of behavior?

(A) Changing environmental demands
(B) Changing the patient's response to the environment
(C) Changing physiologic concomitants of type A behavior
(D) Changing the expectations of the social group or society
(E) Progressive relaxation training

169. Social factors that play a major role in influencing junior and senior high school students to smoke include all the following EXCEPT

(A) peer pressure
(B) cigarette advertising
(C) modeling
(D) social inoculation
(E) experimentation

170. In B. F. Skinner's view, the study of behavior

(A) should be concerned with the fundamental motives that are found in all organisms
(B) should employ factor-analytic procedures to identify the basic dimensions of personality
(C) must be based entirely on an understanding of classical conditioning
(D) cannot make extrapolations about principles of learning from subhuman species to humans
(E) need not make inferences about unobservable organismic states and inner motives

171. Nutritional experts have recommended all the following behavioral tips for weight control EXCEPT

(A) eating slowly
(B) taking small portions of food
(C) waiting 20 min before taking a second helping
(D) watching television or reading while you are eating
(E) recording all food intake in a "dietary diary"

172. Physicians can help patients change their health-related behavior patterns by all the following EXCEPT

(A) discovering and responding to the patient's expectations
(B) simplifying the health treatment plan as much as possible
(C) providing the knowledge to support the recommended behavior
(D) instilling a sense of personal responsibility in the patient for his or her own health maintenance
(E) assuring patients that their health maintenance is solely the responsibility of their physicians

173. Fordyce's classic behavioral approach to pain is based on all the following concepts EXCEPT

(A) behavior in response to pain is significant in its own right
(B) environmental consequences have a strong effect on pain-related behavior
(C) pain behavior is observable and measurable
(D) understanding internal causative factors of conflict or anxiety is crucial
(E) operant conditioning mechanisms are involved

174. Environmental influences on pain and pain-related behavior involve all the following learning mechanisms EXCEPT

(A) operant conditioning
(B) classical conditioning
(C) respondent conditioning
(D) observational learning
(E) latent learning

DIRECTIONS: Each group of questions below consists of lettered headings followed by a set of numbered items. For each numbered item select the **one** lettered heading with which it is **most** closely associated. Each lettered heading may be used **once, more than once, or not at all.**

Questions 175–179

Match each description below with the appropriate learning mechanism.

(A) Contact desensitization
(B) Shaping
(C) Systematic desensitization
(D) Operant conditioning
(E) Classical conditioning

175. Pairs a neutral stimulus with a stimulus that produces a known response until the neutral stimulus alone produces the known response

176. Develops new behaviors and increases the probability of a response by introducing reward or reinforcement

177. Typically pairs muscle relaxation with a hierarchy of imagined scenes associated with anxiety

178. Reinforces successive approximations until the desired response is obtained

179. Combines modeling and guided participation

Questions 180–184

For each description below, match the appropriate mechanism of behavior change.

(A) Contingency management stimulus control
(B) Cognitive restructuring
(C) Thought-stopping procedures
(D) Self-control techniques
(E) Biofeedback

180. Effective in controlling one's autonomic bodily functions by using visual and auditory cues

181. Effective in changing the frequency of behavior by systematically using reinforcement or the n-sequences of behavior.

182. Effective in reducing anxiety

183. Effective in controlling obesity

184. Effective in reducing obsessions

Questions 185–189

For each schedule of reinforcement, select the response pattern with which it is most closely associated.

(A) Concave-upward scallop
(B) Postreinforcement pause
(C) Stable rates of response and highest resistance to extinction
(D) Smooth, stable rates of response inversely proportional to average time interval
(E) Satiation and cessation of response

185. Variable ratio

186. Continuous reinforcement

187. Fixed interval

188. Fixed ratio

189. Variable interval

DIRECTIONS: The group of questions below consists of four lettered headings followed by a set of numbered items. For each numbered item select

A	if the item is associated with	(A) **only**
B	if the item is associated with	(B) **only**
C	if the item is associated with	**both** (A) and (B)
D	if the item is associated with	**neither** (A) nor (B)

Each lettered heading may be used **once, more than once, or not at all**.

Questions 190–194

(A) Classical conditioning
(B) Operant conditioning
(C) Both
(D) Neither

190. An association of a response, which is reinforced by desired consequences, with a stimulus

191. An association of a conditional and an unconditional stimulus

192. Specific reflex responses evoked by specific, identifiable stimuli

193. An increase in the probability of the occurrence of a response after the subject is rewarded

194. A decrease in intensity or probability of a response's occurring (extinction, or forgetting)

Learning and Behavioral Change

Answers

147. The answer is E. *(Kandel, 3/e. pp 997–1007.)* Memory can be divided into short-term and long-term stages. Recently acquired memories are more easily disrupted by such factors as trauma, whereas long-term memories, or older memories, are fairly resistant to disturbance. Short-term memory is transformed into a more permanent long-term store. Thus, the memory process is always undergoing continual change with time. Both short-term and long-term memories are encoded in neural activity that involves a physical change in the brain with apparent alterations of the connections between neurons. It is also clear that the memory traces are not localized to any one brain structure, and that all parts of the nervous system have the plastic properties needed for memory storage. The recall involves an active reconstruction rather than a faithful reproduction of the internal store, and the complex nature of learning itself ensures that the involved neurons are widely distributed in the nervous system. Fortunately, the brain has the capacity to take limited remaining information (memory) and reconstruct a relatively good reproduction of the original memory. The temporal lobes and associated areas and the hippocampus are not registers or banks for memory storage but are actively involved in the storage and retrieval process. Since memory traces are not localized in any one brain structure, trauma to one part of the nervous system can create initial memory loss, but some memory gradually returns even though the lesion or trauma seemed to have caused complete amnesia.

148. The answer is D. *(Schneiderman, pp 162–163.)* The influence of behavior by rewards and punishments has its roots in classical studies of learning. In the earlier classical conditioning experiments, Pavlov investigated the acquired associations between environmental stimuli (food, bell) and smooth muscle responses (salivation). By pairing the food and bell, he elicited salivation using only the bell. This is known as generalization of a response to two or more stimuli. In operant conditioning, the desired behavior is rewarded or reinforced with an object, food, praise, or other reward of pleasing consequence to the learner. Shaping involves rewarding the person's behavior as it begins to approach or approximate the desired or ideal behavior until the desired behavior is reached or mastered. The therapeutic use of this ability to increase or control certain behaviors by reinforcing the desired behavior is the essence of behavioral modification. Behavioral modification has repeatedly demonstrated its efficacy in changing behavior and establishing "good" behaviors in such areas as self-care, social behavior, psychiatric pathology, eating behaviors, smoking, and pain.

149. The answer is D. *(Kandel, 3/e. pp 999–1002.)* Specific behavioral problems, such as shouting obscenities, messiness, or poor hygienic habits, that are often found in institutionalized psychiatric patients can be reduced and replaced with positive and constructive behavior through operant reinforcement by first precisely defining the behavior to be established, then finding an effective reinforcement (e.g., praise, attention, compliments, privileges, money, tokens, food), and finally training the staff to provide the appropriate reinforcement when the desired behavior is emitted by the patient. Punishment is not usually a part of operant reinforcement if one wishes to establish positive and constructive behavior.

150. The answer is B. *(Kaplan, 6/e. pp 109–112.)* Extinction is the gradual reduction of a conditioned response, usually the result of withholding or altering the reinforcement or reward. Extinction is slowed when reinforcement occurs on a variable schedule (i.e., not every response being rewarded) rather than a continuous reinforcement schedule (every response rewarded). Gambling behavior, for example, is maintained powerfully through variable ratio reinforcement, even when there are long periods of nonreinforced responses. A fixed ratio schedule would provide a reinforcement after a specific number of responses or objects were produced (e.g., in a factory worker's schedule). In a fixed interval schedule, a person is reinforced only after a certain time has elapsed, such as with a monthly salary check. Piecework reinforcement is similar to a fixed ratio schedule with a reward being provided after each piece of work is produced.

151. The answer is A. *(Gatchel, 2/e. pp 85–93.)* Repeated instances of noncontingent behavior and outcome can result in learned helplessness, with a person learning and expecting that most events are not controllable or will not be successful. A number of parallels have been drawn between learned helplessness and depression. Although both learned helplessness and depression are very complex phenomena, the characterizations of passive behavior, negative expectations ("I won't be able to do this"), hopelessness, and a feeling of having no control over life's events are present in both. Failing continuously because of one's lack of ability or skill is more apt to relate to depression, while failing because of one's feeling of lack of control over outcomes is more apt to lead to a feeling of helplessness.

152. The answer is B. *(Gatchel, 2/e. pp 217–220.)* Spontaneous recovery, first described by Pavlov, is the return of response strength in due course after extinction. If extinction produced forgetting, then presumably the loss of responsiveness would be permanent. Return of the previously learned material suggests that it is not lost but rather suppressed by some active process resulting from nonreinforcement. Additional support for this concept comes from the finding that responses may return at full strength following a single reinforcement at the end of extinction.

153. The answer is C. *(Gatchel, 2/e. pp 116–118.)* Biofeedback and relaxation training have been used to modify the stress-induced components of hypertension. This results in a small but significant reduction in blood pressure—frequently about 15 mmHg systolic and 10 mmHg diastolic. Meditation and yoga have also been effective in lowering blood pressure. These modest declines in blood pressure have been demonstrated to be especially effective with the person who is at the stage of mild or even moderate hypertension. Weight reduction accomplished by changing one's eating behaviors will also reduce one's blood pressure, even when the salt intake is held constant. Contingency conditioning has not proved effective.

154. The answer is B. *(Linden, pp 221–242.)* Asthma is a very complex respiratory condition. An attack can be triggered or precipitated by a multitude of stimuli and events. The old psychoanalytic explanations and models of several decades ago have been almost completely discredited and even the remaining hope for the efficacy of individual psychotherapeutic treatment lacks sufficient evidence. There is no cure for asthma, but there is considerable evidence that some degree of control can be attained. It is in this context that both sound medical treatment and behavioral self-management can be combined to greatly enhance the control of the disorder. The behavioral self-management program includes education (e.g., mechanics of breathing, use of medications) and self-management training (e.g., self-monitoring and observation of reactions, use of diaries, information processing of own data, decision making with most appropriate options, and self-instruction at all phases of the program). Suggestion can sometimes alter pulmonary function in asthmatic patients, but it has not had adequate success. Even though emotional reactions can act to trigger an asthmatic attack, attempts to eliminate or reduce emotional reactions have proved less effective than self-management in controlling asthma.

155. The answer is C. *(Kandel, 3/e. pp 997–1002.)* Timing is critical in both classical and operant conditioning. In classical conditioning, the conditional stimulus and unconditional stimulus must be presented closely, otherwise learning is poor or slow. In operant conditioning, the reinforcer must follow the desired response without delay, or only weak conditioning will occur. The person or animal must be able to discriminate between the two stimuli (stimuli discrimination) in classical conditioning in order for the second stimulus to be able to elicit the response. Extinction occurs in classical conditioning if the conditional stimulus is repeatedly presented without the unconditional stimulus. Likewise, if reinforcement is not given when the desired response occurs in operant conditioning, the probability of the response's occurring decreases until the response eventually ceases. Simultaneous stimuli presentation is relevant for classical conditioning but not necessary for operant conditioning. Classical conditioning is usually restricted to a specific reflex response (e.g., salivation) that is evoked by a specific stimulus (e.g., food). Operant conditioning involves any behavior that will tend to repeat itself if properly rewarded (reinforced). The learning of predictive relationships between stimuli and behaviors is important in both classical and operant conditioning. In classical conditioning, the person (animal) learns that a certain stimulus (food) predicts a subsequent stimulus (bell) or event. In operant conditioning, the person learns to predict the consequences by his or her behavior as the result of its being reinforced (rewarded).

156. The answer is B. *(Simons, 3/e. pp 608–610.)* The retarded rate of extinction following partial reinforcement in acquisition was labeled the "partial reinforcement effect" by Lloyd Humphreys (1939). This consistent effect was regarded as something of a paradox since resistance to extinction was thought to be a function of response strength built up by reinforcement during training. According to this reasoning, partial reinforcement should produce faster, not slower, extinction.

157. The answer is E. *(Lerner, Psychology, pp 419–425.)* Social learning theory suggests that all the following are methods of attitude change: direct reinforcement—rewarding an expression of the desired attitude or behavior; extinction—denying the rewards that maintain the attitude that is to be changed; and modeling—watching someone else being rewarded for desired responses and punished for undesired ones. Desensitization is a technique for conditioning neutral or positive responses to previously fear-inducing stimuli. It, too, is based on social learning principles. Social learning theory is based primarily on considerations of nurture and has done very little to attempt to integrate considerations of nature (i.e., biologic factors).

158. The answer is B. *(Simons, 3/e. pp 609–610.)* A contingency relationship between response and reinforcement is characteristic of instrumental conditioning. For this form of learning, reinforcement occurs only if the desired response is emitted. Therefore, the occurrence of reinforcement is at least partly under the control of the learner.

159. The answer is C. *(Kandel, 3/e. pp 1001–1002.)* Systematic desensitization was developed by Joseph Wolpe in an effort to decrease neurotic anxiety or phobias that are learned and are usually precipitated by certain environmental situations, such as fear of heights or crowds. The patient is taught muscular relaxation; then, while using the relaxation to inhibit the anxiety, the patient is told to imagine a series of progressively more severe anxiety-provoking situations (e.g., climbing to the second step of a ladder, then the fourth step, and so on) until the anxiety-provoking situation of the highest (strongest) level can be brought to mind without the accompanying anxiety or fear. The anxiety-provoking situation is not brought to mind to be treated by any special form of psychotherapy but becomes paired with the anxiety-reducing relaxation. Most of these anxiety-provoking situations are situation-specific; however, the desensitization often generalizes to other real-life situations that may be potentially anxiety-provoking.

160. The answer is B. *(Simons, 3/e. pp 638–646.)* *Learning disability* is the label given to children who show a discrepancy between their estimated academic potential and their actual level of academic performance. Failure to learn academically does not necessarily imply general impairment in intellectual capacity, but it can seriously affect broad adaptive functioning. Most persons with learning disabilities show a largely selective deficit, despite apparently normal schooling exposure, seemingly normative family settings, appropriate motivational predispositions, intact sense organs, adequate physical status, and normal intelligence, yet they fail to learn with normal proficiency. Research studies show that the criterion of failure to learn to read is the most frequent manifestation of a learning disability. This form of learning disability is generally known as dyslexia and is a problem of major proportions, especially during adolescence.

161. The answer is D. *(Lerner, Human Development, pp 232–262.)* Mastery motivation, achievement motivation, frustration tolerance, level of aspiration, and feelings of competence are traits that begin to develop in early childhood and are directly affected by the encouragement, reward, and expectations of parents and other adults. The old assertion holds true that success breeds expectations of success and failure breeds expectations of failure. These expectations are strongly affected by the expectations and reactions of others. If reaction to the pursuit of goals is positive, then children are more apt to feel satisfied and proud and to develop stronger feelings of personal worth and self-esteem. Greater tolerance for frustration is also developed when a child's efforts are encouraged effectively, resulting in stronger achievement motivation and persistence to set and accomplish higher, but realistic, goals. These goals may be beyond the child's present abilities, but they are eventually within reach. Children who are shamed, ridiculed, or discouraged are more likely to develop feelings of insecurity and inadequacy and fear of failure. Also, they are more apt to set either low goals that they can reach or unrealistically high goals that they may never reach or never try to reach.

162. The answer is B. *(Gatchel, 2/e. pp 231–234.)* Biofeedback is a process of learning to control various components of one's autonomic responses by using visual or auditory feedback of information from one's physiologic functions. The feedback of information about one's physiologic responses and one's ability to learn and practice control can be influenced by such factors as motivation, feelings, attitude, and interpersonal relations, but information feedback is the primary component in the learning process. Just as one learns to improve one's motor skills by feedback of information and observations of distance, time, space, improvement, and so on, one can learn to exert influence on physiologic responses. Formerly these physiologic responses had been regarded as autonomic because we had no visual electronic or mechanical mechanism for feeding back such information.

163. The answer is A. *(Schneiderman, pp 487–489.)* The migraine headache is associated with vascular dysfunction. The headache is typically preceded by intense constriction of the intra- and extracranial arteries in the temporal region. This is followed by a rebound dilation of the vasculature and then a sterile inflammation and edema of the arteries. Medication and psychotherapy are only marginally effective. By using biofeedback of finger skin temperature with the patient imagining a feeling of warmth in the fingers and hands, vasodilation is produced in peripheral blood vessels. The patient learns to control the dilation of peripheral blood vessels, which is also associated with constriction of cranial arteries. Patients taught to constrict their temporal arteries have also reported decreases in headache activity compared with controls. Similar results were demonstrated using EMG biofeedback with the frontalis muscle. Patients using such biofeedback technology have reported fewer and shorter headaches and less use of pain pills. This has not only been effective in the clinic but has been practiced at home without instrumentation. Subsequent research has also demonstrated the effectiveness of relaxation training in reducing general sympathetic tone. Systematic desensitization is also effective and augments the effect of relaxation so that the individual patient can identify and reduce specific stress responses.

164. The answer is C. *(Gatchel, 2/e. pp 177–178.)* The behavioral conditioning process is very active in cancer patients who are receiving chemotherapy. The conditioned response of anticipatory nausea occurs because certain personal, environmental, or situational stimuli may elicit nausea before the administration of the chemotherapy that can cause nausea in its own right. About one-third of cancer patients on chemotherapy develop anticipatory nausea. It also occurs more frequently in patients who are less hopeful and more pessimistic, isolated, and inhibited, and those who have more chronic anxiety. The anticipatory nausea also appears to be related to the severity of the dose of chemotherapy. The major stimuli involved can be the hospital, the clinic, the nurse, or the smells encountered before administration of the chemotherapy.

165. **The answer is C.** *(Rosen, p 24.)* Social learning theory, developed by Bandura, suggests that through observation children acquire certain expectations and learned behavior with regard to smoking. Through media and models they can learn vicariously, for example, that smoking appears to relieve tension or anxiety. Also, when they observe a model appearing to enjoy the behavior, and without negative consequences, a condition of disinhibition results. The young person's learned expectation of negative consequences does not occur, and the expectation of negative consequences becomes weakened. This becomes an important factor in the ultimate decision regarding smoking.

166. **The answer is E.** *(Linden, pp 27–29.)* Evaluations of treatment methods using the classical conditioning model have demonstrated that relapse is more likely to occur in the presence of alcohol-associated stimuli. Thus, the most effective treatment conditions should maintain an environment that is as free as possible of alcohol-associated stimuli, and the patient should be returned to an environment that is different from the one in which dependence was acquired. Since dependence is acquired by the patient's developing alcohol-compensatory conditioned responses, specific, therapeutic strategies should be implemented and practiced over time prior to discharge in order to extinguish these alcohol-compensatory conditioned responses. Aversive affective states, such as depression or anxiety, can also act to increase the likelihood of relapse, so all treatment procedures should attempt to extinguish conditioned associations between aversive affective states and alcohol. The patient will probably experience relief from withdrawal symptoms if allowed to substitute other drugs; thus the very conditioned responses targeted for extinction will be maintained.

167. **The answer is C.** *(Rosen, pp 219–222.)* There is a wide range of intervention strategies and technologies, many of which are very successful (e.g., 50 to 70 percent), but the relapse rate is also high, especially during the first 6 to 9 months after the behavioral change program has terminated. This emphasizes the need to continue some strategy to sustain the behavior, as one might continue to prescribe a drug for hypertension or diabetes. While the behavioral technology for changing behavior is well developed, we are not so well informed about how to prepare and motivate people to decide to adopt risk reduction and health promotion regimens. Outstanding progress has been made on identifying and modifying risk factors and risk behavior, but we know much less about health promotion, since promoting health is far more complex than eliminating risk factors and risk behaviors. Lastly, a far greater percentage of people are able to successfully initiate, complete, and maintain risk-reducing behaviors if they do so on their own. This success appears to be related to self-direction, but little is known about how this occurs, just as medicine knows little about how certain illnesses or conditions abate without medical intervention.

168. The answer is D. *(Rosen, pp 134–140.)* In general, there are three major interactive strategies used in attempting to change type A patterns of behavior: changing the environmental demands, changing the patient's responses to the environment (both behavioral and cognitive), and changing the physiologic concomitants of type A behaviors. Examples of counteracting certain environmental demands or triggers include limiting time spent in the environment, rescheduling deadlines, or avoiding interruptions. Changing one's response is best accomplished by learning to observe one's own type A behaviors (e.g., anger or hostility) and then contracting with oneself to alter those behaviors by practicing new behaviors, coping styles, or reactions. Progressive relaxation, biofeedback, and exercising are effective methods of reducing many of the physiologic responses to stress and anxiety. Attempting to change the expectations of a social group or society is very difficult, especially if the changes are to be directed at one's own personal needs.

169. The answer is D. *(Rosen, pp 26–30.)* The modeling of parents, teachers, and "significant others" has been found to play a major role in influencing a person to smoke. Peer pressure is also a major influence, especially in adolescence. Cigarette advertising, which may use celebrity models and link smoking to such attractions as sports, sex, and prestige, impresses youth with the pleasurable, grown-up, and no-risk aspects of smoking. Social inoculation is a process whereby persons are inoculated with arguments and behavioral skills to reinforce the effects of positive modeling, the social skills to counteract peer pressure to smoke, and various content analyses of the techniques used by advertisers to persuade youth to smoke. Experimentation is a common characteristic of adolescence and smoking is one of the most frequent behavioral trials.

170. The answer is E. *(Kaplan, 6/e. pp 109–112.)* B. F. Skinner's radical behaviorist approach to psychology is based on the idea that behavioral science should restrict itself to the recording and analysis of *observable* behavioral responses. Skinner argued that it is unnecessary to make inferences about such inner states as arousal, need levels, motives, and cognitions. Skinner analyzed behavior in terms of the principles of classic Pavlovian conditioning and, more importantly, operant learning. Operant learning (instrumental conditioning) involves changing the relationship between reinforcement schedules and response outcomes.

171. The answer is D. *(Wilson, 12/e. pp 411–417.)* Empirical studies have revealed a number of changes in eating habits that will significantly discourage the tendency to eat more food than is required by the body. Nutritional experts recommend that we eat more slowly, serve ourselves smaller portions, wait at least 20 min after we have eaten our first serving before taking a second serving, restrict all our eating to one or two places in the home, do not watch television or read while we are eating, and let family and friends know that we are trying to cut down on food intake. In addition we should go grocery shopping only after we have eaten a satisfying meal, not leave food out where we repeatedly see it and can easily reach it many times a day, try to spend less time in the kitchen, get someone else in the family to clear the plates and put away the leftovers, and keep a detailed log or diary of all food intake. Such activities will help to disrupt previously learned, but inappropriate, eating behaviors and establish appropriate environmental conditions and eating behaviors.

172. The answer is E. *(Last, 13/e. pp 1094–1096.)* Physicians have to learn a set of specific educational skills in order to help their patients make significant and lasting changes in their health-related behavior. Several empirical studies have suggested strategies that can be used for improving the effectiveness of health services. Among other strategies, the physician should provide continuity of personalized medical care, discover and respond to the patient's expectations in an individualized manner, simplify the health regimen as much as possible, and provide health knowledge that is necessary to support the recommended behavior and is action-oriented. The physician should also make the health behaviors and motives important to the patient and family, maximize the rewards for the prescribed health-related behavior, minimize the cost and inconveniences, try working slowly into regimens that are unpleasant, and instill a sense of personal responsibility in the patient for his or her own health maintenance.

173. The answer is D. *(Feuerstein, pp 438–445.)* Pain and pain-related behavior can be influenced by the environment via basic learning mechanisms. This concept has made a major contribution to the understanding and management of chronic pain. It recognizes that the pain behavior itself (the overt actions and reactions of the person) is significant in its own right and not necessarily attributed to some underlying anxiety or conflict. Also, it emphasizes operational measurement and observation of the pain behavior itself (e.g., moaning, inactivity, use of medications), not the pain or inferred concepts as to why the person is feeling or reacting to pain. Using these concepts, the pain behavior can be conditioned as separate from the pain itself. Operant conditioning mechanisms are involved as the pain behavior is affected by such environmental consequences as reward (positive) or punishment (negative) factors, which act as reinforcers.

174. The answer is E. *(Feuerstein, pp 438–445.)* The environment can influence pain-related behavior via learning mechanisms, principally operant conditioning, respondent or classical conditioning, and modeling or observational learning. This is referred to as the *learning mechanisms hypothesis.* Certain rewards or secondary gains from the environment (e.g., reduced work or increased attention) are involved in operant behavior mechanisms of reward and reinforcement. The respondent conditioning mechanism involves a specific antecedent; for example, a person may link increased lumbar pain with sleep time so that the pain and preparing for sleep become associated, with the result of anticipatory anxiety and increased pain at bed time. A similar anticipatory or avoidance behavior can maintain such behaviors as limping or decreased activity. Observational learning (or vicarious learning, or modeling) refers to learned reactions to pain as observed in parents, peers, and family or through role expectation. A parent who consistently avoids work when ill can be a model for a child who learns to avoid school or responsibility.

175–179. The answers are: 175-E, 176-D, 177-C, 178-B, 179-A. *(Gatchel, 2/e. pp 217–229.)* Classical conditioning is a basic form of learning. It was first described by Ivan Pavlov working on the conditioned reflex. He was able to take an autonomic reflex (e.g., salivation to food) which was thought to be unconditioned and demonstrated that it could be conditioned to respond to a new stimulus (e.g., a bell) if the new stimulus was presented along with or prior to the unconditioned stimulus (food). After a number of such presentations the new stimulus (bell) would elicit the autonomic unconditioned response. The autonomic response had, in effect, learned to respond to the new stimulus (i.e., a learned association or connection between the two stimuli had occurred). Pavlov called this learned association *stimulus substitution.*

Operant conditioning, sometimes called *instrumental conditioning,* was formulated by Edward Thorndike and later developed by B. F. Skinner. In operant conditioning a new behavioral response is learned, as compared with classical conditioning in which a new stimulus is conditioned (learned) to elicit the same response or behavior. In operant conditioning reinforcement becomes the key stimulus that increases the likelihood that the desired behavior will be repeated or strengthened.

Systematic desensitization is a behavioral technique developed on basic principles of classical conditioning. Joseph Wolpe developed it as a means of alleviating anxiety. Deep muscle relaxation is paired with a series of imagined scenes that depict situations or objects that are associated with anxiety and thus produce anxiety. The scenes or situations are graded into a hierarchy and the pairing with relaxation proceeds from the most simple to the most severe scenes. The patient thus learns to tolerate more and more severe or difficult scenes and becomes desensitized as the relaxation acts to inhibit the anxiety response. The behavioral technique has been especially effective with phobias, insomnia, and stress-related disorders.

Shaping is a reinforcement and learning process wherein a series of successive responses that approximate the desired response are reinforced until the desired response is learned. It is basically an operant conditioning procedure and was originally developed using the bar-pressing response of rats as the act to be learned. The rat was positively reinforced for each of the closer and closer approximations, such as approaching the bar, rising upon hind legs, putting front paws on the bar (lever), and pressing the bar. This is also known as the successive approximation shaping procedure. After the desired behavior has been learned, the experimenter can then introduce different reinforcement schedules to maintain the learned behavior. A discriminative stimulus can also be introduced, such as pressing the bar only when a certain light is on, so that the animal will learn not to press the bar except when the light is on. The shaping technique has been used to train circus and other animals to perform complicated acts used in most zoo and marine animal shows. The process of shaping is considered to be prominent, although greatly modified, in many social and cultural learning situations of everyday life.

Contact desensitization is a variation of systematic desensitization that combines modeling and guided participation procedures. In a fearful person, the therapist (or teacher) models the appropriate behavior and then guides the fearful person through each step of a hierarchy. Contact desensitization has been very effective in the treatment of phobias, such as the fear of snakes. The therapist would model appropriate behaviors, such as approaching the snake, touching the snake, and progressively allowing the snake to crawl around the therapist's arms and shoulders. The fearful person is then encouraged to perform each of these behaviors, beginning with the lowest behavioral task in the hierarchy. With the assistance of the therapist, each behavioral task is repeated until the fear and anxiety associated with the snake are extinguished. This method differs from systematic desensitization in that while a hierarchy is used, relaxation training is not. The procedure is based on extinction rather than depending on relaxation to inhibit the anxiety.

180–184. The answers are: 180-E, 181-A, 182-B, 183-D, 184-C. *(Gatchel, 2/e. pp 227–234.)* From studying a mnemonist and various yogi experts who could control their heart rates, skin temperatures, and other physiologic processes, it was documented that an average person can learn to accomplish the same control by using certain visual or auditory feedback cues. We learn skills and everyday behaviors by using the basic learning principle that we can learn and improve performance by receiving feedback about our response and then making appropriate adjustments. Learning to drive a car, throw a baseball, or perform a venipuncture requires continuous feedback. By providing visual or auditory feedback (biofeedback) of physiologic responses, we can also learn to control voluntarily such physiologic functions. Pioneering experiments by Neal Miller in the late 1950s and early 1960s with animals were extended to demonstrate human subjects' ability to learn to control many responses that were assumed to be "involuntary responses," such as blood pressure, heart rate, activity of the sweat glands, skin temperature, neuromuscular activity, and various brain rhythms. The clinical application of the behavioral technology of biofeedback continues to be explored and effectively applied to certain disorders, such as hypertension, Raynaud's disease, migraine headache, asthma, gastrointestinal disorders, dyskinesias, epileptic seizures, cardiac arrhythmias, anxiety, headache from muscle contraction, and muscular pain.

Contingency management is an attempt to control or manage the contingency between reinforcement (reward) and certain behavior (e.g., pressing a bar) in order to increase the frequency of that behavior. It involves systematically controlling the consequences with appropriate reinforcement. This method is used extensively in everyday activities to encourage or discourage certain behaviors in children, patients, or others with whom we relate. As an example, token economy programs, which give tokens as exchangeable awards, have proved to be very effective in treatment and rehabilitation, especially when the goal is to decrease undesirable behavior, psychotic talk, or the bizarre patterns of behavior of schizophrenics. The contingency management methods are also very effective in increasing the frequency of socially adaptive behaviors, responsibility, and self-reliance.

Cognitive restructuring is a therapeutic technique based on the fundamental discovery by Albert Ellis (1962) that cognitions and faulty or irrational patterns of thinking can produce emotions and other psychological disorders, such as anxiety. By changing the internal or covert sentences that people say to themselves, they can reduce or eliminate negative emotional responses. This became known as cognitive restructuring, and while it may sound deceptively simple, it has added further confirmation to earlier studies showing that not only do attitudes affect behavior, changing behavior also affects attitudes. By integrating the biobehavioral perspective, we can demonstrate how specific thoughts or verbalizations to oneself can give rise to the psychological and physiologic aspects of anxiety. By identifying and modifying (restructuring) these negative verbalizations to oneself and replacing them with more positive statements to oneself, anxiety can be reduced. Similar to systematic desensitization, cognitive restructuring has demonstrated in controlled experiments that it is highly effective in reducing anxiety. Systematic desensitization is more effective with certain phobias, and cognitive restructuring is more effective with multiple fears in interpersonal situations. Thought-stopping is a variation of restructuring. The client concentrates on specific anxiety-producing thoughts, which are then interrupted by a sudden shock statement "stop" by the therapist. After several interruptions, the locus of control is then shifted to the client by the client's learning to emit a subvocal "stop" at any time he or she begins to engage in the self-defeating rumination. In another technique, the client snaps a rubber band worn on his or her wrist when such ruminations occur. Even though this has a slight punishing effect, it does serve to provide an impressive "stop" signal and interrupts the destructive thinking. The thought-stopping procedures are especially effective with clients who have difficulty controlling distressing obsessional thoughts. The techniques of cognitive restructuring mentioned above can be effective in helping patients cope with psychological stressors that are linked to the precipitation exacerbation of physical symptoms. Again, what appears to be deceptively simple and superficial actually works and is based on more recent knowledge in neuroscience and behavioral science than are the traditional psychotherapeutic principles.

There has been much renewed interest in techniques of self-control and self-management for controlling problem behaviors. Some of the more successful techniques have been developed by working with patients attempting to control obesity but can also be applied to smoking, stress, tension, and other problems. Such techniques involve identifying significant rewards and punishments that can be used by patients to reinforce the behavior they are attempting to monitor and control. For example, in the control of obesity there is self-monitoring of daily weight, calories, and exercise; self-reward with extra money, purchases, or privileges; and self-punishment with fines and denial of special privileges or favored activity. Self-monitoring and self-reward are more effective reinforcers than is punishment. Social support is also an effective reinforcement for self-control.

185–189. The answers are: 185-C, 186-E, 187-A, 188-B, 189-D. *(Kaplan, 6/e. pp 109–112.)* The variable ratio (VR) schedule of reinforcement is structured such that a variable and an unpredictable number of responses are required to produce a reinforcement. With time, a steady, smooth rate of response develops. This rate tends to be proportional to the average number of responses required for a reinforcement. VR schedules are sometimes termed "The Gambler's Schedule," reflecting a number of interesting parallels to the behavioral patterns associated with playing slot machines and roulette. It is characteristic of this behavior that it persists after reinforcement is discontinued.

Continuous reinforcement is regarded as the limiting case of all the other schedules. Normally, organisms on this schedule respond rapidly at first in order to accumulate a large number of reinforcements. Behavior then ceases as the reinforcements are consumed. Satiation from the concentrated reinforcement reduces the motivational levels such that responding may not resume for extended periods.

Intermittent responding is generally produced by fixed interval (FI) schedules. In such schedules, reinforcement is produced by the first response after a fixed time period following the previous reinforcement. To maximize the probability of reward, an organism must learn to time this period relatively accurately. The FI scallop appears in the response record when this timing behavior begins to occur. The scalloping effect results from a tendency to response-inhibition during the interval between the reinforcement and the next opportunity for reinforcement. Responding usually resumes slightly before the next reinforcement is available, and it is this sudden rise in response rate that produces the concave-upward scallop in the response tracing.

The fixed ratio (FR) schedule requires that a certain number of responses be emitted for each reinforcement. Normally, there is no restriction on the timing of this behavior. The response pattern generated by FR schedules is characterized by the "postreinforcement pause." This pattern results from an organism's tendency to cease responding, consume the reinforcer, and then wait for an additional refractory period before again responding.

The variable interval (VI) schedule does not show the scalloping that is characteristic of schedules having fixed temporal relationships among reinforcements. In the VI schedule, it is impossible to predict the time that must elapse between successive reinforcements. Organisms therefore tend to respond with a smooth, steady rate that is inversely proportional to the average time interval in the schedule.

190–194. The answers are: 190-B, 191-A, 192-A, 193-B, 194-C. *(Kandel, 3/e. pp 997–1002.)* Classical conditioning involves the pairing (or association) of a conditional stimulus, such as a light or bell, with an unconditional stimulus, such as a shock or food. The conditional stimulus (light or bell) originally produces no response, while the unconditional stimulus (shock or food) produces a response called the *unconditioned response* (e.g., withdrawal or salivation). By repeatedly presenting the conditional stimulus just before the unconditional stimulus, the conditioned response can then be elicited by the conditional stimulus alone, as though the unconditional stimulus was being anticipated or predicted.

Operant conditioning (sometimes called instrumental conditioning or trial-and-error learning) is also associational learning in that it is the association between a response and a stimulus. While classical conditioning is the formation of an association between two stimuli, the conditional and unconditional stimuli, and is generally restricted to specific reflex responses, operant conditioning involves the reinforcing of behaviors that either occur spontaneously or with no recognizable eliciting stimuli. When such behaviors are either rewarded or result from the removal of noxious stimuli, they tend to reoccur and increase in the probability of occurrence. This process is known as *reinforcement*.

In classical conditioning, the conditioned response will decrease in intensity or probability of occurrence if the conditional stimulus is presented repeatedly without also presenting the unconditional stimulus. This is known as *extinction*, or *forgetting*, and also occurs in operant conditioning if the reinforcement does not occur. Behaviors followed by aversive or noxious consequences tend not to be repeated.

Historically, classical and operant conditioning have been regarded as dissimilar; however, classical and operant conditioning appear to be controlled by remarkably similar laws. The two kinds of learning appear to be manifestations of a common underlying neural mechanism.

Life-Span Development

DIRECTIONS: Each question below contains five suggested responses. Select the **one best** response to each question.

195. Erik Erikson views the stage of young adulthood as being best described by a crisis of

(A) trust versus mistrust
(B) intimacy versus isolation
(C) identity versus role confusion
(D) initiative versus guilt
(E) autonomy versus dependence

196. All the following statements about aging are true EXCEPT

(A) the maximal life span has increased in populations over the past 20 years
(B) the risk of death increases exponentially with time
(C) life expectancy would increase only 20 years if heart disease and cancer were eliminated
(D) the biomedical model is becoming increasingly inapplicable in accounting for death in the elderly
(E) the $\dot{V}_{O_2 \, max}$ can be used as an integrated measure of the functional limits of the whole body

197. The environmental factor with the most underused potential for developing cognitive and interpersonal competence in children is the

(A) school
(B) family setting
(C) community mental health center
(D) health care system
(E) child welfare agency

198. Educational stimulation of disadvantaged children results in a subsequent improvement in cognitive and academic performance when stimulation includes all the following EXCEPT

(A) daily rather than occasional activity
(B) maintenance for an extensive period of time
(C) very early institution of aid
(D) a focus on cognitive, language, and number skills
(E) attempts to separate these children from the influence of their family

199. According to current research, a daughter is most likely to have traditional vocational aspirations if she has a

(A) nonworking mother
(B) working mother
(C) mother in a traditionally masculine occupation
(D) working father
(E) father with high occupational status

200. Compared with pregnant women aged 20 to 25, pregnant adolescents are more apt to have all the following EXCEPT

(A) infants of lower birth weight
(B) inadequate prenatal care
(C) higher rates of infant mortality
(D) similar rates of birth defects and mental retardation
(E) higher degree of poverty

201. Sequential studies of human development suggest that the growth of intelligence may continue through

(A) late adolescence
(B) early adulthood
(C) middle adulthood
(D) late adulthood
(E) old age

202. All the following research findings on adult development are true EXCEPT that

(A) significant developmental changes continue to occur throughout adulthood
(B) as people age, there is an increasing range of differences between individuals
(C) changes in adulthood occur in all areas of development (cognitive, physical, and social-personal)
(D) adult cognitive changes may show quantitative reduction on an ability test, but a qualitative acquisition of a different form of intelligence
(E) just as is the case in childhood and adolescence, there are predominant and universal developmental stages in adulthood

203. In the theory developed by Jean Piaget, the first unit to appear in cognitive development is

(A) language
(B) schema
(C) concepts
(D) rules
(E) images

204. According to Freud, children pass through all the following psychosexual stages of development EXCEPT the

(A) oral
(B) anal
(C) phallic
(D) autoerotic
(E) genital

205. A prominent "embracing" response that can be elicited in a newborn infant by a sudden change in the head position is called the

(A) sign of Babinski
(B) startle (Moro's) reflex
(C) convulsive reflex
(D) infant carry response
(E) primate hug

206. In comparing health behaviors of younger and older people, older people report all the following EXCEPT

(A) more symptoms
(B) less positive health status
(C) more vulnerability to health threats
(D) decline in regular physical activity
(E) improvement of eating habits

207. Recent studies concerned with alcohol use and abuse in adolescence have found all the following to be true EXCEPT that

(A) alcohol is the most widely used drug by youth between the ages of 12 and 17
(B) adolescent problem drinkers are less likely to use illicit drugs than are nondrinkers
(C) heavy drinking during adolescence is typically accompanied by other antisocial behaviors
(D) the most frequent cause of death and disability among youth today is traffic accidents, many of which are directly related to alcohol
(E) adolescent problem drinkers are more tolerant of deviance

208. Erik Erikson's theory of the life cycle and growth of the ego is reflected in which of the following statements?

(A) Sexual drive is crucial in determining the development of a sense of identity
(B) Ego maturation is genetically predetermined; cultural influences are of minor importance
(C) There are eight stages characterized by crises whose satisfactory resolution is essential to the development of a healthy sense of identity
(D) The phases of development are characterized in turn by aggressive, affiliative, achievement, nurturance, and power motives
(E) People are burdened with too many ego functions; society would benefit from stricter and more economic processes of socialization

209. The most rapidly increasing rate of mortality is found in

(A) infancy
(B) childhood
(C) adolescence
(D) middle age
(E) old age

210. All the following statements about prenatal and perinatal development are true EXCEPT that

(A) the developmental consequences of prematurity are resolved within the first 18 months
(B) prematurity is more frequent in mothers from lower socioeconomic groups
(C) maternal anxiety is associated with incidence of colic in the neonate
(D) marital conflict during pregnancy may affect the quality of early mother-child interaction
(E) the incidence of neonatal retardation is highest in mothers who are less than 20 or more than 35 years of age

211. Institutionalization during infancy often involves all the following consequences EXCEPT

(A) poor linguistic organization during early childhood
(B) deficits in concept formation and abstract thinking
(C) later impairment of motor skills
(D) anaclitic depression
(E) abnormal behavioral patterns

212. In René Spitz's classic study of sensory deprivation, he found all the following to be true EXCEPT that

(A) social interaction with other humans is essential in infant development
(B) in the first 4 months, infants in the foundling home (having less contact with other people) scored better on several developmental indices than those in the nursing home (where mothers visited)
(C) by 1 year, the foundling home infants had fallen far below those in the nursing home on developmental indices
(D) after 2 or 3 years, most infants in the foundling home could not walk or talk
(E) children in the nursing home had a higher incidence of infection than those in the foundling home because of the many social contacts

213. The complex of symptoms characteristic of children who are deprived of their mother or of a mother substitute during infancy and often extending into the first years of life is known as

(A) stranger anxiety
(B) anxiety neurosis
(C) autism
(D) childhood schizophrenia
(E) anaclitic depression

214. Which of the following statements about dependency behavior patterns in the preschool years is true?

(A) The degree of dependency on peers does not change significantly between 2 and 4 years of age
(B) Boys usually exhibit greater dependency than do girls
(C) Help-seeking behavior ("instrumental dependency") is constant from 3 to 5 years of age
(D) Intense dependency at age 5 or 6 portends dependency conflicts in adolescence and adulthood
(E) By age 5 or 6, dependency becomes an unstable personality trait with girls

215. Stages in the child's normal development of speech are characterized by all the following statements EXCEPT that

(A) between 1 and 6 months, infants invent new noises and experiment with them
(B) infants 4 to 5 months old will repeat sounds they hear
(C) infants between 12 and 18 months will intentionally use a word appropriate to the situation
(D) between 24 and 36 months, infants use 200 to 300 words in phrases and two-word sentences
(E) by 48 months of age, the child should have a vocabulary of about 1500 words

216. All the following factors are included in gender identity EXCEPT

(A) gender role behavior
(B) parental and cultural attitudes
(C) external genitalia
(D) sexual behavior
(E) genetic influence

217. Which of the following statements about the development of moral standards during childhood is true?

(A) Only at puberty do a child's moral standards become independent of external rewards and punishments
(B) The development of guilt as a reaction to transgressions is fostered by parental warmth
(C) Children of 11 or 12 years of age are more likely to make inflexible, absolute moral judgments than those 7 or 8 years of age
(D) Older children are more likely than younger children to judge behavior as right or wrong in terms of its reinforcement outcomes
(E) The development of moral reasoning is independent of general intellectual maturation

218. Research findings on early gender-role identification and behaviors show that all the following statements are true EXCEPT

(A) gender-related differences in play behavior are evident as early as 13 months
(B) males are generally more aggressive in their play and problem-solving activities than are females
(C) children who experience gender reassignment after the age of 2 are considered to be high-risk candidates for psychological disorders
(D) children between 3 and 4 years of age are able to make gender-appropriate choices according to Western stereotypes
(E) females 3 to 5 years old appear to be more concerned about gender-appropriate play activities than are males of a similar age

219. In comparing overweight adolescent boys and girls, girls are more apt to experience all the following EXCEPT

(A) parental pressure to restrict food intake
(B) inclination to eat in response to negative and positive moods
(C) blame by their parents for their weight status
(D) presence of other people as a signal for eating
(E) inclination to take more drastic measures to control their weight

220. The most common presenting feature of Alzheimer's disease is

(A) change in personality
(B) loss of memory
(C) difficulty in learning new information
(D) impairment of orientation to time
(E) loss of intellectual skills

221. In Piaget's theory of child development, the processes that allow a child to move from one stage of cognitive development to the next include all the following EXCEPT

(A) reinforcement
(B) representational ability
(C) equilibration
(D) assimilation
(E) accommodation

222. The phenomenon of parent-infant bonding proposed by Kennell and Klaus produces all the following EXCEPT

(A) enhancement of infant's language development
(B) enhancement of infant's cognitive development
(C) increase in parental touching and fondling
(D) decrease in amount of crying done by infant
(E) increase in unwarranted maternal concern

223. Major obstacles for children in the creative solving of problems include all the following EXCEPT

(A) failure to understand or grasp a problem
(B) forgetting certain aspects of a problem
(C) more concrete thinking than adults
(D) fear of failure
(E) insufficient knowledge

224. Children develop identification with a parent as a result of all the following EXCEPT

(A) perception of similarities, physical and behavioral
(B) communication from others concerning similarities
(C) imitation of parental mannerisms
(D) attractiveness of the parent
(E) obedience to parental authority

225. Language development in childhood is characterized by which of the following?

(A) Infants 15 to 20 weeks of age use different patterns of vocalization to identify discomforts such as hunger, fright, and pain
(B) Most children master all consonant sounds by the age of 3 to 3½ years
(C) The first words spoken are usually verbs
(D) Vowels emerge in hierarchical order between ages 3½ and 7 years
(E) None of the above

226. Intelligence and cognitive development during adolescence are usually characterized by each of the following EXCEPT

(A) the emergence of hypothetico-deductive reasoning
(B) attitudes and reasoning that tend to be egocentric
(C) a growing capacity for probabilistic thinking
(D) a type of reasoning that subordinates reality to possibility
(E) less attention to and ability to infer what others are thinking and feeling

227. Perinatal gonadal hormones have a developmental impact on all the following EXCEPT

(A) sex-linked neural differentiation
(B) sexuality in adulthood
(C) neural morphology
(D) the permanent organization of parts of the nervous system
(E) hermaphroditism in genetic males

228. Cognitive skills of early childhood show all the following patterns EXCEPT

(A) at 18 months, a child begins to follow simple one-part directions, begins many questions with "what," imitates people in his or her environment, and infers causes from observing effects

(B) at 2 years, the child begins to learn about time sequences, matches simple shapes and sizes, attempts new solutions to old problems, and may arrange several words in grammatically incorrect sentences

(C) at 3 years, the child asks many "why" questions, talks in sentences using four or more words, can give his first and last name, and may talk about his fears

(D) at 4 years, the child may begin many questions with "how," knows the days of the week, can identify coins correctly, and can follow a three-step direction in proper order

(E) at 5 years, the child asks the meaning of words, talks more, and is more externally focused

229. Significant changes in physiologic and cognitive functioning develop with age. Studies of aging show that

(A) intraindividual variability is decreased with aging

(B) interindividual variability is decreased with aging

(C) there is more age-related decline found in longitudinal methods than in cross-sectional methods

(D) life-style and experiences play a major role in retention of various cognitive functions

(E) sustained attention is reduced considerably by age 80

230. Biologic changes in the adolescent years include all the following EXCEPT

(A) a growth spurt for girls with peak velocity at 14 years of age

(B) menarche at any time between 10 and 16½ years of age; the average now is just over 12 years of age

(C) a growth spurt for boys with peak velocity about 2 years later than girls

(D) growth of testes beginning as early as age 9½ or as late as age 13½ and ending at any time between ages 13½ and 17 years

(E) a historical rate of decreased age of menarche of about 4 months each decade

231. True statements regarding childhood dreams include all the following EXCEPT

(A) there is substantial proof that dreaming begins at 1 to 1½ years of age
(B) they are experienced as pleasant more often as the preschooler grows older
(C) they increase in frequency as the child approaches the age of 5
(D) in the form of frightening nightmares they occur at a relatively young age (3 to 4)
(E) dreaming is closely linked to the ability to talk

232. True statements concerning aging include which of the following?

(A) Twenty percent of aged persons live in long-stay institutions (nursing homes, mental hospitals, homes for the aged)
(B) The majority of old people feel bad most of the time
(C) Aged drivers have more accidents per person than drivers under age 65
(D) All five senses tend to decline in old age
(E) Personality traits become unstable in the elderly

233. Concepts of death and pain at various stages of child development include all the following EXCEPT

(A) between birth and 2 years of age, separation is more apt to be experienced as synonymous with death
(B) children 3 and 4 years of age believe that a toy feels pain when it is broken
(C) children 5 to 6 years old fantasize that the dead person continues to experience emotion and biologic function in the grave
(D) children 7 to 9 years of age realize the inevitability of death for all living things, no longer feel responsible for the death of others, and yet feel that death can be avoided
(E) at 10 to 12 years of age children see death as the result of aggression or trauma and can accept the concept of nonexistence

DIRECTIONS: Each group of questions below consists of lettered headings followed by a set of numbered items. For each numbered item select the **one** lettered heading with which it is **most** closely associated. Each lettered heading may be used **once, more than once, or not at all**.

Questions 234–237

For each description of a child's behavior below, select the age with which it is most closely associated as part of the growth and development sequence.

(A) 18 months
(B) 2 years
(C) 3 years
(D) 4 years
(E) 5 years

234. Cuts around pictures with scissors; buttons a small button; can copy a square

235. Can drink from a cup without much spilling; turns several pages of a book together; builds a tower of four or five blocks

236. Can copy a circle; can wash and dry hands; can brush teeth—but not adequately; begins to use blunt scissors

237. Can turn doorknobs that can be reached; can drink from small cup using one hand; builds a tower of six or seven blocks

Questions 238–240

Match each view of illness with the developmental age at which it is characteristic.

(A) Preschool age
(B) Elementary school age
(C) High school age
(D) Adult
(E) Elderly

238. Person views self as immortal or immune to external agents (e.g., germs)

239. Person regards illness as a consequence of "bad" behavior

240. Person fears loss of control

Life-Span Development
Answers

195. The answer is B. *(Lerner, Psychology, pp 334–343.)* Erik Erikson's stage theory of psychosocial development provides descriptions of personality development that are consistent with a life-span perspective. It has served as a major basis for research on human development. Erikson viewed the individual as having to develop the capacities (the ego functions) to meet the expectations of society. At each of the eight stages of psychosocial development there is an accompanying "ego crisis." These stages are trust versus mistrust (birth to 1½ years), autonomy versus shame or doubt (1½ to 3 years), initiative versus guilt (3 to 6 years), industry versus inferiority (6 years to puberty), identity versus role confusion (adolescence), intimacy versus isolation (young adulthood), generativity versus stagnation (adulthood), and integrity versus despair (maturity). During intimacy versus isolation in the stage of young adulthood, there is psychosocial pressure for a person to form a close, stable interpersonal relationship. Thus, to the extent that one can attain an unconditional interchange and relationship, one will feel a sense of intimacy in feelings, ideas, and goals. If one cannot share and be shared, then one will feel a sense of isolation.

196. The answer is A. *(Hazzard, 2/e. pp 3–18.)* In spite of advances in medical science, there has been no extension of the limit of the life span, although a greater proportion of the population is reaching the apparent biologic limit of 85 plus or minus 10 years. It is estimated that life expectancy would increase only about 20 years if all heart disease and cancer were eliminated. In effect, prevention and intervention have improved cohort survival as specific causes of fatal diseases have been conquered. In general, the risk of death in the elderly increases exponentially with time. However, the biomedical model for diseases is not as applicable today since death increasingly occurs in the absence of disease. One series of studies has shown that some cells are apparently programmed for a fixed and limited number of reproductions, and then they die. This has provided some new concepts on aging and death. The $\dot{V}_{O_2\,max}$ has been determined to be an integrated measure of the functional limits of the whole body. Furthermore, the relative impairment and functional age of a person can be evaluated by the use of a simple nomogram.

197. The answer is A. *(Hamburg, Selected Perspectives, pp 81–89.)* Cognitive and interpersonal competence are valued by society and incompetence can predispose to the development of psychopathology. Prevention and treatment through environmental factors have been shown to be effective in assisting the development of cognitive and interpersonal competence. The school environment is considered to have the most potential as a focus for intervention, but it is also the most underused resource at present. Schools can be effective as a buffer against negative or destructive environments, especially if they emphasize expectations of high achievement, provide positive feedback, allow children to assume responsibility within the school system, provide adequate discipline, and avoid physical punishment in dealing with learning or behavioral problems.

Intervention in discordant family settings, some types of institutionalization, community mental health centers, and the health care system can achieve limited success, but they are generally costly, isolated, and without the potential for multidisciplinary efforts.

198. The answer is E. *(Schuster, 2/e. pp 291–295.)* Over the past 2 decades, many programs have attempted to improve the school performance of children from lower-class or disadvantaged homes. Most such studies have focused on developing competencies and motivational patterns that would provide the skills necessary to improve cognitive and academic performance. In general, they have demonstrated considerable success in improving subsequent cognitive and academic performance, including IQ. The degree of success is most often related to instituting the educational stimulation as early as possible; focusing directly on cognitive, language, and number skills; maintaining the effort over a prolonged period of time (years); and providing the stimulation on a daily basis rather than occasional exposure. These studies have also shown the importance of recognizing the powerful forces exerted on children by the values of the family and the community and the patterns of identification with social class and ethnic groups, so that a few isolated months or years of intervention cannot always offset the conditions and influences of the socioeconomically disadvantaged child. Programs that have been declared as unsuccessful in enhancing the intellectual functioning and academic success of such disadvantaged children have most often failed to provide one or more of the four listed components.

199. The answer is A. *(Lerner, Psychology, pp 388–391.)* When females develop within a family in which their mother is employed, they have less stereotyped views of female roles than do daughters of nonworking mothers, have a broader definition of female roles, and are more likely to emulate their mothers. It is hypothesized that homes with working mothers have different family interactions than do homes with nonworking mothers. The modeling influence for working and the development of achievement orientations appear to be major factors in developing nontraditional vocational aspirations.

Also, fathers of high occupational status are more apt to promote nontraditional vocational achievement in their daughters. Interaction in such family settings may promote the development of vocational role orientations and behaviors that are nontraditional. In contrast, the daughter of a nonworking mother will be more influenced by the traditional model of the nonworking mother and will develop achievement orientations more consistent with the traditional female roles.

200. The answer is D. *(Lerner, Psychology, pp 446–453.)* Children born to adolescents are more likely to be of low birth weight than children born to older women. These children also have higher rates of infant mortality, mental retardation, and birth defects. All the tendencies apply across different races. Pregnant adolescents are also less likely to have had adequate prenatal care, the maternal death rate for adolescents is higher, and they are more apt to suffer from medical complications such as toxemia and anemia and from poor nutrition. They are also more apt to suffer from a higher degree of poverty and have a limited economic and educational future.

201. The answer is E. *(Lerner, Psychology, pp 229–232.)* Studies of intelligence suggest that a person's IQ score is somewhat variable in the early years, becomes increasingly stable through middle adolescence, and at about age 18 reaches a maximum score that is maintained for some time. Early cross-sectional studies indicated a decrease in IQ scores from middle adolescence into adulthood, but data from later longitudinal research indicated more stability or actual increases in scores. In 1956, Schaie began to study 500 people ranging in age from 21 to 70. When the data were analyzed cross-sectionally, the adolescent-to-adulthood decline typically seen in such studies was observed, but when the data were looked at longitudinally within each of the birth cohort groups in their sequential design, a decline on only one of the four measures (visual-motor flexibility) of intelligence was found. Knowledge attained through education and socialization (e.g., verbal comprehension, number skills) and the ability to organize and process visual information resulted in a systematic increase in scores for all age groups. Clearly, the course of intellectual change from adolescence onward is not just an age-related phenomenon. One may expect that many of the levels and types of ability present in adolescence will be maintained or enhanced in the adult and aged years, in large part depending on such factors as education, experiences, and cognitive activities.

202. The answer is E. *(Lerner, Human Development, pp 7–18, 93–113.)* Although significant developmental changes continue to occur throughout adulthood, there is an increasing range of differences, or variability, between individuals of the same chronologic age. Hence, there are no predominant and universal developmental stages in adulthood as one finds in childhood and adolescence. Even if such predominant stages could be defined, the age at which people experience such stages or the sequence in which they occur is much more variable. In adulthood, changes occur in all areas of development (cognitive, physical, and social-personal). These changes may be a quantitative change in level, rate, or degree or a qualitative change in the nature or type. Thus, an aging adult's level of performance on an ability test may be reduced quantitatively, but qualitatively different forms of intelligence unique to adulthood, such as wisdom, may be acquired. Positive growth and change are expected and encouraged in childhood and adolescence, but in adulthood society does not provide such expectations and encouragement. The full potential for adult development has not begun to be realized.

203. The answer is B. *(Lerner, Human Development, pp 179–185.)* A schema is an abstract or mental representation of the original elements of an event and their relation to each other. Piaget viewed children as continually trying to make sense of their world by dealing actively with objects and people. An infant's schema for another person's face, for example, is most likely to emphasize a circular outline containing other circular elements that represent the eyes. As soon as a schema for an event is established, the child tends to show prolonged attention to those events and to show even more attention to those events that are a little different, but not extremely different, from the one that created the original schema. A new idea or object is thereby incorporated into an idea or schema the child has already developed.

204. The answer is D. *(Lerner, Human Development, pp 64–69.)* Sigmund Freud believed that children pass through psychosexual stages that are characterized by the erogenous zone that gives the greatest pleasure during a specific stage. For example, during the oral stage in the first year of life, oral activities of feeding and biting supposedly supply the greatest pleasures. Gratification occurs by bowel movements in the anal stage during the second and third years. During the fourth and fifth years, the phallic stage, the genital area becomes a primary source of pleasure. The genital stage occurs in adolescence, when the genitals mature and love objects are formed. It is asserted that if the emotional experiences associated with a given zone or stage are too intensely pleasurable, children may develop a fixation at the corresponding stage of development. In such cases, emotional development is retarded. *Autoerotic* refers to sexual self-stimulation and not a Freudian stage.

205. The answer is B. *(Lerner, Human Development, pp 150–154.)* Moro's reflex, known as the startle reflex, is an innate response to unexpected changes in head position, or sometimes to any surprising event. The reflex involves extension of the arms laterally, extension of the fingers, and then return of the hands to midline as if grasping someone. Developmentally, this reflex begins to disappear at 3 to 4 months and is usually gone by 6 months of age. It is believed that the disappearance of Moro's reflex coincides with functional maturation of the neocortex. Presumably, the cortex inhibits brainstem centers that mediate such early reflex responses.

206. The answer is B. *(Rosen, pp 205–214.)* In general, there is a gradual improvement of health behaviors with age. In children aged 8 to 15 there is a decline in health behaviors with decreasing regularity in eating and sleeping, and an increase in new risk behaviors such as smoking and drinking. In young adulthood, this pattern reverses itself with gradual improvements in health behavior, including eating habits. The health behavior that does not improve with age is physical exertion. This is unfortunate since lack of exercise shows the highest level of association with illness and mortality in the aged. In spite of the fact that older people report more symptoms, they also report themselves as being in more positive health status, especially people over the age of 60.

207. The answer is B. *(Rosen, pp 42–45.)* Alcohol is clearly the most widely used drug by youth between the ages of 12 and 17, and the problem drinkers are more likely to use illicit drugs than are nondrinkers and typically exhibit other antisocial behaviors. These behaviors appear to make them more tolerant of deviance, especially since problem drinkers are less religious ,ess successful in school, and more concerned with independence than with academic pursuit. Traffic accidents, one-half related to alcohol use, are the most frequent cause of death and disability of youth.

208. The answer is C. *(Lerner, Human Development, pp 69–70, 205–209.)* Erik Erikson's theory of ego development defines eight "crises" during the life cycle. Each crisis is critical to the development of a sense of personal identity. Although these crises are partly related to the five stages of psychosexual development delineated by classic psychoanalysis, Erikson tends to give greater emphasis to the growth of ego functions as independent of libidinal drive and more related to psychosocial than psychosexual development. As such, they are related to adaptive demands placed on the individual by society and involve a life-span perspective. The eight crises are basic trust versus basic mistrust, autonomy versus shame and doubt, initiative versus guilty functioning, industry versus inferiority, identity versus role confusion, intimacy versus isolation, generativity versus stagnation, and integrity versus despair.

209. The answer is C. *(Hamburg, Frontiers of Research, p 130.)* In general, the mortality for adolescence is relatively low. However, adolescence is the only age period in which the mortality is actually rising. The potential loss is even greater for adolescents and for society when one calculates the years of life lost and loss of potential productivity over the life span. Among males, the leading cause of death is accidents, especially motor vehicle accidents.

210. The answer is A. *(Lerner, Human Development, pp 119–140.)* Developmental differences between premature and full-term children may still be evident at 4 to 6 years of age. The effects of prematurity include decrements of height and weight, as well as slower acquisition of motor and cognitive skills. Prematurity is more frequent with women from lower socioeconomic groups than with women in more fortunate circumstances, and premature babies born to such mothers recover less quickly from developmental deficits than do children from higher socioeconomic families. Prematurity, low birth weight, and infant mortality are of higher incidence among blacks than whites.

211. The answer is C. *(Simons, 3/e. pp 140–147.)* Many psychological and behavioral deficiencies are associated with institutionalization and inadequate primary caretaking during infancy. There is frequently an initial motor retardation, but permanent impairment of motor skills is not usually observed. However, absence of primary caretakers and inadequate institutional arrangements have been implicated in deficiencies of emotional responsiveness and general intellectual functioning, particularly conceptual reasoning, as well as abnormal behavioral and emotional patterns. The irreversibility of such impairments caused by early deprivation is a matter of some controversy.

212. The answer is E. *(Kandel, 3/e. pp 946–947.)* In the 1940s, René Spitz compared the development of infants in a foundling home (much less contact with other human beings) with those in a prison's nursing home (where the mothers were allowed to spend time with their children). Both facilities provided good medical care and nutrition. After 4 months the foundling home infants actually scored better on several developmental indices (perhaps a genetic influence), but by 12 months the foundling home children had fallen far below the nursing home children. Further, many of the foundling home children had developed an anaclitic depression, were withdrawn with little curiosity or happiness, and were prone to infection. The nursing home children were similar to children raised in normal families after 2 or 3 years— walking well and talking actively. Of the 26 foundling home children, only 2 were able to walk or speak, and they could only say a few words. Spitz's findings have been confirmed by subsequent investigators, demonstrating that social interaction with other humans is essential in development, and that severe social and sensory deprivation in early childhood can have catastrophic consequences for later development.

213. The answer is E. *(Kaplan, 6/e. pp 29–30, 106–107.)* *Anaclitic depression* refers to the complex of symptoms exhibited by young children who are deprived of their mother or of a mother surrogate during the first few years of life. This reaction is made up of a number of stages. On first being separated from its caretaker, an infant will protest vigorously. If the caretaking figure is not restored to the infant, the infant enters what is known as the phase of despair and ceases protesting. This phase can be followed by a refusal to eat, which sometimes is fatal, or by a phase of detachment in which the infant withdraws from any interaction and engages in various forms of self-stimulation.

214. The answer is D. *(Lerner, Human Development, pp 197–203.)* By 5 or 6 years of age, dependency is a moderately stable personality trait. Recent studies validate its predictive validity—thus, an overly dependent 5 year old is liable to have dependency conflicts during adolescence and adulthood. However, the predictive value of this trait is much stronger for girls than for boys. In this respect, dependent behavior at 5 years of age manifests the obverse pattern to aggressive behavior: aggression is a more stable personality trait for boys than for girls, whereas dependency is more stable for girls.

215. The answer is B. *(Schuster, 2/e. p 272.)* In order to assess the normal development of a child, it is important to understand the complex process and sequence of developmental skills that are involved in acquiring speech. Starting in the first 6 months of life, babies invent new noises and appear to experiment with them. Cooing usually begins around 2 months of age and occurs especially when the babies appear to be happy. By 4 or 5 months, babbling occurs. This is the practice of expressing alternative vowel and consonant sounds such as "baba." Babbling is an important skill to acquire before a child can learn to repeat sounds heard from other humans. Between 6 and 9 months of age, babies begin to repeat sounds or sound combinations that they have heard and advance to the lalling stage. Within the next several months, the babies attempt to imitate any and all sounds they hear. They begin to select those sounds that help them communicate their wants or that amuse them. Between 24 and 36 months of age, infants will be able to use 200 to 300 words in phrases and two-word sentences. By the age of 48 months, a child should have a vocabulary of about 1500 words that can be used in short sentences with almost 100 percent intelligibility.

216. The answer is D. *(Kaplan, 6/e. pp 438–440.)* A person's sense of maleness or femaleness is known as gender identity. It is both biologic and social. One's biologic sex of physique, including external genitalia and genetic influence, interrelates with a complex series of rewards, punishments, parental and cultural attitudes, and gender roles to influence gender identity. Gender role behavior is learned and is also derived in part from gender identity. A normal and healthy developmental outcome requires a reasonable congruence of gender identity and gender role behavior.

217. The answer is B. *(Schuster, 2/e. pp 362–374.)* While the cognitive development the child undergoes brings about a great awareness of moral values and standards, orientation to abiding by them depends on other factors, primarily identification with the parents and the experiencing of guilt for violation of guidelines. The development of conscience can be seen in internal reactions to transgressions in the form of guilt or by the child's taking up of standards that the child feels personally responsible for maintaining. A number of studies indicate that conscience development is fostered by the presence of parental love and warmth of a degree adequate for positive identification and modeling. Such positive identification and modeling more readily occur if the parents' own conscience and moral standards are mature and reasonable rather than either deficient or overly strict, harsh, and inflexible.

218. The answer is E. *(Schuster, 2/e. p 321.)* Significant gender-role identification and behaviors are learned early in life. Gender-related differences in play behaviors are evident as early as 13 months of age. Males are generally more aggressive in their play and problem-solving activities than are females. These early behaviors are apparently so critical to one's core gender identity that children who experience gender reassignment after the age of 2 are high-risk candidates for psychological disorders. Recent research involving choices in child play indicates that children 3 to 4 years of age are able to make gender-appropriate choices according to Western stereotypes. Three-to five-year-old male children appear to be more concerned about gender-appropriate play activities than are females at that age. This continues into adolescence, as adolescent males also appear to be more conscious of gender roles than are females of that age.

219. The answer is D. *(Rosen, pp 96–98.)* Puberty is associated with important biologic and psychological changes, especially in females with proliferation of fat cells, and general shifts in body image in reference groups from family to peers and in perceived identity. Parents attempt to exert considerable pressure to restrict adolescents' food intake, more so for girls than boys. Parents are unlikely to blame their sons for a weight problem but regard their daughters' obesity in terms of problematic eating behavior and actively attempt to restrain their eating behaviors. Attempting to apply strict parental restrictions on eating tends to minimize options for learning self-control skills. Daughters are generally more apt to eat in response to both negative and positive moods. Exposure to more restraint may lead weight-conscious females to regard the presence of other people as a signal for not eating or for eating smaller portions. Adolescent girls are more concerned with their weight and more apt to take drastic measures to control their weight (e.g., starvation diets or vomiting).

220. The answer is B. (*Hazzard, 2/e. pp 934–937.*) Alzheimer's disease is a progressive, disabling, degenerative disease and the most common cause of dementia in the elderly. The most common presenting feature of Alzheimer's disease is loss of memory. It is also usually accompanied by a gradual decline in intellectual function and impairment of orientation to time and place, judgment, problem solving, language, perception, and learning. Personality change often involves alteration or accentuation of premorbid traits, delusions, apathy, or depression.

221. The answer is A. (*Lerner, Human Development, pp 179–182.*) Assimilation is the addition of a new concept or object into a cognitive scheme already possessed by a child. Generally, this process involves the application of known rules to new objects and situations. Accommodation is the process of adapting or changing one's rules or schemes to include new information, objects, or ideas. Each successive accommodation is a step toward cognitive maturity. Equilibration is the process of changing one's ideas about the world through accommodation to make them consistent with reality. Representational ability involves the ability to represent an absent object internally and to know that it continues to exist. While reinforcement does occur, it is not a major factor in Piaget's theory of cognitive development.

222. The answer is E. (*Schuster, 2/e. pp 667–670.*) While background variables of economic status, race, culture, housing, education, parity, and age may be more important variables in determining subsequent behavior of infants, the phenomenon of parent-infant bonding has recently been shown to be important also. The bonding that occurs during the critically sensitive period from the first hours and weeks of life has been shown to enhance such factors as language development, cognitive development, length of breast feeding (which may be both a cause and an effect), and touching and fondling by parents. The lack of parent-infant bonding tends to increase the amount of crying done by the infant, failure to thrive, and subsequent child abuse or neglect. While cause and effect may be interacting here, there are extensive animal studies that demonstrate the importance of biologic bonding. These findings have had a humanizing effect on physicians and hospital policies.

223. The answer is C. *(Schuster, 2/e. pp 473–476.)* Common barriers to the creative solution of problems by young children include failure to understand or grasp a problem or forgetting certain aspects of it, fear of failure, and insufficient knowledge. Such barriers may produce solutions that are novel but not creative; that is, their solutions may be unique but impractical or inefficient. Experience seems to be important in facilitating problem solving. Children are more concrete in their thinking and in problem solving than either adolescents or adults. Because they are more concrete, they are less apt to consider more options and alternatives.

224. The answer is E. *(Schuster, 2/e. pp 359–366.)* Children identify with their parents because they want to and, involuntarily, because of a perception of similarities. Insofar as most parents are seen by a child as having desirable attributes (e.g., power, freedom, ready access to pleasures, mastery over the environment), the child, wishing to become the same, identifies with his or her parents. If the parents should provide such poor models that the identification process is hampered, the child is then likely to identify with other significant adults in his or her environment. Parental authority is a powerful force; obedience is quite different and distant from identification.

225. The answer is A. *(Schuster, 2/e. pp 264–265.)* Before a child begins to talk, he uses a variety of vocalizations to express himself and to communicate with others. The 15- to 20-month-old child frequently emits long vocalizations that are qualitatively differentiated to communicate discomforts such as hunger, pain, or fright. Vocalizations of very young infants generally consist of vowel sounds. Most children master all the vowel sounds of American English by the age of 3 to 3½ years. Consonants emerge in hierarchical order as mastered phonemes between ages 3 and 7. Some consonants are more difficult to produce than others and are mastered later in the development sequence. The first words spoken are usually nouns.

226. The answer is E. *(Conger, 4/e. pp 143–156.)* Many of the cognitive and personality changes that characterize adolescence may be related to the emergence of formal operational thought during puberty. Formal reasoning enlists cognitive structures that enable adolescents to subject real occurrences to speculative yet systematic thinking about probable consequences. Such thinking, essential to hypothetico-deductive methods, underpins certain adolescent views relating to idealism, romanticism, and egocentrism. The ability to infer what others are thinking and feeling (social cognition) actually becomes much more advanced during adolescence, in spite of adult perceptions that adolescents seem to be much less concerned with the feelings and thoughts of others.

227. The answer is E. *(Kandel, 3/e. pp 960–972.)* Recent evidence has shown that there are morphological and functional differences in the nervous system of males and females. It is known that hormonal deficiencies during early development may result in two syndromes: Turner's syndrome, an anhormonal state in which gonadal tissue does not form (resulting in a phenotypic female, but one who fails to show pubertal changes), and androgen insensitivity syndrome, which is primarily associated with genetic males. (This latter syndrome was formerly called "testicular feminization," but persons afflicted with it do not have feminizing testes and do not secrete estrogen-type hormones; they possess abnormal genes and are indistinguishable from phenotypic females in external appearance and psychosexual orientation and libidinal interests.) It is thought that this genetic disorder prevents or blocks responsiveness to androgens throughout development. It is also known that fetal exposure to heterotypical steroid hormones (hormones of one sex given to or influenced by the hormones of another sex) can cause hermaphroditism in genetic females, but it has not been demonstrated in genetic males. If, during the fetal period, the female fetus is exposed to an unusual amount of male hormone, the female organ development is distorted, partially reversing the differentiation of the peripheral sex apparatus. The adult sexual behavior of hermaphroditic females is also altered. Thus, the effect is not only on the differentiation of external genitalia, but also on the differentiation of neural tissues that mediate later patterns of sexual behavior. The developing nervous system of both genders is considered to be bipotential. While the female anatomic and behavioral patterns can develop in either an anhormonal or maternal-dominated prenatal environment, the active influence of androgens is required for the development of a male pattern. Furthermore, there is a critical time period during which specific interactions between the developing brain and its environment (internal and external) will mold neuronal and behavioral capabilities. There is increasing evidence that the effects of the perinatal male hormones upon subsequent sexual behavior are more upon the developing central nervous system than upon the peripheral sexual apparatus.

228. The answer is D. *(Schuster, 2/e. p 230.)* Cognitive skills in children develop in a fairly predictable pattern. Most cognitive behaviors can be expected to emerge chronologically. In comparing average age with expected behaviors of early childhood, one can expect the average 18-month-old child to begin many questions with "what," imitate almost everything in his or her environment, understand space only from his or her own activity of moving through it, begin to follow simple one-part directions, and begin to infer causes from observing effects. The average 2 year old can be expected to begin to learn about time sequences (e.g., "after lunch"), may arrange several words together in grammatically incorrect two- or three-word sentences, matches simple shapes and colors, attempts new solutions to old problems, and demonstrates a beginning cooperation in toilet training by anticipating a need to "go." By the age of 3, the child can be expected to ask many "why" questions, talks in sentences using four or more words, may talk about his fears, can give his first and last name, and may explore the environment outside the home if given the chance; in addition many retain urine through a night's sleep and wake up dry. By the age of 4 years, the child begins many questions with "where," may talk with an imaginary playmate, may threaten to "run away from home," can give opposites (up-down, hot-cold, and so on), and can associate familiar holidays with their seasons. Asking questions with "how," knowing the days of the week, identifying coins correctly, and following a three-step direction in proper order usually do not occur until the age of 5 years. At 5 years, the child may also begin asking the meaning of words, talks more "constantly," and may need to be reminded to eat or go to the bathroom because attention is so externally focused that he may fail to recognize subtle internal physiologic cues. Knowing the average age at which certain cognitive skills can be expected to develop can be of great assistance in helping the physician monitor the normal, or typical, growth or development of individual children.

229. The answer is D. *(Hazzard, 2/e. pp 913–917.)* There are significant changes in cognitive and physiologic functioning that develop with age. Most studies of aging use cross-sectional methods, which usually show greater age-related declines than do longitudinal methods, which show the age-related declines to occur at an older age. The result has been to recognize that there is a great degree of individual variability to be found in cognitive and in physiologic functioning. Inter- and intraindividual variability have been found to increase with aging. Therefore, group or normative data do not reveal results as valid as those of longitudinal data, nor are group norms or cross-sectional data as valid a measure of an individual's variability. For example, various cognitive abilities show a decline in the group means in cross-sectional studies, whereas longitudinal studies show individuals to experience cognitive decline at different ages and at different rates. One's life-style and educational, intellectual, and other growth experiences have been found to play a major role in the retention or delayed decline of various cognitive functions. Tests of sustained attention show that the elderly perform extremely well into old age with less than one standard deviation of change between ages 20 and 80.

230. The answer is A. *(Conger, 4/e. pp 70–89.)* Growth spurts occur for both boys and girls. A growth spurt for girls usually has its peak velocity at about 12 years of age, whereas the growth spurt for boys will have a peak velocity at 14 years of age. Although the adolescent growth spurt for girls typically begins at age 10½ and ends at age 14, it can start as early as age 9½ and end as late as age 15. Similarly, menarche can come at any time between the ages of 10 and 16½ and tends to be a late event of puberty. The adolescent growth spurt of boys can begin as early as age 10½ or as late as 16 and can end anywhere from age 13½ to 17½. Growth of the testes can begin as early as age 9½ and as late as 13½ and end at any time between the ages of 13½ and 17. In the United States, the rate of decreased age of menarche has been about 4 months per decade.

231. The answer is A. *(Schuster, 2/e. pp 226–227.)* Piaget and his associates report that the youngest age at which definite proof of dreaming is observed ranges from 21 months to 2 years of age. The evidence indicates that dreams do not occur until the child is able to talk and thereby symbolically manipulate events. The frequency of dreams, as well as their content, tends to change in different phases of the development process. Dreaming appears to increase in frequency as children approach the age of 5. Nightmares occur at a relatively young age (3 to 4). Pleasant dreams occur more often as the preschooler grows older and gains more experience.

232. The answer is D. *(Hazzard, 2/e. pp 102–106, 119–123, 146–154.)* A major problem in attempting to provide health care for the elderly is understanding and counteracting some of the common stereotypes of aging. Although it is generally true that all five senses tend to decline in old age, it is not true that most old people feel miserable most of the time. In fact, recent studies show that the majority of the aged see themselves as being as happy as they were when they were younger. Boredom and lack of meaningful activity do become major factors with some aged, however. Another misconception is that a high percentage of the aged population live in long-stay institutions, such as nursing homes, mental hospitals, and homes for the aged. Actually, only about 5 percent of persons 65 and over, and about 10 percent of persons age 75 and over, are in long-stay institutions. Attempting to retain one's social, physical, and cognitive independence is a dominating factor and priority among the aged. Also, contrary to the stereotype that older drivers have a high automobile accident rate, older drivers have about the same accident rate per person as middle-aged drivers and a lower rate than drivers under age 30. Longitudinal research has demonstrated that personality traits are highly stable after about age 30.

233. The answer is E. *(Schuster, 2/e. pp 407–413.)* Although a child's discovery of death is a private and individual experience, it is closely related to cognitive and affective developmental stages. Cognitively, a child must be able to conceptualize animate versus inanimate objects, comprehend cause-effect relationships, and deal with concrete factors before dealing with the abstract. Affectively, sufficient ego-strength, separateness, uniqueness, vulnerability, and coping skills must be developed. The infant must develop a concept of self before being able to comprehend "me—not me."

Between birth and 2 years of age, the infant is aware of separation through object loss and separation anxiety. This deprivation is an early form of experiencing separation as something synonymous with death. Children 3 and 4 years of age believe that all things think, feel, and experience things as they do. Thus they think that a toy feels pain when it is broken and that it must feel hurt when it is repaired. Also, they consider death as another form of life. At 4 and 5 years of age, they believe that death is a cessation of movement but that the dead person or animal continues to experience feelings. Cross-cultural studies have identified many primitive peoples who conceptualize death on this level, since many of them place food, drink, and other objects at the grave or in the tomb of the deceased. Our custom of placing flowers and other adornments on graves may, in part, be a remnant of this level of conceptualizing death. Children at this age are also apt to associate death with retaliation or punishment, which may lead them to fear, anger, and aggression toward others. Physicians must be aware of this possible interpretation of the 5- and 6-year-old child as a reaction to death, especially in the child's own family.

At 5 or 6 years of age children are apt to feel that death can be avoided and that they are not responsible for another person's death. They also begin to realize that their own significant others can die, and this can lead to notable uncertainties and insecurities. Children at 7 to 9 years of age begin to accept the inevitability of death for all living things, but believe that somehow it is external to oneself. By 10 to 12 years of age, death begins to be accepted as a biologic finality and understood in relation to natural laws, rather than being perceived as the result of aggression or trauma. Children at this age can see illness and accidents as causative agents and also that death originates within us and is not just external to us. No longer does the child feel that the dead person continues to live and feel in the grave. Adolescents spend much time in abstract thought about death and try to integrate the past, present, and future experiences into a philosophy of life. They still find it difficult to accept the concept of nonexistence, and this difficulty may extend into adulthood or even old age.

234–237. The answers are: 234-D, 235-A, 236-C, 237-B. *(Schuster, 2/e. p 200.)* The development of both gross and fine motor skills has been clearly observed and scientifically documented for various ages and stages of development. At the age of 18 months, a child can run, climb, throw a small ball, drink from a cup without much spilling, turn several pages of a book together, unzip a large zipper, scribble with a pencil, and build a tower of four or five blocks.

At 2 years of age, a child can try to jump, can turn doorknobs that can be reached, can drink from a small cup using only one hand, turn pages of a book one at a time, unbutton large buttons, and build a tower of six or seven blocks.

At 3 years of age, a child can peddle a tricycle, jump from a low step, begin to use blunt scissors, copy a circle, wash hands and brush teeth (but not adequately), and imitate a bridge made of three blocks.

At age 4, a child can hop forward on one foot, walk backward, cut around pictures with scissors, copy a square, button side buttons, and may bathe self with assistance.

At 5 years of age, a child can jump rope, stand up without using hands, may be able to print own name, copy a triangle, dress without assistance, eat with a fork, and put toys away neatly.

238–240. The answers are: 238-C, 239-A, 240-E. *(Schneiderman, pp 257–275, 547–548.)* A person's developmental level directly affects cognitive, social, emotional, and behavioral factors in illness. Chronologic age is of less value to the health professional in assessing and anticipating problems in treatment and prevention. Persons with mental or physical handicaps can be particularly difficult to assess and predict.

Preschool children generally see being sick as the result of some external agent (e.g., germs). They believe that getting well depends on strict adherence to rigid health rules. They are also more apt to view hospitalization as a punishment for bad behavior. This makes preparatory procedures especially important prior to and during hospitalization in order to deal with anxiety and stress. Because of close ties between the preschool child and parents, separation from parents can be an extreme source of stress for both the child and the family.

In adolescence, the complexities of illness and health and the more sophisticated interaction of internal and external factors become more prominent. The long-range consequences of an illness are not apparent, however, and the adolescent views himself or herself as indestructible or immortal. Peer group activities are of extreme importance. Adolescents will deny or neglect their medical care or health so as not to appear "different." Diabetes provides special difficulties. Peer pressures to drink or smoke can also undermine present or future health.

A major concern of the elderly is the possibility of developing a debilitating illness. The fear is that they might lose control of their mental and physical abilities and become dependent on or rejected by significant others. Other concerns are possible disfigurement or handicap, impending death, extended pain, chronic hospitalization, and invalid status.

Communication and Interaction

DIRECTIONS: Each question below contains five suggested responses. Select the **one best** response to each question.

241. Interpersonal relationship studies have concluded that the most critical element to assure compliance behavior in a physician-patient relationship is

(A) the exchange of accurate information and facts
(B) the congruence of expectations of physician and patient
(C) similarity of physician's and patient's age
(D) recognition and down-playing of social class differences between physician and patient
(E) allowing for the patient to be rewarded in some way for compliance

242. Mothers rate their satisfaction with their children's physicians as higher when the physicians are seen as demonstrating each of the following EXCEPT

(A) understanding
(B) provision of information the parents expect
(C) good communication skills
(D) efficiency and businesslike demeanor
(E) caring

243. The type of information that is most effective in helping patients cope with anticipated surgery is information about

(A) procedures to expect
(B) complications that can occur
(C) sensory experiences to expect
(D) other patients' experiences
(E) medications before and after surgery

244. In opening an initial interview with a patient, it is important to do all the following EXCEPT

(A) ask the patient why he or she has come
(B) state what you already know concerning the problem
(C) refrain from duplicating questions already gathered in the chart
(D) ask open-ended questions
(E) project an image of knowledge and authority

245. The highest patient adherence (compliance) can be achieved by

(A) communication that is technical and authoritative
(B) the patient's belief that his or her health is influenced by internal control
(C) the patient's belief that his or her health is influenced by external control
(D) explanations of need for prophylactic medicine
(E) patients being treated for chronic disease

246. All the following are important in informing a patient or a patient's relative of the patient's serious illness EXCEPT

(A) establishing clearly that you would prefer to talk about it only after you have all the facts, tests, and other relevant information
(B) finding out what the person thinks or knows about the illness
(C) finding out what the person wants to know about the illness
(D) giving honest answers in such a way as to leave the person with some realistic hope
(E) determining the person's understanding of what you have discussed

247. Transference may be characterized by all the following statements EXCEPT that it

(A) may represent strong positive feelings
(B) can provide cues to the unconscious
(C) is often accompanied by countertransference
(D) may express itself as opposition
(E) is a fairly rare phenomenon

248. In preoperative patients, which type or types of information will be most effective in reducing stress?

(A) Sensory information
(B) Procedural information
(C) Coping information
(D) Sensory and procedural information
(E) Sensory and coping information

249. In judging facial expressions, all the following emotions can be easily recognized and differentiated in most cultures EXCEPT

(A) happiness
(B) disgust
(C) sadness
(D) surprise
(E) anger

250. The intervention style that is most effective in relieving the stress of surgery and enhancing the outcome is to provide the patient with

(A) problem-focused information
(B) emotion-focused information
(C) a match between personality factors and treatment style
(D) maximum family support
(E) as much preparatory medical information as can be understood

251. Statements about patients' or physicians' perceptions of symptoms that are generally true include all the following EXCEPT

(A) physicians tend to focus on symptoms that have serious implications for future health
(B) physicians usually focus on symptoms according to visibility or recognizability
(C) patients often focus on symptoms that interfere with usual activities or routines
(D) patients tend to focus on the degree of discomfort rather than the amount or degree of tissue damage
(E) patients tend to deny symptoms they fear may be related to a severe illness

252. Which of the following interventions has been found to be most effective in reducing preoperative distress and facilitating recovery?

(A) Procedural information
(B) Reassurance
(C) Interpersonal support
(D) Hypnosis
(E) Relaxation training

253. Common attitudes and feelings of others about cancer patients include all the following EXCEPT

(A) fear they might catch the disease
(B) tendency to attribute disease to past behavior or undesirable traits of the patient
(C) fear that discussion about cancer will make the patient uncomfortable
(D) ambivalent feelings about patients with cancer
(E) feeling that they should tell the patient the "truth" about their prognosis

254. Which of the following is considered the most powerful nonverbal communication?

(A) Touch
(B) Gesture and posture
(C) Dress and grooming
(D) Physical distance
(E) Facial expression

255. Patients who are ill are LEAST likely to use denial when

(A) they view their social roles and expectations to be threatened
(B) they have detected symptoms that they fear to be potentially serious and life-threatening
(C) their fears are not matched by their capacities to take meaningful action
(D) there is increased opportunity for secondary gain
(E) they view their personal desires to be threatened

256. The length of the typical physician-patient interaction time is

(A) correlated with patient satisfaction
(B) positively correlated with patient compliance
(C) about 15 min for office-based specialists
(D) about 15 min for office-based internists
(E) about 15 min for office-based pediatricians

DIRECTIONS: Each group of questions below consists of lettered headings followed by a set of numbered items. For each numbered item select the **one** lettered heading with which it is **most** closely associated. Each lettered heading may be used **once, more than once, or not at all**.

Questions 257–261

Match the body language behaviors below with the correct interpretation.

(A) Not willing to enter into a communicative interaction
(B) Angry, hostile, or upset
(C) "I'm interested in you. Notice me"
(D) Assertive and domineering
(E) Submissive and fearful

257. Stroke one's own hair, rearrange clothing, push hair away from face

258. Lower the eyebrows

259. Visually notice someone but then quickly withdraw visual contact

260. Cross arms and press knees together

261. Reach up and touch one's own throat

Questions 262–266

Match the statements or descriptions below with the appropriate forms of nonverbal communication.

(A) Facial expressions
(B) Emblems or symbols
(C) Illustrators
(D) Self-manipulators
(E) Display rules

262. Movements that amplify or emphasize verbal communications

263. Movements involving one part of the body doing something to another part of the body

264. General universality in occurrence and meaning

265. Body movements that transmit a highly specific message

266. Sex difference in recognition and use

Communication and Interaction
Answers

241. The answer is B. *(Gatchel, 2/e. pp 185–190.)* Low rates of compliance appear to result from defective relationships between patients and health care providers. The most crucial element in the physician-patient relationship is the nature of role expectations that each has and the congruence and mutuality of such expectations. The exchange of information and facts, similarity of ages, social class differences, and patient rewards are relevant at times but are usually of less importance than the congruence of expectations between the physician and the patient.

242. The answer is D. *(Gatchel, 2/e. pp 188–189.)* Variables in communication were found to be most important when mothers consulted physicians about their children. Also, mothers rated their satisfaction as higher when they were provided with information and discussion that met their expectations, including an expected diagnosis or a discussion of causes of the illness. Physicians perceived as understanding and caring provided greater satisfaction, while those perceived as efficient and businesslike provided less satisfaction.

243. The answer is C. *(Kaptein, pp 24–25.)* Significant behavioral interventions have been devised to help moderate a patient's anxiety and distress over anticipated surgery or other threatening medical procedures. In addition to the patient's concern about the disruption of his or her normal routine, travel to the hospital, time off from work, child care arrangements, and so on, there are very real worries about the surgical procedures themselves and their outcome. Information about the procedures to expect, complications that can occur, other patients' experiences, and medications that may be necessary are usually important and helpful to the patient, but studies have demonstrated that information about the sensory experiences that will be or can be associated with the procedure is the most helpful. This allows patients to evaluate the threats realistically so that they are not overwhelmed by unexplained and unfamiliar feelings and sensations that might be misinterpreted by the patient as dangerous sensory signals.

244. The answer is E. *(Gatchel, 2/e. pp 200–202.)* The opening statement in initiating an interview with a patient is important and sets the tone as well as direction of the interview. It is important to learn directly from the patient why he or she has come and to state what you know in a frank and honest manner, recognizing the information the patient has given and encouraging a forthright relationship. The temptation to play the role of an authority may actually inhibit the exchange of information and encourage a dependency role. In general, one must look for interactions that facilitate rather than restrict the interview. Therefore, open-ended rather than yes-or-no questions will usually allow the patient to speak more freely, provide more information, and put the patient more at ease.

245. The answer is B. *(Kaptein, pp 21–23.)* Some studies have shown that about 50 percent of patients fail to follow advice or treatment prescribed. The lowest rates for adherence (compliance) are found in situations where prophylactic medication or advice is prescribed, especially for patients with chronic diseases. Significant levels of nonadherence occur where the symptoms are not seen or felt by the patient and there are no immediate adverse consequences experienced, e.g., in glaucoma, lung cancer, diabetes, or hypertension. The quality of the patient-physician communication is one of the most important factors; the highest adherence occurs when the communication is more open and shared with sufficient opportunities to discuss ideas and concerns. Adherence is low when the information presented is extensive, complicated, technical, and easily forgotten or misunderstood. Another important factor is patients' perceived control of their own health matters (locus of control). There is less adherence if patients feel that they have almost no control and that their health is primarily influenced by external factors, powerful others, or chance. Adherence is higher if patients believe that they have a high degree of internal control and can take responsibility for their own health.

246. The answer is A. *(Wilson, 12/e. pp 2–5.)* Asking a patient "What do you think?" and then correcting or qualifying the answer is an important part of informing a patient or helping the patient to understand the illness and the prospects for the future. It is important to find out what the patient or relative thinks or knows or wants to know about the illness and to give honest answers that will leave the patient or relative with a realistic hope. It is also important to determine the patient's or relative's understanding of what you have discussed and to leave the communication channel open for further questions. A frequent error is for physicians to avoid giving any information or discussing the illness, especially the diagnosis or prognosis, by stating that they prefer not to talk about it until they have all the facts, tests, and so on. Many times the physician is fearful that he or she will only raise the patient's fear or anxiety or appear not to know what the illness is, or perhaps look bad in the patient's eyes by discussing the illness before all the data are in. Yet, the patient and family most often have a whole series of rational and irrational ideas about the illness and its prognosis that should be explored by the physician. The patient must know that the physician will be supportive, regardless of what he or she will be going through.

247. The answer is B. *(Simons, 3/e. pp 21–23.)* Transference is the development in the patient of unconscious feelings toward the doctor. It is a ubiquitous phenomenon and is most often related to past experiences and relationships with physicians or authority figures. Transference can be positive in terms of strong positive feelings toward the doctor, or negative in terms of resentment and negative feelings toward the doctor. Similarly, doctors can develop positive or negative feelings toward patients; this is called *countertransference* and is likewise related to the unconscious and to previous experiences. It is important for the physician to be aware of transference and countertransference and to understand how they can affect the doctor-patient relationship and influence the outcome of the illness and the treatment.

248. The answer is E. *(Gatchel, 2/e. pp 167–170.)* Sensory information alone (what one can expect to feel) has been found to be the most effective type of information. Coping information (e.g., teaching coping skills, ways to relieve pain and discomfort) is the next most effective because it provides the patient with some sense of control. Procedural information (what procedures will be done) makes the surgery more predictable, but does not address the sensations one should expect. The most effective reduction of stress is achieved by combining sensory and coping information so that the patient is able to predict when pain will occur, how it will feel, and how to cope with it. Studies confirm that it is important for the patient to be able to establish or retain some sense of control.

249. The answer is D. *(Vander Zanden, 4/e. pp 89–91.)* Basic emotions, as expressed by facial behavior, are relatively constant across cultures. Of the six basic emotions—happiness, sadness, anger, surprise, disgust, and fear—all the different facial expressions can be recognized and differentiated across cultures except surprise and fear, which appear to be very similar. Even though different cultures establish and teach their own "display rules" that regulate the expression of various emotions, it appears that the central nervous system of humans is genetically prewired for the expression of emotions through certain facial behaviors (fixed motor patterns). Thus, the face is a very important vehicle for the nonverbal expression of human experience and emotion.

250. The answer is C. *(Gatchel, 2/e. pp 174–177.)* Attempts to match a patient's personality style and treatment or health care style have been found to be most effective in minimizing the stressful situation of surgery and maximizing favorable medical outcomes. Patients are individuals, each with different personality dimensions and needs and with different coping styles. Extensive problem-focused information (informing about surgical procedures and sensations) will be helpful to certain patients but anxiety-producing to others. Likewise, some will respond favorably to emotion-focused information or technical medical information, but others will become anxious, confused, or upset. Family support is usually helpful, but again, it can become overwhelming. Listening to a patient and understanding a patient's personality and coping style will help the communication in this very complex process.

251. The answer is B. *(Last, 13/e. p 978.)* People evaluate and make decisions with respect to their symptoms according to a wide variety of influences. In general, two types of variables define a person's estimate of the impact of these symptoms: perceived seriousness and extent of disruptiveness. Physicians ordinarily focus most on symptoms that have serious implications for the patient's future health status. Patients more often focus on symptoms that tend to interfere in some obvious way with usual activities and routines and on the degree of discomfort rather than the amount or degree of tissue damage.

252. The answer is E. *(Gatchel, 2/e. pp 167–170.)* Behavioral intervention prior to surgery has been found to reduce both pre- and postoperative distress and to facilitate recovery. Various interventions have been compared, and it has been demonstrated that relaxation training among preoperative patients reduces distress and facilitates recovery more than hypnosis, interpersonal support, reassurance, or information about procedure. Each of these interventions, however, has been shown to be more effective than no intervention.

253. The answer is E. *(Lindzey, 3/e. pp 823–825.)* Cancer patients generally receive ambivalent responses from others in their own social support networks. Feelings are likely to be negative toward cancer patients and to arouse fear and feelings of their own vulnerability and the possibility they might catch the disease. People are often strongly motivated to protect themselves by attributing the disease to the patient's undesirable characteristics or past behavior. They also fear that any discussion about cancer or death or their negative feelings will make the patient uncomfortable. Therefore, they avoid discussing their feelings and try to assume a "cheerful" role. Under these circumstances, the frequency and quality of the time spent with the patient are most apt to decrease and a certain amount of anxiety is likely to be evoked. Because most people avoid discussing cancer, they will shy away from discussing a hopeless prognosis and will fall back into cheerful but irrelevant chatter that represents a tragic waste of what could be meaningful and quality time for both the patient and the family.

254. The answer is A. *(Vander Zanden, 4/e. pp 71–92.)* All channels of communication between persons other than the literal meaning of words spoken are designated as nonverbal communication. All the following can be considered as nonverbal communication: gesture and posture; touch; dress and grooming; physical distance; facial expression; skin color (e.g., pale, blushing); body hygiene; and even voice inflection, tone, and volume. Nonverbal communications communicate more emotions and feelings than other types of information, and they are important in placing verbal communication into a context. Physicians must be especially sensitive to nonverbal communication in order to secure the maximum communication, information, feelings, and context. It is also important to recognize that differences in cultural and ethnic backgrounds are often expressed in different nonverbal communication patterns. Touch is considered to be the most powerful of the many forms of nonverbal communication as it can communicate such messages as caring, support, and intensity of feelings. It is also regarded as having significant curing power in its own right. Furthermore, touching can communicate valuable information to the physician about the patient, such as tension, temperature, anxiety, and muscle tone.

255. The answer is D. *(Gatchel, 2/e. pp 180–185.)* What patients know, believe, and think about their illness affects the symptoms they think to be important, what they see as serious, and what they think they should do. Their social roles and personal desires often lead them to deny an illness. They often ignore symptoms for a long period before taking action. Fear about particular illnesses that may be of life-threatening character often causes them to deny the existence of the symptoms or their seriousness. Also, when their level of fear exceeds their capacity to cope, denial is a very likely result. The psychological process of secondary gain will also produce a postponement of action but is not usually associated with denial. Health educators need to help people bypass the usual hypothesis-testing of the cause of symptoms and help them take action by consulting a physician.

256. The answer is D. *(Rosen, p 344.)* Physicians frequently claim they are limited by lack of time to spend with patients, and patients cite this as one of the most important factors in their decision to change doctors. Yet research does not support this contention. The length of the physician-patient interaction is not correlated with patient satisfaction. Also, there is a negative correlation between the length of the interaction and patient compliance with treatment, with the shorter interactions resulting in higher compliance, and longer interactions yielding lower compliance. One study indicated that the average time spent with office-based internists was only 8 min, and that across specialties the average time was only 15 min. Another study indicated that the average office-based time spent by a pediatrician was 5 min. While much time can be wasted with ineffective communication, such brief encounters may not be sufficient to address important behavioral data, patient concerns, and family history, which may be at the root of the patient's health problem (e.g., smoking, environment, diet, or stress).

257–261. The answers are: 257-C, 258-D, 259-A, 260-B, 261-E. (*Vander Zanden, 4/e. pp 83–91.*) A man may straighten his hair or adjust his clothes if he wants to signal "I'm interested in you" or "notice me." Likewise, a woman may stroke her hair, adjust her clothes, check her make-up, or push her hair away from her face. These are called preening behaviors.

If we feel positive toward a person we are more apt to lean toward them, stand closer to them, and look them more directly in the eyes. By looking a stranger in the eyes once or twice, we signal that we are willing to enter into some sort of communicative interaction. If we notice someone, look at them, but then quickly withdraw visual contact, we signal that we are emitting a negative signal that we do not wish to establish a communicative interaction. This has been called *civil inattention.*

We also perceive the lowering of brows as an assertive and domineering signal and the raising of brows as receptive and submissive.

The closed body position—holding in the elbows, crossing arms, pressing knees together—is a frequent signal emitted by persons who are apt to be angry, hostile, upset, or nonreceptive. In an open body position the elbows are held away from the body, hands and arms are extended outward, legs are stretched out, and one ankle is crossed over the other knee.

Submission and fear are also communicated by body language. The submissive role tends to be represented by such actions as crouching slightly, assuming self-protective stances, reaching up and touching one's own throat, standing pigeon-toed, or not sitting until the dominant person sits.

Physicians must be able to decipher a patient's body language in order to get the full message. Nonverbal patterns signal inner attitudes and feelings, and many researchers conclude that nonverbal cues provide a more salient and valid message than verbal cues.

262–266. The answers are: 262-C, 263-D, 264-A, 265-B, 266-A. (*Lindzey, 3/e. pp 283–285. Vander Zanden, 4/e. pp 71–92.*) The ability to read and interpret nonverbal expressions is of critical importance to physicians, since such expressions reveal both intentional and unintentional feelings.

Illustrators are movements that amplify or emphasize words as they are being spoken. These can be movements of the hands to illustrate or emphasize the emotion (e.g., easy or flowing versus jerky or rapid) or they can be facial movements, called *speech illustrators,* which usually involve the brow, forehead, and eyelids to accent, emphasize, or supply emotion to words being spoken. The type of illustrator used is often related to a person's ethnic background or culture. Clinically, depressed patients have a low use of illustrators; as their depression lifts, their use of illustrators increases. Other observations include the following: there is a decrease in use of illustrators when a patient is attempting to hide his or her feelings; as illustrators decrease, the average voice pitch level increases; and, in general, people who show a high rate of illustrators are regarded by others to be outgoing, sociable, and expressive.

Self-manipulators are movements involving one part of the body doing something to another part of the body. Examples include such movements as scratching one's head, picking one's nose, wringing one's hands, and licking one's lips. They differ from emblems in that they usually occur with little awareness and are not deliberate attempts to convey a message to another person. Also, observing them can be useful to the physician in learning more about a patient, although the message is often diffuse rather than specific. Anxious patients have a high incidence of self-manipulators, and self-manipulators are often regarded as an index of discomfort of a person ill at ease or tense.

Facial expressions, as a form of nonverbal communication, appear to be universal in both occurrence and meaning, particularly in regard to the six basic emotions of happiness, sadness, surprise, fear, anger, and disgust. Cross-cultural studies have demonstrated that people display similar expressions when experiencing a given emotion, even though there are cultural and other learned variations with regard to such dimensions as stoicism or intensity of emotional response that are governed more by display rules and that can mask or conceal universality of facial expressions.

An emblem is a gesture or movement that communicates a specific message or meaning within a given culture. In the United States the following are examples of emblems: crossing the index finger and middle finger as a sign of hope that something will happen or, occasionally, to indicate one is lying; holding the hand upright with the palm outward and fingers together and moving the hand toward another person to indicate "stop"; clenching the fist at shoulder level with elbow bent and moving the hand back and forth toward another person as a sign of protest, anger, or determination to "get even" or aggression toward the other person; forming a circle by joining the end of the thumb and the index finger while holding the arm upright to indicate "OK," or agreement. A wink is considered to be a facial emblem; a head nod "yes" or "no" is a head emblem; a shrug of the shoulders is a body emblem, and so forth. Emblems do vary from culture to culture, but the emotion conveyed is generally clear. One study found less than a hundred emblems for Americans compared with a few hundred for Israelis and Iranians.

A growing body of research demonstrates that women are generally superior to men in both the reading and transmission of nonverbal facial communications. This does not appear to be innate but is related to certain child-rearing practices in which girls are encouraged to pay attention to nonverbal cues and boys are actively discouraged. When comparing four different types of nonverbal cues (facial expressions, body movements, changes in voice tone, and discrepancies between different nonverbal cues), women were clearly superior in the recognition and use of facial expressions, but showed decreasing superiority with regard to body cues and voice tone, with about equal ability to recognize and use discrepancies.

Group Processes

DIRECTIONS: Each question below contains five suggested responses. Select the **one best** response to each question.

267. According to studies of attitude change, communicators can increase their persuasiveness by

(A) discussing only one side of an issue when an audience is hostile
(B) presenting only one side of an issue when a competing persuader will get a chance to present the other side
(C) discussing one side of the argument when it is not important to achieve long-lasting attitude change
(D) de-emphasizing their own expertise
(E) allowing an audience of limited intelligence to draw its own conclusions

268. Accurate statements regarding changes that can occur in individuals' attitudes include all the following EXCEPT

(A) individuals strongly attracted to a group are less likely than other members to change their attitudes in response to facts conflicting with group norms
(B) individuals are more likely to change a privately held attitude than a publicly disclosed one
(C) attitude change is more likely to occur if individuals participate in a group discussion than if they listen to lectures
(D) the influence of a group's attitudes on an individual is weakened only if more than one person openly disagree with the group
(E) a disliked person is more persuasive in writing than on videotape

269. The view that leadership is a reciprocal process of social influence with leaders and followers being influenced by each other is known as

(A) situational leadership
(B) contingency model
(C) social facilitation
(D) collective behavior model
(E) transactional leadership

270. Social support provides all the following EXCEPT

(A) a means for interpretation of situations
(B) a good substitute for engaging in health-promoting behaviors
(C) the ability for social comparison and validation
(D) models for behavior
(E) access to significant others

271. Which of the following statements is true regarding a person's performance of a task in an isolated environment versus in the presence of others?

(A) Performance of all tasks is improved in social situations
(B) Performance of all tasks is impaired in social situations
(C) Performance of all tasks is essentially the same in social and solitary situations
(D) Performance is facilitated on easy tasks by the presence of others but impaired by such presence on complex tasks
(E) Performance is facilitated on complex tasks by the presence of others but impaired by such presence on easy tasks

272. In an emergency, all the following variables will influence a bystander to help EXCEPT

(A) perception that the other person is intoxicated
(B) proximity to the other person
(C) knowledge of what to do
(D) few others in the immediate area
(E) male gender of bystander

273. The most successful primary and secondary prevention strategy against drug abuse has been

(A) an appeal to fear
(B) education regarding the dangers of drugs
(C) affective underpinning
(D) long-term hospitalization
(E) social resistance skills

274. Persons who have social supports experience all the following results EXCEPT

(A) longer life
(B) less practice of denial
(C) fewer somatic illnesses
(D) more dependency
(E) fewer crises

275. The Hawthorne effect is best illustrated by which of the following situations?

(A) Of a group of factory workers who volunteer for a study of productivity and piecework payment, more than 80 percent quit the project because of the influence of nonvolunteer workers

(B) A group of factory workers who volunteer for such a study demonstrate an improvement in work rate greater than that associated with changed working conditions because they feel specially treated

(C) Work rate increases when workers are allowed frequent brief rest periods

(D) Productivity increases when workers have more opportunity to participate in the organization of their daily routine

(E) Although many workers initially are reluctant to have their routines changed and are suspicious of managerial motives, such changes are quickly accepted if their connection with improved working conditions is demonstrated

276. Recent evidence has indicated that a person in a group will be perceived by its members as a leader if that person's communication is

(A) high in quality, regardless of the quantity

(B) high in quality and low in quantity

(C) high in quality and high in quantity

(D) high in quantity, regardless of the quality

(E) low in quantity, regardless of the quality

277. In the study of group behavior, deindividuation has been found to produce all the following effects EXCEPT

(A) weakened restraints against impulsive behavior

(B) inability to monitor or regulate one's own behavior

(C) decreased sensitivity to immediate cues

(D) lessened concern about evaluations by others

(E) lowered ability to engage in rational planning

278. Successful leadership is most contingent on which of the following?

(A) The leadership style of a particular leader

(B) The interpersonal relationship between leader and followers

(C) The type of task situation in which a leader is involved

(D) The amount of power available to a leader

(E) The training of the leader

279. One might expect the socio-emotive leader in a group, as opposed to the task leader, to utilize primarily

(A) expert power
(B) coercive power
(C) informational power
(D) referent power
(E) political power

280. In a small group situation, departures from norms are most likely to be tolerated if

(A) the group enjoys strong leadership
(B) the norms have been stated frequently and clearly
(C) there is consensus and cohesion
(D) a dissenting member possesses resources or talents prized by the group
(E) the setting is private

281. Studies on attitude change show that people are LEAST strongly influenced by

(A) facts and information
(B) comparison of their own attitudes and beliefs with those of others
(C) their own personal and social needs
(D) the need to reduce unpleasant motivational states
(E) the attributes of the communicator who is recommending change

Group Processes
Answers

267. The answer is C. *(Vander Zanden, 4/e. pp 194–204.)* Hovland, Janis, Kelley, McGinnies, and McGuire drew a number of conclusions concerning effective communication. For instance, the most effective communicators are those perceived to have both high expertise and credibility. With very intelligent audiences, communicators are more effective if they let their audiences draw their own conclusions; with other audiences, they achieve more attitude change by stating their conclusions explicitly. One-sided arguments are most effective when audiences start out agreeing with the communicator or when there is little chance that an audience will be exposed to the other side of an issue. Although one-sided arguments may be immediately effective, the resulting attitude change is not always enduring. Nevertheless, the studies demonstrated that communicators can increase their persuasiveness by presenting one side of an argument when the audience is generally friendly, or when their position is the only one that will be presented, or when they want immediate, though temporary, opinion change.

268. The answer is D. *(Vander Zanden, 4/e. pp 194–204.)* Publicly held opinions are much more resistant to persuasive effects than are privately held opinions. In his action-oriented research, Kurt Lewin argued that group discussion and decision-making are much more conducive to attitude change than simply listening to the same information from speakers and lecturers. Solomon Asch's dramatic research on conformity demonstrated that a majority opinion could lead an individual to give erroneous responses on very simple perceptual tasks. However, Asch also showed that this majority power could be considerably weakened by the presence of even a single individual who openly disagreed with the majority. Other investigators studying group influence have shown that members who are most strongly attracted to a group are least likely to be swayed by communications that are inconsistent with group norms. A likable communicator is more persuasive in changing attitudes if the communication is on videotape or audiotape rather than written. On the other hand, a disliked communicator is more persuasive with a written message.

269. The answer is E. *(Lindzey, 3/e. pp 501–504.)* The transactional view of leadership is of a reciprocal process of social influence. The leaders are both directing the followers and being influenced by them. The focus is on the perception of and the relationship between the leaders and followers. Other important considerations in the transactional model are whether followers perceive the leader's position as legitimate or illegitimate, whether leaders perceive their groups in a positive or negative light, and the nature of the task faced by the group. This transactional view relates directly to the doctor-patient relationship and aids in achieving optimal communication. It is much more complex and interactive than former views, such as the situational view it replaced. The situational theory regarded the task faced by the group and the general situation within which it must operate as the most important factors, rather than the personality traits of the leader or group members as even earlier theories had proposed. The contingency model of leadership analyzes effective leadership in terms of two major factors: the leader's personal traits or characteristics and certain features in the situation that play an important role in the leadership process. This model is consistent with the transactional view but attempts to restrict the more fluid components by identifying task-oriented authoritarian leaders and contrasting them with less directive, warm, and relaxed leaders. The situational factors are the leader's personal relationships with other group members, the clarity of the group task, and the power of the leader over the group members. Social facilitation refers to the effects on performance caused by the presence of others; that is, the presence of certain persons can both facilitate and impair the performance of the group on a particular task. Collective behavior refers to the actions of unrelated persons who happen to be at the same place at the same time and who are responding to the same stimuli. Examples would be commuters waiting for a bus or train, persons fleeing a burning building, or persons at the scene of an accident. Under these conditions, group behavior and leadership may be quite different from that of organized or intentional gatherings.

270. The answer is B. *(Lindzey, 3/e. pp 820–826.)* Studies on the effects of social support have demonstrated that social support provides the ability for social comparison, for interpretation of situations and feelings, and for modeling behaviors and is a mechanism for access to significant others. Social comparison or social validation provides an important source of information on how others experience the same phenomenon. The social support group helps patients interpret their situation, their feelings, and what is happening to them. Members of a support group in a similar situation can also serve to model behaviors so patients can learn more about the meaning and appropriateness of their own behaviors. Support groups also provide easy access to significant others so that the patient can maintain and enhance personal relationships. Patients without social support are more apt to increase their reliance on drugs or other substances and have less motivation to engage in health-promoting behaviors.

271. The answer is D. *(Lindzey, 3/e. pp 492–496.)* Social facilitation has the effect, in minimal social situations, of improving individual task performance on easy or familiar tasks and of deteriorating performance on more difficult tasks. In general, social facilitation produces an increase in activation levels. Increased arousal level usually results in improved performance on familiar tasks but tends to inhibit the acquisition of new skills or performance on tasks that are complex and unfamiliar.

272. The answer is A. *(Lindzey, 3/e. pp 956–959.)* Many people avoid taking action in an emergency situation. The farther away the bystander is and the more people present, the less likely is a bystander to get involved. One is more apt to help the more one knows what to do, the fewer people present, if one is a male, if the victim does not appear to be responsible for his or her mishap (e.g., stroke victim vs. drunk), if the negative consequences to the bystander are minimal and the positive consequences reasonable, if the bystander's freedom is not limited by helping, if the bystander is somehow forced to get involved, if someone else is acting as a helping model, and if the victim is dependent or without resources or has helped the bystander in the past. Altruism is most easily learned through positive reinforcement and imitation.

273. The answer is E. *(Last, 13/e. pp 778–780.)* Over the past 25 years, a number of programs for prevention of drug abuse have been tried. Even though most of them have a high "face validity," the appeal to fear, drug education, attempts to understand our affective selves, and long-term hospitalization have proved to be relatively ineffective in preventing initial or repeated drug dependency and abuse. The teaching of social resistance skills has been more effective than any of the other strategies. The development of general social skills for managing social interactions and overcoming social pressures to use and abuse drugs has shown 35 to 75 percent effectiveness compared (on 2-year follow-up) with 15 to 25 percent for other methods.

274. The answer is D. *(Lindzey, 3/e. p 859.)* Social support serves to buffer and protect healthy and ill persons from the negative effects of crisis and change. It also helps them with the coping and adaptation process. They live longer, have fewer somatic illnesses, possess higher morale, and have a more positive mental health. The physiologic impact of social support appears to affect cardiovascular disease; that is, it appears to affect positively serum cholesterol, catecholamine responses, and severity of coronary artery lesions. Most recently, an association has been found between social support variables and cancer. The pathophysiologic mechanisms mediating this relationship are not yet identified. Social support encourages independence and self-confidence and less denial since coping and adaptation are more effective.

275. The answer is B. *(Rosenthal, 2/e. pp 112–113.)* In a piece of classic research at the Hawthorne plant of the General Electric Company, it was found that participation by employees in a special research project had a greater effect on work output than did any of the changes in pay scales, rest periods, and working conditions that the investigators initially wished to study. This phenomenon, in which research participation has greater influence on behavior than do the particular manipulations involved in the investigation, became known as the Hawthorne effect. It suggests that one of the most effective forms of social influence results from making individuals aware that they have been selected for special attention. Such influence is used in a wide variety of social investigations, including most forms of experimental research.

276. The answer is D. *(Lindzey, 3/e. pp 505–507.)* The more actively individuals participate in a group, the more they will be perceived as group leaders. This is found to be true regardless of the quality of participation, apparently because quality and quantity indicate different things to group members. Although quality gives some indication of the ability of the contributor, quantity is seen as an index of motivation. Persons who are regarded as highly motivated toward the group are likely to be perceived as the leaders of the group by its members.

277. The answer is C. *(Lindzey, 3/e. pp 27, 57.)* Deindividuation is a psychological phenomenon that exists in groups where the presence of many other persons appears to weaken the restraints against impulsive or wild behavior, such as destructive vandalism, mob violence, or looting. Their sense of self-awareness is reduced, thus reducing their restraints against impulsive behavior or decreasing their ability to monitor their own behavior. Anonymity, whereby a person feels submerged in a large, undifferentiated group, appears to be the most influential factor leading to a state of reduced self-awareness and deindividuation, thereby allowing the individual to engage in impulsive behavior. Other factors contributing to deindividuation are feelings of close group unity (which act as an external stimulus), a high level of arousal (which can be physiologic or emotional), and a focus on external events and goals (which detracts from or overpowers internal control and rational behavior). Various studies have demonstrated that the psychological results of deindividuation are a weakened restraint against impulsive behavior, inability to monitor or regulate one's own behavior, a lessened concern for evaluations by others, and a lowered ability to engage in rational planning and other cognitive processes. Studies also show that instead of blocking out or decreasing their sensitivity to immediate cues, as might be expected, people actually experience an increase in sensitivity and reaction to these immediate cues and their current emotional state.

278. The answer is B. *(Lindzey, 3/e. pp 513–516.)* In his contingency theory of leadership, Fred Fiedler presents three situational factors that are important for predicting both leadership style and who will be an effective leader. Of these factors, he considers leader-group relationships the most important, that is, whether the leader is liked by the members of the group. Another situational factor is the type of task structure—whether the requirements of a situation are clear or ambiguous, for example. To complete the definition of a leadership situation, the power available to a leader must also be determined.

279. The answer is D. *(Vander Zanden, 4/e. pp 444–445.)* Exercising influence on the basis of one's status as an expert may further successful completion of the task confronting a group but runs the danger of increasing the social distance between leader and group members, a consequence that would be of more concern to a socioemotive leader than to a task leader. Coercive power may achieve compliance, but only at the expense of a leader's rejection by the group. Informational power, like expert power, also would be more consistent with the task leader's purposes than with the socioemotive leader's, again because of the distancing produced by these power sources. Political power can be utilized with considerable persuasion but is distracting and can compromise a group's cohesion and motivation. Referent power, by appealing to shared elements among group members, generally tends to promote closer relationships between leader and follower than do the other forms of power. Thus, referent power is the primary form of social power available to a socioemotive leader.

280. The answer is D. *(Vander Zanden, 4/e. pp 218–234.)* Group members may wish to ignore a norm if it is burdensome or a source of punishment. Norm rejection is more easily achieved in the absence of enforcement and more readily tolerated if the rejecting member possesses strengths and abilities needed by the group. A norm that has been frequently and clearly stated is more difficult to avoid because members cannot then claim ignorance or misinterpretation. The threat of censure or punishment is a strong deterrent to violation of group norms, especially if the group is very cohesive and if the setting is one of privacy.

281. The answer is A. *(Vander Zanden, 4/e. pp 194–203.)* Many studies have been done on the impact of group influences on attempts to change people's attitudes and behavior. These studies view people as social beings with considerable dependence on others to provide them with knowledge about the world and about themselves. Persuasive facts and information are not nearly as effective in changing attitudes as are attempts to satisfy various personal and social needs, the need to reduce unpleasant motivational states, and the process of comparing one's own attitudes and beliefs with those of others. Other group factors that influence attitude and behavior include the communicator's credibility, the patterns of communication, and other attributes of the communicator and the situation.

Family and Community

DIRECTIONS: Each question below contains five suggested responses. Select the **one best** response to each question.

282. All the following statements about fertility and attitudes toward childbearing in the United States are true EXCEPT that

(A) the percentage of young married women who did not plan to have children more than tripled between 1967 and 1973
(B) infertility is personally more serious for women than for men
(C) the age of greatest fertility for women is from 15 to 20 years
(D) in approximately one-third to one-half of infertile marriages it is the man who is sterile
(E) about 10 percent of married couples below the age of 40 will have no children

283. Adolescent delinquency in boys can be predicted most accurately on the basis of

(A) IQ
(B) physique or body type
(C) family size
(D) socioeconomic status of parents
(E) relationship with parents

284. Effective parental discipline of children requires all the following EXCEPT

(A) consistency—no significant change in expectations should occur through time
(B) follow-through—parents should pay attention to the child's response to discipline
(C) immediate feedback—the quicker the consequences of an action are experienced, the more learning takes place
(D) self-disclosure—children need to know that parents are human and make mistakes
(E) corporal punishment—when accompanied by love, this is the only truly effective discipline

285. Most mental health care authorities agree that the recent trend toward community-based treatment of patients who have emotional disorders, as opposed to their incarceration in public mental institutions, can be ascribed principally to

(A) improved therapeutic results when treatment is available within a patient's community
(B) the development of preventive measures for various mental illnesses
(C) the use of new drugs that allow many emotionally disturbed patients to function outside an institution
(D) an increasing willingness by general hospitals to accept mentally disturbed patients
(E) the 1961 report of the Joint Commission on Mental Illness and Health, which strongly recommended community mental health programs

286. All the following statements about the development of independence during adolescence are true EXCEPT that

(A) sex differences in the age at which independence is achieved tend to be greater in societies whose economy depends on the male's physical strength and motor skills (e.g., hunting and herding versus food-gathering cultures)
(B) compared with the majority of other cultures, independence training in contemporary America begins relatively early but also is relatively protracted
(C) in general, the shift of parental attitudes toward permissiveness that occurs during adolescence is greater in fathers than in mothers
(D) in general, authoritarian parental attitudes are viewed by adolescents as more appropriate in fathers than in mothers
(E) confidence and self-esteem are enhanced by parental attitudes that encourage autonomy yet express interest in an adolescent's behavior and opinions

287. A Stanford University community health education study evaluated the effects of an educational campaign on reduction of cardiovascular risk factors. One community was exposed to mass media education, another received both mass media education and behavior modification training, and a third served as a control group. The most impressive results included which of the following?

(A) Cigarette smoking, egg consumption, and cholesterol levels declined equally in both test communities

(B) The control community made important achievements

(C) The mass media campaign plus the behavioral modification training achieved the most significant results

(D) It is better to focus on one public medium of communication at a time

(E) The mass media campaign had the most impact

288. All the following statements about child abuse are true EXCEPT that

(A) fathers abuse their children more often than do mothers

(B) child-abusing parents often were abused by their own parents

(C) prematurely born children are more often abused than are normal-term children

(D) parents are more likely to abuse one "scapegoat" child than to abuse all their children

(E) younger children are more often abused than are older children

289. Which of the following hypotheses can LEAST account for reported inconsistencies between the attitudes people express and their actual behavior?

(A) Attitudes often are measured very imprecisely

(B) Norms, expectations, and situational demands can alter people's readiness to behave in accordance with their attitudes, while leaving unchanged the basic underlying attitude

(C) Attitudes are more often based on education and knowledge

(D) Attitude questionnaires often measure orientation toward some general category, whereas behavioral assessments often involve only one facet of that category

(E) Attitudes and behavior are reciprocally influential

290. Women with high rates of heavy drinking include each of the following EXCEPT

(A) young women with small children

(B) women with alcoholic husbands

(C) employed women in stressful occupations

(D) women with a high rate of amenorrhea

(E) women in the presence of men

291. The most efficacious way to actually reduce automobile accidents and deaths among teenagers is to

(A) provide driver education
(B) raise the legal age for drinking
(C) increase insurance costs (increase the penalty for reckless driving)
(D) raise the legal age for driving
(E) require use of seat belts

292. All the following statements are true about those 75 years of age or older EXCEPT that

(A) 10 percent have never had a child
(B) 68 percent of women are widows
(C) 23 percent of men are widowers
(D) 9 percent of women are divorced or never married
(E) 9 percent of men are divorced or never married

293. The two main functions of the family in America today are which of the following?

(A) Socialization of children and nurturance and security of adult personalities
(B) Achievement of economic security and regulation of sexual behavior
(C) Socialization of children and regulation of sexual behavior
(D) Achievement of economic security and perpetuation of lines of inheritance
(E) Perpetuation of lines of inheritance and stabilization of adult personalities

294. The loss of a mate is often followed by a loss of all the following EXCEPT

(A) social validation
(B) decision-making responsibility
(C) task performance
(D) social support
(E) social protection

295. The most consistent parental behavior found in cases of child abuse is

(A) inconsistency in discipline
(B) employment of harsh mental punishment
(C) rejection
(D) parents treating the child as they were treated by their parents
(E) persuasiveness

296. Ethnocentrism is the

(A) belief that ethnic groups should remain geographically segregated
(B) tendency to think that one's own group or way of life is preferable or superior
(C) belief that ethnic groups should not intermarry
(D) belief that values held by marriage partners should be in accord
(E) belief that multiple cultural practices should be incorporated into marriage and the family

297. Research results show that all the following statements are true EXCEPT that

(A) married persons have a significantly longer life expectancy than nonmarried persons, especially when compared with formerly married persons
(B) separated or divorced men have a much higher admission rate to state and county psychiatric hospitals than do married men
(C) widowed women have a higher admission rate to state and county psychiatric hospitals than do widowed men
(D) widowed women have a higher admission rate to state and county psychiatric hospitals than do separated or divorced women and never-married women
(E) death rates for heart disease and cancer of the respiratory tract are twice as high for divorced white men compared with married white men

298. Absence of the father in the home has all the following effects on children EXCEPT that

(A) it has a more detrimental influence on the child's personality in early development than when the absence occurs after 5 years of age
(B) for male children, absence of the father because of divorce, separation, or desertion is not as detrimental as absence because of death
(C) for female children, the earlier the absence of the father, the more mothers are apt to display overprotection
(D) in cases of absence of the father because of divorce, adolescent girls actively and aggressively seek the attention of men
(E) in cases of absence of the father because of death, the reaction of adolescent girls is active avoidance of male peers and a preference for other girls as companions

299. The percentage of married women who were employed rose from 5.5 percent in 1900 to what percentage in 1987?

(A) 26 percent
(B) 36 percent
(C) 46 percent
(D) 56 percent
(E) 66 percent

300. Research on the relationship between marital success and the birth order of the partners shows that all the following are true EXCEPT

(A) first-born male and later-born female partnerships have high marital success
(B) first-born male and first-born female partnerships have low marital success
(C) youngest male and youngest female partnerships have low marital success
(D) later-born male and first-born female partnerships have low marital success
(E) middle-born male and middle-born female partnerships have a higher chance of success

301. The most common reason for cohabitation outside of marriage is

(A) temporary convenience
(B) trial marriage
(C) permanent alternative to marriage
(D) overt and covert rebellion
(E) experimentation with a new lifestyle

302. Daughters of mothers who were employed during some period of the daughters' childhood or adolescence tend to do all the following EXCEPT

(A) aspire to a career outside the home
(B) pursue a more feminine occupation
(C) aspire to more advanced education
(D) get better grades in college
(E) have less stereotyped views of female roles

303. A greater likelihood of marital adjustment and stability exists

(A) the lower the social class of the couple
(B) the younger the couple are when they marry
(C) if the two are of different levels of intelligence
(D) the higher the educational level of the couple
(E) if the wife has a higher educational level

304. An early study by Pauline Bart looked at the "empty nest" syndrome. Subsequent studies of this syndrome have shown that women who have launched their last child most often report

(A) a less meaningful existence
(B) more feelings of depression
(C) less positive self-concepts
(D) less stress
(E) fewer social activities

DIRECTIONS: Each group of questions below consists of lettered headings followed by a set of numbered items. For each numbered item select the **one** lettered heading with which it is **most** closely associated. Each lettered heading may be used **once, more than once, or not at all**.

Questions 305–308

Select the type of parental behavior that would be expected to result in each of the types of children characterized below.

(A) Cold-rejection with autonomy-permissiveness
(B) Warmth-acceptance with autonomy-permissiveness
(C) Cold-rejection with control-restrictiveness
(D) Warmth-acceptance with control-restrictiveness
(E) None of the above

305. Dependent, extremely cooperative with peers and adults, does not show extreme behaviors

306. Rebellious, acting-out behaviors, patterns of delinquence

307. Passive, shy, follower, anxious to win approval of peers and adults

308. Self-centered, often "spoiled," inadequate impulse control, relationships with peers impaired

Questions 309–312

The ethnic background of the family may have a significant influence on children's school success. For each pattern of school performance, select the ethnic background with which it is most closely associated.

(A) Black
(B) Jewish
(C) Chinese
(D) Hispanic
(E) Native American

309. Children tend to show good verbal abilities but relatively poorer numerical scores

310. Children tend to show consistently high skills in reading, numerical, and spatial activities, but poorer performance in verbal areas

311. Children tend to show more skill in verbal tasks and poorer performance on problems of reasoning and spatial relations

312. Children tend to perform better on spatial tasks and more poorly on tasks of verbal ability

Questions 313–316

For each description relating to community health, choose the factor with which it is most closely associated in the United States.

(A) Personal income
(B) Economic and social class structure
(C) Age
(D) Religious beliefs
(E) Health beliefs

313. The nature and distribution of health care services

314. The overall health status of an individual

315. The widest gap between need and provision of health care services

316. The perception of patterns of disease and their relative importance

Family and Community

Answers

282. The answer is C. *(Kammeyer, pp 288–321.)* Ultimately, about 10 percent of all couples will have no children. In the 1960s only about 1 percent of all couples preferred to remain childless; however, between 1967 and 1973 the proportion of wives who stated they did not expect to have children more than tripled from 1.3 percent to 4 percent. There is also strong evidence that those who do have children will have fewer in the future because of sociocultural changes, such as the increase of women in the work force and the delay in starting one's family. One study showed that in 1968, 41 percent of the public declared their ideal number of children to be four or more, whereas by 1974, the ideal of four or more children was professed by only 19 percent. Fertility problems and the possibility of not having children are more personally serious for women than for men because the mother role is more basic to a woman's sense of self. Until recently, it has been generally assumed that the inability to conceive was the "fault" of the woman; however, it is now estimated that about one-third to one-half of all infertile marriages are due to the sterility or other problems of the man. The fertility rate in both women and men is related to age. Women reach their highest potential fertility from about age 18 to age 25. After the mid-20s there is a gradual decline in fertility until age 35, when there is a sharper decline to age 49. Male fertility also declines with age, but the decline is not as rapid or as definite.

283. The answer is E. *(Conger, 4/e. pp 529–531.)* The nature of an adolescent boy's relationship with his parents is the single factor most predictive of juvenile delinquency. In the most extensive study of the subject, J. G. Bachman found that the better a boy reported he got along with his parents, the less likely he was to engage in delinquent behavior. Other studies have found that delinquency is related to overly severe and overly lax home discipline as well as to an atmosphere of mutual hostility and rejection between parents and children. Despite the widely held belief that most delinquents come from broken homes, recent evidence indicates that the incidence of delinquency among boys of unhappy, though intact, homes is greater than that among boys of broken homes.

284. The answer is E. *(Schuster, 2/e. pp 373–374.)* The most effective parental discipline of children uses several basic principles that apply in all situations to all children. If properly used, these principles help children by guiding them toward the goal of becoming self-actualized, self-directed, socialized adolescents and adults. Parental expectations must be consistently maintained through time. The principle of follow-through entails parental attention to the child's response to discipline. If a certain form of disciplinary punishment is stated, then it must be carried through. Discipline should be paced with the maturational level of the child. The quicker the consequences of an action are experienced, the more learning takes place. This is the principle of immediate feedback. Delayed consequences are usually ineffective in changing behavior. Adults must be truthful with children at all times. Effective child-rearing practices involve mutual trust. Children need to feel that their parents are human and fallible just as they are. They need to know that parents often can and do make mistakes. The most important principle of discipline is genuine love. Adults and parents who really love their children rarely fail in raising autonomous, socialized, self-actualizing children. Genuine love is not an accident; it must be learned and pursued.

285. The answer is C. *(Kaplan, 6/e. pp 144–145.)* The old approach of treating mentally ill people in large, isolated institutions is becoming outmoded largely because of the effectiveness of new psychotropic drugs that enable many disturbed persons to function normally. The success of these drugs resulted in the recommendations in 1961 of the Joint Commission on Mental Illness and Health to increase the use of community facilities in treating mental illness. Congress passed the Community Mental Health Centers Act in 1963 to provide funds for the construction of community mental health centers. As a result, general hospitals became more active in mental health therapy and community mental health centers developed to support mental patients in a functional atmosphere, in addition to taking steps at a local level to prevent mental illness. Cuts in the federal budget over the past 10 years have significantly restricted the programs and reduced the number of community health centers. As a result many of the patients who have regressed while in the community are not receiving the much needed social support, vocational counseling and training, a paying job, or psychiatric treatment. Thus, the potential benefits from new medications have been lost because of a failed public policy of deinstitutionalization.

286. The answer is C. *(Conger, 4/e. pp 195–212.)* Most societies stress independence more in male than in female adolescents; however, the sex difference is greatest in hunting and herding cultures. Independence training in American culture begins early but is prolonged, leading to the phenomenon that Erik Erikson has termed the "psychosocial moratorium." In contemporary America, parents usually shift toward more permissive attitudes as their child matures; however, this shift is more pronounced in mothers than in fathers.

287. The answer is C. *(Gatchel, 2/e. pp 306–307.)* The Stanford University community health education study evaluated the relative effects of an intensive multifactor health education campaign on the reduction of cardiovascular risk factors. The study developed a multimedia campaign to encourage people to lose weight, increase exercise, stop smoking, and change their diet. One town was exposed to a large-scale mass media campaign, another received the mass media campaign coupled with behavioral modification training for high-risk individuals, and a third served as a control community. Both test communities decreased cigarette smoking, egg consumption, and cholesterol levels. The community with the mass media campaign plus behavioral modification training achieved the most impressive results. The findings of the study clearly indicate that health beliefs and attitudes can be modified in natural settings as well as in research laboratories. Two problems were emphasized: the powerful countervailing pressures in society that promote smoking and eating of nonnutritional foods and the resistance to change created by the sedentary state of our highly automated society.

288. The answer is A. *(Conger, 4/e. pp 194–202.)* Certain children are singled out for abuse by their parents; these children frequently were born prematurely and were slower to develop than were their siblings. Child abuse is committed most often on children below the age of 3. A principal finding in studies of the personality of parents who abuse their children is that such parents usually were abused by their own parents. Mothers abuse their children more often than do fathers, probably because mothers have more contact with their children. Most children who are abused come from poor homes and their families tend to be socially isolated. About 1 million children are maltreated each year; this maltreatment accounts for 2000 to 4000 deaths each year.

289. The answer is C. *(Vander Zanden, 4/e. pp 174–182.)* For many reasons, attitudes are never measured precisely. For example, test items may be ambiguous, or respondents may attempt to describe themselves in more favorable, rather than more accurate, terms. Behavior may be consistent with attitudes if situational norms and expectations favor consistency, but not if they do not. Researchers often use questionnaires that tap attitudes toward some general category, but measure behavior toward only one aspect of that category. Thus, a researcher might devise a scale to measure attitudes toward blacks, then ask respondents to pose for a picture with a specific black person. In a recent discussion of the attitude-behavior controversy, H. A. Alker has suggested that consistency may itself be an individual variable—that is, some people may show more consistency between attitude and behavior than others. In general, attitudes influence and are influenced by three components: the cognitive, the affective, and the behavioral.

290. The answer is E. *(Rosen, p 39. Wilson, 12/e. pp 2146–2151.)* Studies of the drinking habits of women have found that the highest rates of heavy drinking are among young women with small children, women with alcoholic husbands, and employed women, especially women in stressful occupations. On the average, women tend to drink less than men, but in the presence of men they tend to drink even less. Effects of high ethanol intake particular to women include amenorrhea, decreased size of ovaries, absence of corpora lutea with associated infertility, and spontaneous abortion.

291. The answer is D. *(Rosen, p 16.)* While behavior change is most often the most effective means of promoting health, technological or regulatory measures can be more successful in certain instances. If the goal is to reduce automobile accidents and deaths among teenagers, raising the legal age for driving is more effective than driver's education or encouraging the use of seat belts. Raising the legal age for drinking or adding punitive insurance costs will have some reducing effect, but not as much as raising the legal age for driving. An aggregate strategy of mixing education, technology (safety devices), and regulation is the most effective.

292. The answer is A. *(Hazzard, 2/e. pp 146–154.)* A significant number of the elderly do not have a close family member on whom they can rely. Sixty-eight percent of women and 23 percent of men at the age of 75 or older are widowed. In addition, 9 percent of the women and 9 percent of the men are divorced or have never married. Add to this the 20 percent of the 65-and-older population who have never had a child and an increasing number who have outlived their children, and it becomes apparent that the elderly do not have the family resources to help them in failing health. This is particularly true for women, who are at much greater risk of being a widow and of living alone. Neighbors and friends can help but do not approach the level of help of family.

293. The answer is A. *(Conger, 4/e. pp 160–189.)* The American family has progressively lost a number of its previous functions, such as educating its offspring and serving as a center of recreational activity. Two major functions are left to the family: socialization of offspring and stabilization of adult personalities. The influence of parents during their children's early years suggests that socialization is still one of the family's primary functions, despite the fact that other agencies (e.g., schools) have attempted to take over some aspects of this task. The second function, that of stabilization of adult personalities, is accomplished when men and women succeed in adjusting themselves to roles of parental responsibility and sharing nurture and security. The changes occurring in marriage, women's roles and child care and the factors of poverty, single-parent families, divorce, and remarriage are having a major impact on the socialization function, and particularly on the function of nurturance and security of adult personalities.

294. The answer is B. *(Lindzey, 3/e. pp 823–825.)* There is an increase in mortality following the loss of a mate and the subsequent bereavement. The loss of a partner leads to a deficit in the areas of social validation, social support, task performance, and social protection. The loss of social validation means loss of support for one's confidence in one's own judgments, assessments, and appropriateness of ideas and behavior. The survivor also recognizes the loss of routine and special tasks that were provided by the deceased. The loss of social support and unconditional positive regard seriously reduces a major source of self-esteem and self-regard. Not only is there a great deal of disruption, but it often fosters a sense of helplessness. Decision-making responsibility is increased, even though a sense of helplessness may occur. There are dramatic increases in health risks, such as those of suicide, accidents, alcohol and drug dependency, and tuberculosis.

295. The answer is A. *(Lerner, Human Development, pp 295–297.)* Studies on child abuse have found that inconsistency in discipline is the most common parental behavior. Also, abusive parents often use harsh physical punishment in controlling their children. Another repeatedly observed finding is that abusive parents tend to have been abused by their own parents. This creates a generation effect whereby the harsh discipline practices of one generation may serve as a model for the next generation. Thus physicians attempting to work on cases of child abuse should focus on breaking the cycle of parental behaviors for one generation. Many child-abusive parents may be rejecting and cold toward their children, but they are more apt to be overcontrolling than permissive.

296. The answer is B. *(Vander Zanden, 4/e. pp 409–410.)* Ethnocentrism is the tendency to consider one's group or way of life (usually national or ethnic) superior to other groups and to use one's own group as the frame of reference against which other groups are judged. Americans are sometimes considered ethnocentric because of the relative isolation of American families from persons of different cultures and their ways of life. This can often cause us to have a very narrow view of marriage and family life.

297. The answer is C. *(Last, 13/e. pp 687–695.)* There are significant relationships between marital status and health status. The married have a significantly longer life expectancy than the nonmarried, especially when compared with the formerly married (widowed, divorced, or separated). Married persons have less chronic illness, especially mental illness, than the formerly married and make fewer requests for health care service. Children raised in single-parent families have more illness and make more demands on the health care service system than children in families where both parents are present. Death rates comparing divorced and married white men show that divorced white men have twice as many deaths from heart disease and cancer of the respiratory tract as married white men. Separated or divorced men have a higher admission rate to state and county psychiatric hospitals. Widowed men have a higher admission rate to state and county psychiatric hospitals than do widowed women, but widowed women have a higher admission rate than separated or divorced women and never-married women.

298. The answer is B. *(Lerner, Psychology, pp 596–598.)* Research on factors that influence children's personality development has often been directed at studying the effects of the absence or withdrawal of specific factors. Thus, to understand the effects of the absence of the father from the home, situations of separation, desertion, divorce, or death have been studied. Results have shown that the effect on the child's personality depended on the sex of the child and the timing of and the reason for the father's absence. A father's absence during a child's early development has a more detrimental effect than when the absence occurs after the child is 5 years old. For males, the absence of the father caused by death is not as detrimental as absence caused by divorce, separation, or desertion. For females, absence of the father caused by death seemed to interfere more with overall adjustment than for males. Absence of the father alters the interaction of adolescent girls with other males, producing one of two extreme reactions. In cases of absence caused by divorce, girls actively and aggressively seek social and physical attention of men. In cases of absence caused by death, however, girls are more apt to react with avoidance of male peers and a preference for other girls as companions. Other studies have shown that the absence of fathers from either divorce or death caused girls to express more insecurity about their ability to relate to males: divorce more often led to overinvolvement, and death typically led to avoidance. Also, the earlier the absence of the father had occurred, the more mothers were likely to have displayed overprotection. Other studies of boys with absent fathers showed a tendency for conflict and uncertainty as to appropriate masculine orientations—sometimes resulting in a "supermacho" role as overcompensation and in other instances a more feminine orientation.

299. The answer is D. *(Last, 13/e. pp 571–572.)* In 1900, 20 percent of all adult women were in the labor force. Married women and women with children in the labor force significantly increased so that by 1972 there were 40 percent and by 1987 there were 56 percent in the work force. Fifty-six percent of married women with children are employed and married women with children under the age of 2 represent the fastest growing group in the work force. In 1950, 1.5 million families were headed by women, compared with 11 million in 1988, and 88 percent of these women are in the work force. The poverty rate of these families maintained by women is three times the rate for all families. The gender wage gap continues to exist and most women are still trapped in traditional women's jobs, which fosters job insecurity and job-related stress and health problems. These conditions are gradually changing for the better.

300. The answer is D. *(Schuster, 2/e. pp 352–353.)* Research indicates that the combination of birth orders of partners in terms of marital success is as follows: high marital success is associated with first-born male and later-born female, later-born male and first-born female, and middle-born male or female and any birth order. Medium marital success is associated with only child, male or female, with first-born. Low success is associated with first-born male and first-born female, youngest male and youngest female, and only child male and only child female. Obviously, birth order is only one of many factors involved in adjustment to adulthood and to marriage, but it is important to recognize that children within the same family have different social learning experiences and differential reinforcement of behavior patterns, which, among other factors, can foster independence, leadership, dependence, or other characteristics and interpersonal skills.

301. The answer is A. *(Kammeyer, pp 160–178.)* Cohabitation, usually defined as an unmarried male and an unmarried female living together, has become more frequent in recent years. It is especially evident on college and university campuses (where most of the research on this phenomenon has been conducted), but it is also becoming more common in other communities in the United States. The most frequent reason for cohabitation is as a temporary matter of convenience or choice without any necessary commitment to marriage. The second most frequent reason given for cohabitation is as a "trial marriage" in which couples may anticipate marriage but live together to test compatibility or to await more favorable personal circumstances for marriage. Another reason for cohabitation is as a permanent and lasting alternative to marriage. Although cohabitation generally involves persons in their late teens and in their twenties, increasing numbers of people in their thirties and forties are cohabitating, particularly after a divorce or separation. Overt or covert rebellion plays a role in a small minority of cohabitations, as does experimentation with a new life-style.

302. The answer is B. *(Lerner, Human Development, pp 573–574.)* One of the most consistent and well-documented correlates of vocational departure from traditional feminine roles is maternal employment during childhood and adolescence. Daughters of mothers who were employed during some period of the daughters' childhood or adolescence generally aspire to a career outside the home, aspire to more advanced education, get better grades in college, and have less stereotyped views of female roles than do daughters of nonworking mothers. Also, daughters of working mothers are more apt to choose a traditionally masculine occupation than those of nonworking mothers. Daughters of working mothers have a broader definition of the female role and are more likely to emulate their mothers and more often name their mother as the person they aspire to be like. Working mothers also appear to promote independence rather than dependency in their daughters. Thus, it has been shown that family settings having particular characteristics can promote the development of vocational roles that vary from the traditional.

303. The answer is D. *(Kammeyer, pp 245–247.)* There is a greater likelihood of poor adjustment in marriage and higher potential for subsequent divorce the younger people are when they marry. When women marry in their teens and men marry under the age of 22, they are about twice as likely to obtain a divorce as persons who marry when they are older. In general, the lower the social class of persons marrying, the less stable the marriage. Persons from upper-class backgrounds are more apt to have marriages that are better adjusted and less prone to divorce, possibly reflecting higher financial resources. Also, the higher the educational level, the greater the marital adjustment and stability. A higher educational level is also correlated with a later age at marriage and a higher income. Marital stability appears to be negatively affected when the educational level of the wife is higher than that of the husband. Difference in intelligence and difference in education are not necessarily concomitant as lack of education is not proof of lack of intelligence. The dangers of differences in intelligence are that the partners may grow apart, intellectual isolation may be unsatisfying to the one with superior intelligence, and they may discover that intellectual stimulation and exchange of ideas can be as important as emotional and physical stimulation.

304. The answer is D. *(Kaplan, 6/e. pp 47–48.)* An earlier study by Pauline Bart argued that the role of full-time mother leaves women in a difficult and depressed state when their children reach adulthood and leave home. This was designated as the "empty nest" syndrome. Subsequent studies have shown that this conventional wisdom is misleading; that women report less stress; that many newlyweds visit or telephone their parents, use their cars, and so on; that with delayed marriage, getting children to leave home is becoming a bigger problem; that middle-aged women who had not launched their children reported much less positive self-concepts than those who had, especially in interpersonal relationships; and that, in general, women look forward to the freedom and opportunity acquired by having their children launched. The increase in divorce at this age is more often related to the departure's unmasking of an empty marriage than to the empty nest syndrome.

305–308. The answers are: 305-D, 306-A, 307-C, 308-B. *(Lerner, Human Development, pp 282–285.)* Most parental behavior can be categorized somewhere between the four extremes of warmth-acceptance versus cold-rejection and autonomy-permissiveness versus control-restrictiveness. In general, warm-accepting parents provide understanding and emotional support, respond positively to a child's appropriate behaviors, express physical affection, and provide an explanation for their disciplinary actions. The cold-rejecting parent demonstrates the opposite behaviors. Restrictive-controlling parents typically impose a large number of rigidly enforced rules involving almost every aspect of the child's behavior. They expect obedience, no "back talk," and no aggression. Parents who engender autonomy-permissiveness are the opposite. Most parental behavior can be categorized as a combination of these more extreme positions. Various studies have found that when the more extreme cold-rejection is combined with autonomy-permissiveness, the children are more apt to show acting-out behaviors, rebelliousness, and patterns of delinquency. They also are apt to be "loners," immature, and have emotional problems thought to result from excessive freedom, noncaring parents, and feelings of rejection.

Combining warmth-acceptance with autonomy-permissiveness is more apt to result in children who are self-centered and "spoiled" and who have inadequate impulse control and impaired ability to get along with their peers. This is thought to result from combining freedom with emotional concern; i.e., the parents combine an unwillingness to set limits for their children and love.

Cold-rejection with control-restrictiveness is associated with conforming and submissive children who are more passive, shy, and anxious to win and maintain approval of peers and adults. The children do not feel warmly loved or accepted by their controlling and distant parents and do not appear to develop the independence and self-sufficiency they need to be leaders rather than followers.

Combining warmth-acceptance with control-restrictiveness produces many of the characteristics described for cold-rejection with control-restrictiveness, except that the children perceive their parents as loving and concerned, but perhaps too overprotective, leading to dependence and extreme cooperation with peers and adults. They are often regarded as model children, not too compliant or too rebellious, too loud or too quiet, just moderate, but not generally independent or creative.

Most authorities stress that parents should provide an atmosphere of warmth-acceptance coupled with moderate autonomy-permissiveness that would allow and foster traits of responsibility, self-initiative, achievement, goal direction, and independence. Another generalization from research is that inconsistency of parental discipline has a detrimental influence on a child's personality and social development.

309–312. The answers are: 309-A, 310-C, 311-B, 312-D. *(Lerner, Human Development, pp 236–243.)* In our society, one of the best predictors of school success is the family's position in the social structure. Middle-class children are much more successful in school than are children from the lower social classes. The ethnic background of the family may have a significant influence on children's school success. On studying verbal abilities, general reasoning skills, numerical abilities, and spatial relations skills of Chinese, black, Jewish, and Hispanic first-grade children, it was found that Chinese children tend to show consistently high skills in reading, numerical, and spatial tasks but poorer performance in verbal areas. Black children tend to show good verbal abilities but relatively poorer numerical abilities. Jewish children tend to show more skill in verbal tasks and poorer performance on problems of reasoning and spatial relations. Hispanic children tend to perform better on spatial relations and poorer on tasks of verbal ability.

313–316. The answers are: 313-B, 314-A, 315-C, 316-E. *(Williams, SJ, 3/e. pp 51–71.)* Several major characteristics of a community are directly related to health status and to health care systems or other approaches devised to meet perceived health needs. The nature and distribution of the present system of medical care in the United States are products of a political process determined in turn by economic and social class structure. These determinants of the health care system place power in a community's dominant individuals to decide how and to whom health services are distributed.

Personal income has a direct relationship to health. Such critical measures of community health as maternal mortality, prenatal and infant mortality, life span, disability, and hypertension are worse in all age categories among people who are poor. Unlike the affluent, the poor cannot buy good health services. When the data are adjusted for health status, the lower socioeconomic groups still have fewer visits to physicians than do higher socioeconomic groups. Primary care programs reach less than one-third of the medically underserved.

The elderly at every income level in every social class demonstrate a proportionally higher need for health services than do other population groups. Increasing expenditures for Medicare relate to increasing costs. The elderly and the poor continue to suffer disproportionate neglect on the basis of income, needs, and services available.

People's perceptions of their own health status can be influenced by sociocultural factors, including their particular community's technologic prowess. Indeed, all these factors shape a person's attitude toward health, an attitude that, in turn, eventually governs that person's response to his or her own health needs and use of the health services available. Level of education and income is related to the use of preventive services and preventive behavior.

Sociocultural Patterns of Behavior

DIRECTIONS: Each question below contains five suggested responses. Select the **one best** response to each question.

317. The F-scale developed by Theodore Adorno and coworkers was intended to be a measure of

(A) fear
(B) fixation
(C) frustration
(D) fascism
(E) none of the above

318. Behavioral signs and symptoms of alcoholism include all the following EXCEPT

(A) conservative religious practice
(B) problems on the job
(C) patterns of accidents
(D) marital difficulties
(E) driving-related difficulties

319. The risk for hypertension is greatest among

(A) whites of lower socioeconomic status
(B) blacks of lower socioeconomic status
(C) whites of higher socioeconomic status
(D) blacks of higher socioeconomic status
(E) upwardly mobile middle-class whites

320. Dieting induced by social and cultural pressures results in all the following EXCEPT

(A) a raised basal metabolic rate
(B) hormonal changes that promote fat storage afterwards
(C) net long-term weight gain
(D) plateaus in the process of weight loss
(E) increasingly compulsive strategies in the pursuit of an ideal weight

321. Biologic responses are most adversely influenced over time by

(A) regressiveness
(B) interpersonal conflict
(C) confusion
(D) uncontrollability
(E) fearfulness

322. All the following are characteristics of heavy alcohol drinkers in college EXCEPT

(A) they tend to come from large metropolitan rather than rural areas
(B) they are more likely to major in the social than the natural sciences
(C) they tend not to be deeply religious
(D) they use nonalcoholic drugs less frequently than nondrinkers
(E) their parents are more likely to use alcohol

323. An important therapeutic aspect of *curanderismo* often lacking in Western scientific medicine is the

(A) ability to "cure" psychosomatic illnesses
(B) cultural congruence between healer and patient
(C) extensive use of symbolism
(D) laying on of hands
(E) use of herbal preparations

324. In comparing the effects of consumption of alcohol on Caucasians and Asians, Caucasians exhibit all the following EXCEPT

(A) a higher rate of alcoholism
(B) lower levels of acetylaldehyde
(C) more reactivity of heart rate and blood pressure
(D) less subjective discomfort
(E) less facial flushing

325. A *social norm* is best defined as

(A) a rule
(B) average behavior
(C) an individual's expectations of another
(D) shared expectations about behavior
(E) recommended behavior

326. Each of the following statements about minorities and the use of alcohol and the incidence of alcohol problems is true EXCEPT

(A) Asian Americans tend to drink less than non-Asian Americans
(B) rates of alcoholism among Hispanic Americans tend to be higher than the national average
(C) when American Indians enter an urban environment, the rate of alcoholism becomes much worse
(D) alcoholism among blacks appears to be increasing
(E) the incidence of alcoholism among homosexuals appears to be greater among females

327. The most effective method of reducing racial prejudices in an individual is through

(A) interracial contact
(B) introducing black studies into elementary school curricula
(C) psychotherapy for black-white confrontations
(D) improving the black image in the mass media
(E) campaigns to counteract stereotypes

328. Considering the characteristics of the population over age 65, all the following statements are true EXCEPT

(A) the older population has been getting larger
(B) the older population is expected to level off in numbers by the year 2000
(C) about 5 percent are residents of nursing homes
(D) the female population has increasingly outnumbered the male population
(E) of the 85-and-older segment, the number of men per 100 women is expected to decrease from about 45 to about 39 by the year 2000

329. A person becomes more vulnerable to conditions of psychological and physical distress if he or she is

(A) aware of results of diagnostic tests
(B) receiving medical information
(C) denying the illness
(D) introspective
(E) receiving counseling

330. The basic technology of Native-American medicine uses all the following EXCEPT

(A) drugs
(B) surgery
(C) religious or spiritual practices
(D) blood-letting
(E) mineral springs bathing

331. Studies of pain response among different American ethnic groups disclosed that, for disorders of equivalent objective severity, the degree of open and vocal response to pain was greatest in which of the following groups?

(A) "Old American" and Jewish
(B) Italian and Jewish
(C) Irish and "Old American"
(D) Jewish and Irish
(E) Italian and "Old American"

332. In comparing alcohol consumption in women and men, each of the following is true EXCEPT that

(A) women and men who are heavy drinkers are equally susceptible to alcohol-related morbidity and mortality
(B) at comparable levels of alcoholism, alcoholic women would pose a greater cost to society
(C) in mixed company, women drink less
(D) the amount of alcoholism among men is greater
(E) social norms display less tolerance of heavy drinking in women

333. Ethnic differences in response to pain are attributable primarily to

(A) differences in pain threshold
(B) differences in subjective experience of pain
(C) intellectual ability to grasp the significance of a disease
(D) cultural traditions of stoicism or emotionalism
(E) experimental bias

334. All the following statements about teenage use of alcohol are true EXCEPT

(A) 80 percent of teenagers (12 to 17 years of age) report having tried alcohol
(B) since 1966, the number of high school students who report they become intoxicated at least once a month has doubled from 10 to over 20 percent
(C) more than 30 percent of teenagers report they drink alcohol once or twice a week
(D) 3 percent of male high school seniors report they drink alcohol each day
(E) nearly 80 percent of male high school seniors report that they drink at least once a month

335. The World Health Organization has stated that the most serious worldwide drug problem is use of

(A) cocaine
(B) alcohol
(C) marijuana
(D) amphetamines
(E) opium

336. Research has established all the following gender-related differences in development EXCEPT

(A) females have greater verbal ability
(B) females are more emotional
(C) males have better visual-spatial skills
(D) males excel in mathematical skills
(E) males are more aggressive

337. The basic symbol of Chinese-American medicine is the

(A) mandarin hat and coat
(B) dragon
(C) dog
(D) snake
(E) yin-yang

338. In Talcott Parsons's formulation of the "sick role," which of the following statements is true?

(A) The sick person has the right to refuse to cooperate in the process of getting well
(B) The sick person has the right to be defined as "not responsible" for his or her condition
(C) The sick person has the right to take advantage of any secondary gains involved in being sick
(D) The sick person has the right but not the obligation to define the state of being sick as undesirable
(E) None of the above

339. Among spiritual healers, the most common theory of disease is that

(A) disease is a spiritual malaise resulting from sinful acts
(B) disease results from psychological stress
(C) disease is caused by parapsychological phenomena
(D) disease is caused by germ-mechanical factors
(E) disease is caused by invasion of the body by evil spirits

340. All the following statements about persons of lower socioeconomic status and their attitudes toward health are true EXCEPT

(A) their medical needs are greater
(B) they are less concerned about their health
(C) they have a chronically low utilization rate of health services
(D) their health-seeking behaviors do not change even when financial barriers are removed
(E) they are more alienated from society and medical institutions

341. Patients who are ill and facing death are LEAST likely to exhibit reactions to the loss of

(A) independence
(B) appetite
(C) self-image
(D) control
(E) financial resources

342. True statements about reporting of symptoms and seeking help for them include which of the following?

(A) Women are more likely to report symptoms
(B) Men are more accurate in their reporting of symptoms
(C) Women are less likely to seek medical help
(D) Lower social status is associated with lower reporting of symptoms
(E) None of the above

343. The factor that has the LEAST influence on the outcome of teenage pregnancy is

(A) maternal intake of protein calories
(B) maternal age at conception
(C) maternal educational level
(D) prenatal medical care
(E) paternal identity

344. Which of the following statements regarding pregnant adolescents is true?

(A) They show a positive relationship between weight gain of pregnancy and infant birth weight
(B) They retain nitrogen more efficiently than do pregnant adult women
(C) They have an incidence of growth-retarded children similar to that of pregnant adult women
(D) The birth weight of their babies is somewhat higher due to an excess carbohydrate diet
(E) Malnutrition in pregnant adolescents is rarely seen in the United States

345. Which of the following statements about infant mortality is true?

(A) Black infant mortality in the U.S. is about twice as high as white infant mortality
(B) Finland has one of the highest infant mortalities of all European countries
(C) Infant mortality in the U.S. is lower than in Canada
(D) Infant mortality in the U.S. is lower than in Spain
(E) Infant mortality in Hong Kong is higher than in the United States

346. A patient is more apt to comply with a physician's recommendations if the treatment

(A) interferes with the patient's personal behavior
(B) is rather complex
(C) is long term
(D) is expensive
(E) is for a minor illness

347. In aging, the response to lost roles or activities is most often

(A) redistribution of energy
(B) disengagement
(C) substitution of similar activities
(D) disorganization
(E) depression

348. Studies on the sexual behavior of adolescent females show that

(A) the youngest are most likely to use contraceptives
(B) an adolescent who has had an abortion is more likely to be pregnant again within 2 years than one who has given birth
(C) parental involvement in a teenager's abortion reduces the probability of subsequent unwanted pregnancies
(D) each year about 40 percent of the 1 million pregnant adolescents obtain abortions
(E) median age for initiation of sexual activity is 14

349. True statements about poverty among older groups include

(A) poverty acts as a survival stimulus and helps to persuade the elderly to adopt a healthier lifestyle
(B) Social Security policy has increased poverty among older adults in the past 2 decades
(C) in 1984 more than 40 percent of older unmarried women were in poverty
(D) women are two and a half times more likely than men to be poor or near poor
(E) the life expectancy differential between lower and middle classes has decreased with Medicare

350. True statements regarding health beliefs include which of the following?

(A) The majority of people with hypertension are able to monitor their own blood pressure with signs and symptoms

(B) Patients assign more validity to their physician's instructions than to their self-assessment of their health

(C) Patients who believe they can control their health outcome are more apt to change their health-related behavior

(D) Younger patients are more apt to believe that controlling their emotions and staying mentally active are important preventive actions

(E) Older patients place more value on vigorous exercise to promote health and prevent illness

351. When the importance of social ties for health in the elderly is compared with that in younger populations, the elderly

(A) are more apt to experience significant life changes that separate them from social connections

(B) benefit increasingly from marriage as a factor that decreases mortality

(C) are more likely to maintain multiple sources of social contacts

(D) have less of a dependence on the support of friends and relatives

(E) are more stressed when not married

DIRECTIONS: Each group of questions below consists of lettered headings followed by a set of numbered items. For each numbered item select the **one** lettered heading with which it is **most** closely associated. Each lettered heading may be used **once, more than once, or not at all**.

Questions 352–356

For each of the descriptions below, match the appropriate term.

(A) Authoritarian personality
(B) Discrimination
(C) Ethnic group
(D) Prejudice
(E) Minority

352. A group distinguished on the basis of socially or culturally acquired lifeways

353. An attitude of aversion or hostility toward members of another group simply because they are members and presumed to have the same objectionable characteristics attributed to the group

354. Denial of power, privilege, or status to members of one group whose qualifications are equal to those of the dominant group

355. Rigid, conventional thinking, highly judgmental values, and a cynical and "fascist" mind-set

356. A social aggregate or group that has hereditary membership and a high degree of in-group marriage and suffers oppression by a dominant segment

Questions 357–361

For each description below, match the most appropriate model or theory related to compliance.

(A) Defense mechanism model
(B) Health perception model
(C) Health opinion survey model
(D) Health belief model
(E) Naive health theory (common-sense model of illness)

357. Identifies aspects of the doctor-patient communication that can influence the patient's subjective perception of his or her own health

358. Asserts that the patient connects an apparently unrelated symptom with a disorder and complies only when the symptom arises

359. Measures a patient's preferences for more or less active participation

360. Links denial to recovery

361. Ties recovery and rehabilitation to a patient's perception of his or her own health

DIRECTIONS: The group of questions below consists of four lettered headings followed by a set of numbered items. For each numbered item select

A	if the item is associated with	(A) **only**
B	if the item is associated with	(B) **only**
C	if the item is associated with	**both** (A) and (B)
D	if the item is associated with	**neither** (A) nor (B)

Each lettered heading may be used **once, more than once, or not at all**.

Questions 362–365

(A) Traditional, or disease, model of alcoholism

(B) Behavioral model of alcoholism

(C) Both

(D) Neither

362. Alcoholism is a function of antecedent and consequent events

363. Alcoholism is physiologic or genetic in origin

364. Organismic variables are involved

365. Neuropsychological deficits are included in etiology and treatment

Sociocultural Patterns
of Behavior
Answers

317. The answer is D. *(Rosenthal, 2/e. pp 190–191.)* Following World War II, many social psychologists studied the causes of fascism and anti-Semitism. Theodore Adorno and coworkers developed the F-scale (for fascism), which they believed to be a measure of the authoritarian personality. Persons scoring high on the F-scale generally are very rigid in their thinking, very aware of status differences between themselves and others, highly deferential to superiors, very strict with subordinates, and generally prejudiced toward ethnic and minority groups. Such a person is seen as aligning with authority figures, protective in-groups, nationalism, and rigid moralism and to perceive most things in absolute terms.

318. The answer is A. *(Wilson, 12/e. pp 2148–2151.)* One of the most important aspects of identifying a person with a problem of alcoholism is to do an adequate social history. If the patient is having problems on the job, marital difficulties (which could also be with other members of the family), certain patterns of accidents, and driving-related difficulties, these can be considered behavioral markers for suspicion of excess drinking. There is a simple 25-item form (the Michigan Alcohol Screening Test, MAST) to be answered by the patient that explores other behaviorally related areas and is of great help in identifying the patient with alcohol-related problems. Often, the patient's complaints, such as insomnia or hypertension, can serve as a way of beginning to gain the patient's collaboration to do something about the alcohol problem. Other findings, such as multiple bouts of pneumonia, unexplained cardiac arrhythmias, cirrhosis, and pancreatitis, can also raise suspicions.

319. The answer is B. *(Gatchel, 2/e. pp 114–116.)* Genetic factors alone cannot account for the high prevalence of hypertension among various racial, social, and cultural groups. Compared with that among whites, the prevalence of hypertension among blacks is significantly higher. Hypertension is more prevalent among poor American blacks, however, than among blacks of middle and upper classes.

320. The answer is A. *(Rosen, pp 97–98.)* Dieting induced by social and cultural pressures initiates a process of biologic, cognitive, and behavioral dis-

regulation. The first effect of reducing the intake of calories is a lowered basal
metabolic rate, which does not immediately increase after the dieting has
ceased; this results in a net increase in calories and weight. Also, hormonal
changes occur after dieting, especially after severe dieting, that actually promote fat storage. Other biologic changes induced by dieting include plateaus
in weight loss, cravings, or binges, and the frequent development of increasingly compulsive strategies in attempts to lose weight. These mechanisms can
actually result in weight gain, especially over the long term, since external
pressures are generally not effective for maintenance of weight loss.

321. The answer is D. *(Lindzey, 3/e. pp 858–859.)* While fearfulness, confusion, interpersonal conflict, and regression can generate stress that can have
a direct effect on biologic responses, the loss of perceived control can take
an even greater toll on the body. Excessive workload and job responsibility
are stressful factors in terms of coronary risk, but they become even more
powerful and biologically more destructive when they approach the limit of a
person's capacity to control his or her own work. Whether the stress is from
employment, unemployment, finance, family, disease, or other factors, the
threat of loss or actual loss of control over one's being or activities appears
to be the most devastating influence. Different people also have considerable
variability in their responsiveness to a lack of or loss of control; this responsiveness then has a subsequent effect on their biologic processes.

322. The answer is D. *(Conger, 4/e. pp 428–430.)* College students who do
not drink alcohol tend to come from rural, conservative, and deeply religious
(usually Protestant) backgrounds. Heavy use of alcohol is found more frequently among social science majors from metropolitan areas, particularly
those who are pessimistic about their future. Heavy drinkers are more likely
than nondrinkers to use nonalcoholic drugs and have a higher rate of academic failure and drop-out. Their parents are more likely to drink, as well as
their friends and best friends.

323. The answer is B. *(Twaddle, 2/e. pp 175–176.)* *Curanderismo* is a
Mexican-American conception of disease that identifies imbalances of heat
and cold within the body as the major cause of disease or illness. Certain
diseases are considered hot and others cold. Hot foods (e.g., rice, pork,
beans, onions, beer, and goat's milk) are used to cure cold illnesses (e.g.,
measles and ear infections), and cold foods (e.g., lamb, corn, tortillas, peas,
cow's milk, and oatmeal) are used to cure hot illnesses (e.g., bleeding and
skin disorders). Foods and herbs are considered hot or cold on the basis of
their relationship to hot and cold forces within the body, not according to
actual temperature. *Curanderos* practice as soloists and are respected and
valued because they reflect and reinforce the culture of the *barrio*—the com-

munity. They share the same value system, norms, and symbol systems. The healer is truly of the people. This cultural congruence between healer and patient produces a close healer-patient relationship of the type that is all too rare in Western scientific medicine.

324. The answer is C. *(Linden, pp 22–24.)* Many Asians exhibit a general flushing response to the ingestion of alcohol. This aversive effect of alcohol has been attributed to genetics and results in an exaggerated sensitivity. They also have a lower rate of alcoholism than do Caucasians. Asians and Caucasians do not differ in the oxidation rate of alcohol. Many Asians, however, develop higher levels of acetylaldehyde after consumption. Japanese subjects, in particular, have been shown to develop an atypical form of alcohol dehydrogenase (ADH) enzyme that more rapidly produces acetylaldehyde, resulting in higher levels of accumulation. This particular allele is found in 85 percent of Asians and only 6 percent of Europeans. Many Asians have demonstrated a stronger reactivity in heart rate. Blood pressure, as well as facial flushing, is also increased to a greater extent than in Caucasians. And Asians report that they experience more subjective discomfort following alcohol consumption than do Caucasians.

325. The answer is D. *(Vander Zanden, 4/e. pp 213–215.)* Most sociologists consider a norm to be a shared expectation concerning the behavior of a group or a particular person in a particular role. If a norm is violated, some type of sanction or punishment generally will be imposed on the violator. Although average behavior may be considered "normal," it is not normative unless it meets shared expectations and is subject to enforcement.

326. The answer is E. *(Rosen, pp 46–49.)* Alcoholism among both male and female homosexuals is estimated to be between 20 and 32 percent. Although there is considerable variation among races and nationalities, Asian Americans tend to drink less alcohol than non-Asian Americans. They also metabolize ethanol more quickly. Rates of alcoholism among Hispanic Americans appear to be higher than the national average and are thought to be related to sociocultural norms and values. Alcoholism among American Indians and native Alaskans is high, and the rate of alcoholism becomes even higher when American Indians from reservations enter the urban environment. Alcoholism among blacks appears to be increasing with little recognition of its threat. In terms of prevention, all minority groups suffer from a lack of targeted treatment and prevention programs; they also tend not to use the few existing programs.

327. The answer is A. *(Vander Zanden, 4/e. pp 468–470.)* Racial prejudice is often so thoroughly learned that it is extremely difficult to modify. However, the most effective means of reducing racial prejudice has been found to be interracial contact. Since most black-white prejudices are formed in the context of lack of contact, prevention and attitude change can best be accomplished by multiple opportunities for blacks and whites to get to know each other. It is also important to recognize that the interracial situation should consist of equality of black-white status, a need for cooperation, very few members with negative stereotypes about each other, intimacy of interaction, and antiprejudice social norms and expectations. Introducing black studies into elementary school curricula, improving the black image in the mass media, legislating against prejudiced behavior, campaigns to counteract stereotypes, and the use of psychotherapy in treating black-white confrontation have all been of assistance in reducing prejudice but have not proved as powerful as interracial contact. There is still considerable controversy as to whether legislating against prejudiced behavior is an even more effective method of reducing racial prejudices. The old adage "a person convinced against his will is of the same opinion" still has some validity, but legislating against prejudiced behavior also has much validity. Perhaps at the interpersonal level the interracial contact is most important, while legislating has more social or societal importance.

328. The answer is B. (*Hazzard, 2/e. pp 146–154.*) The number of persons over the age of 65 has continued to increase in this century from 3.1 million in 1900 to 24.1 million in 1978. The proportion of the over-65 age group also rose from 4.1 percent to 11 percent. By the year 2000, the over-65 age group was expected to increase to 32 million and 12 percent of the population, but present declining mortality could result in 38 million and about 14 percent of the total population by the year 2000. In 1978, the over-75 age group was 38 percent of the total over-65 age group, and it is estimated that by 2003 the over-75 age group will have increased to about 47 percent. Thus more of the population has been reaching the 65-and-older age group, and living longer, and will continue to do so. Also, among the elderly the female population has progressively outnumbered the male population. The 80 men per 100 women in the 65-to-69-year-old group decreases to 45 men per 100 women in the 85-and-over population. While the 80 men per 100 women in the 65-to-69-year-old group is expected to rise slightly to 82 by the year 2000 and 83 by 2020, the men per 100 women in the 85-and-over group is expected to fall to 39 in 2000 and slightly below 39 by 2020. Only about 5 percent of the over-65 age group are in institutions (e.g., long-term facilities and nursing homes), which means that about 95 percent of the elderly are attempting to live with some measure of independence. A disproportional number of the institutionalized elderly are white (94 percent), and there are twice as many females as males.

329. The answer is D. (*Rosen, pp 13–15.*) Persons who tend to focus more on feelings and bodily changes have been shown to be more likely to experience disturbing and distressing states. Self-awareness achieved through such acts as being aware of test results and receiving medical information or counseling is positively correlated to psychological and physical health. Introspectiveness, however, emerges as the strongest predictor of distress, overshadowing all other predictors.

330. The answer is D. *(Twaddle, 2/e. p 178.)* In contrast to Western scientific medicine, practitioners of Native-American medicine never considered blood-letting to be of medical value. They have employed a wide variety of drugs, however, such as astringents, emetics, sedatives, stimulants, antibiotics, and even pharmacologic contraceptives. Mechanical treatments have included quarantine, sweat baths, bathing in mineral springs, surgery, and immobilization of broken limbs. Spiritual methods employed in Native-American medicine and carried out by a shaman include group singing, incantations, and facilitation of communication with the spirits by smoking the peace pipe.

331. The answer is B. *(Twaddle, 2/e. pp 131–132.)* Studies by Zborowski (1952, 1969) revealed that American Italians and Jews were much more likely to be open and vocal about their discomfort than were Americans of Irish or "Old American" descent (the classification "Old American" refers to persons having several generations of ancestors born in the United States). The Italians focused on the pain itself, whereas the Jews worried about what the pain portended for the future. The Irish seemed to deny the existence of the pain, whereas the "Old Americans" described the pain in detail in a detached and scientific manner. Pain was measured both by a person's subjective ratings of discomfort on a scale from 1 to 10 and by responses on a standardized questionnaire.

332. The answer is A. *(Rosen, pp 38–41.)* Scandinavian, Canadian, and American studies comparing the alcohol drinking patterns of women with those of men show that women have significantly higher morbidity and mortality as a result of alcohol consumption. For example, they are more successful with suicide and more apt to die from both accidents and cirrhosis of the liver. The more toxic effect of alcohol on the hypothalamic-pituitary-gonadal axis in women and genetic predispositions are thought to be prominent factors. Women are known to drink less than men in general, and even less in mixed company. The overall severity of alcoholism in women is less than in men. Some of this is attributed to the fact that social norms are less tolerant of heavy drinking in women. Because of the effects of alcohol on such factors as fertility, miscarriage, cirrhosis, suicide, and sexual dysfunction, the cost to society of comparable levels of alcoholism appears to be even greater for women than men.

333. The answer is D. *(Twaddle, 2/e. p 132.)* There are no ethnic differences in *threshold* for the sensation of pain. The ethnic *response* to pain, however, is highly variable and is conditioned by cultural factors. The ethnic significance and traditions of emotionalism or stoicism regarding pain are major factors in accounting for this variable response to pain.

334. The answer is D. *(Lerner, Experiencing Adolescence, pp 204–207.)* There has been a great increase in teenage use of alcohol. About 80 percent of those 12 to 17 years old report having had a drink in the past; more than 50 percent report drinking once a month; more than 30 percent drink once or twice a week; and 3 percent report drinking each day. Since 1966, the number reporting that they become intoxicated at least once a month has doubled, from 10 to 20 percent. Of the male high school seniors, 80 percent report that they drink once a month, and more than 6 percent report daily drinking. Alcohol-related accidents are the leading cause of death in those 15 to 24 years old, and 60 percent of all alcohol-related highway fatalities are among young people.

335. The answer is B. *(Hamburg, Selected Perspectives, p 207.)* Alcohol use and abuse is thought to be the most serious worldwide drug problem. It affects many millions of adult problem drinkers, as well as their families, friends, coworkers, and innocent victims of alcohol-related accidents and violence. About 50 percent of motor vehicle deaths are related to alcohol and it is estimated that about 10 percent of all deaths in developed nations are the result of misuse of alcohol. It is also a causal factor in damage to the liver and brain and is involved in some cancers. Cocaine, opium, marijuana, and amphetamines are major problems in the world, but they tend to be more localized in certain regions or cultures, whereas alcohol use is ubiquitous.

336. The answer is B. *(Schuster, 2/e. p 321.)* Many misconceptions have developed regarding gender-related differences, often to justify role stereotyping. In actuality, only four gender-related differences have been established through empirical research in the United States. The differences that have been found consistently in development are as follows: females have greater verbal ability, males have better visual-spatial skills, males excel in mathematical skills, and males are more aggressive. It is important to recognize that these are normative gender-related differences and that in normal development there is much crossing-over and overlap. In fact, research has determined that persons with a dynamic, flexible orientation toward life make the most positive adjustments to life. The interaction of sociocultural learning with individual biologic activity must obviously be considered an important aspect and modulator of the development of gender-related differences.

337. The answer is E. *(Twaddle, 2/e. pp 179–180.)* Chinese-American medicine assumes that each person has a vital force. In each person's life force there is a conflict between yin and yang, the cold and hot forces, respectively. Many treatments are associated with restoration of the appropriate balance of yin and yang. Foods and herbals are most commonly used for this purpose.

338. The answer is B. *(Twaddle, 2/e. pp 146–147.)* Talcott Parsons's formulation of society's expectations concerning the "sick role" sees that role as consisting of norms defining two rights and two obligations that are attached to persons defined as being sick. These persons have the right to be exempt from normal social activity and the right to be defined as "not responsible" for their condition. They have the obligation to define the state of being sick as undesirable, which implies that they must seek to get well and not take advantage of any secondary gains involved in being sick, such as gaining attention from others. They have the obligation to seek technically competent help and cooperate in the process of trying to get well.

339. The answer is B. *(Twaddle, 2/e. pp 172–174.)* Most spiritual healers consider disease to be a result of psychological conflicts. Stress produced by this conflict ultimately yields symptoms that are identified as a disease entity. Healers believe that the conflict and stress will be relieved once affected patients submit to the larger plan of God. Some spiritual healers explain disease as the result of original sin or the disenchantment of heavenly spirits. The parapsychological perspective speculates that there is a radical interchange of energy between body, mind, and the psychoid or Jungian collective unconscious. The healing process involves a large-scale exchange of energy and equates an emotionally charged atmosphere with energy transfer and rapid resolution of illness. Some healers recognize a germ-mechanical theory of disease in which germs cause a deterioration of physical systems and recommend that patients seek resolution of the germ problem before spiritual healing can succeed. Few spiritual healers subscribe to the notion that disease results from the invasion of the body by evil spirits.

340. The answer is B. *(Last, 13/e. pp 638–639.)* People of lower income have a chronically low rate of utilization of medical care facilities. They have a greater need for medical care and are more concerned about their health, yet they exhibit greater tolerance for or endurance of symptoms. The lower rates of utilization are often explained on the basis of the inadequate financial resources; the "culture of poverty," in which the poor are more apt to be alienated from society and medical institutions; and the barriers that the poor encounter, such as the greater distances from medical care facilities, the longer waits and impersonal care, the fragmented services, and a lack of understanding of how to use the system. An interesting finding is that the provision of financial assistance packages and improved access to prepaid programs does not significantly change the health-seeking behavior patterns. This would suggest the role of certain social, psychological, and cultural factors in the problem.

341. The answer is B. *(Hazzard, 2/e. pp 354–355.)* Patients facing the threat of death most often exhibit physical and emotional reactions to loss. The most frequent losses are of independence, self-image, control, and financial security. The loss of independence is particularly upsetting to persons who have always taken care of their own physical needs but who now need help with simple daily tasks. The dependency generated by intense pain is of great concern to dying patients. Earning power, mobility, and family or job role are also important parts of independence. Loss of self-image through change of personal appearance, weakness, disfigurement, and embarrassingly altered body function is also disturbing. Loss of control is one of the most upsetting conflicts and often results from the control and authority assumed by the medical profession. Patients often fear that they will be abandoned if they do not relinquish complete control over their lives. The loss of financial resources engendered by illness, e.g., the threat of financial hardship or loss of one's entire life savings, is also of major concern for the dying patient. Dying patients usually are not hungry and do not express concern for food.

342. The answer is A. *(Gatchel, 2/e. pp 172–173.)* The interpretation and reporting of symptoms is influenced by complex psychosocial and cultural factors. Studies comparing men and women in terms of their reporting of symptoms and their seeking help have found that women are more likely to report symptoms and to seek medical attention for them. Also, women are more accurate in reporting their symptoms. Persons of lower socioeconomic status are also more likely to report symptoms. Whether one seeks help is even more complex and depends on several intervening factors such as prior medical or psychological history, distress, social support, and economic factors.

343. The answer is E. *(Hamburg, Selected Perspectives, pp 134–136.)* It is now known that the intake of protein calories is a major determinant of the outcome of teenage pregnancy, yet many pregnant adolescents are malnourished in this regard and produce an increasing incidence of low–birth-weight babies and fetal wastage. The younger the age at conception, especially for mothers under 16 years of age, the greater the number and severity of risk factors. Postnatal medical care is important, but prenatal care has been demonstrated to be even more crucial. This is especially true from the standpoint of prevention of some risk factors that can be modified or averted. Adolescent pregnancy is positively linked to low educational status in that education is often interrupted or terminated, which significantly reduces the life options of the adolescent mother and results in low-paying jobs throughout adult life. The result is most often a single-parent household, stress, and greatly reduced educational and psychological growth. These socioeconomic and behavioral factors can result in outcomes for both the pregnant adolescent and the developing child more destructive than the potential physical and biomedical problems. The children of adolescent mothers have a higher percentage of developmental, behavioral, and cognitive difficulties than children of older mothers. While the identity of the father could play a role in terms of identifying genetic factors, transmission of sexually transmitted diseases, and potential source of marriage and support, it is not as important a factor as nutrition, age, educational potential, or prenatal care.

344. The answer is A. *(Hamburg, Selected Perspectives, pp 132–136.)* Malnutrition plays a major role in pregnancy at any age; it can be even more important, however, for a pregnant teenager, who is still growing and developing at the same time as the fetus. There are areas in all parts of the U.S. where pregnant teenagers, as well as other adolescents and children, are subjected to significant malnutrition and undernutrition. Protein-energy malnutrition and iodine and iron deficiencies are major health concerns. Socioeconomic and political factors, life-style, and ignorance play important roles. Studies of nutrition and weight gain during pregnancy have shown a strong relationship between the weight gain of pregnancy and infant birth weight. Mothers who were initially underweight and who gained less than 7 kg during pregnancy had a 40 percent risk of delivering a child of lower birth weight. Adolescent mothers had a greater risk of delivering an infant of low birth weight, and adolescents between 10 and 16 years of age delivered infants who were even more retarded in growth than those of older adolescents. Also, pregnant adolescents retain nitrogen less efficiently than do pregnant adult women.

345. The answer is A. *(U.S. Public Health Service, pp 1, 58.)* Infant mortality in the U.S. is now about one-third the rate it was in 1950 (29.2 per 1000 births in 1950 versus 10.1 in 1987). Infant mortality for both black and white births in the U.S. has decreased at about the same rate since 1950, but black infant mortality remains about twice as high as that for white infants (12.7 versus 6.6). Internationally, the U.S. ranks twenty-fourth among all countries. Japan has the lowest infant mortality of all countries (5.0 deaths per 1000 births) and is followed by Sweden, Finland, Switzerland, Canada, Singapore, Hong Kong, Netherlands, France, and Ireland. Canada ranks fifth among all nations. Availability and quality of prenatal and neonatal care are obviously major factors in comparing these countries with the United States.

346. The answer is D. *(Steptoe, pp 201–203.)* Physicians must consider the values held and conditions experienced by patients if they expect the patient to comply with recommended actions. In general, the more complex the recommended actions, the longer the duration of time required for the treatment, and the more the patient sees the treatment as interfering with his or her own personal behavior, the less complete compliance one can expect. Compliance is most often related to such factors as threat to health, disabling symptoms, social support, personal and continuous source of care, cooperative relationship with health professionals, and a knowledge of the nature and rationale for the specific treatment recommendations. The cost paid for treatment is more apt to be positively than negatively related to compliance. A major or life-threatening disease will assure more compliance, but a minor illness will result in less compliance, especially if the treatment is as inconvenient as having the illness.

347. The answer is A. *(Lerner, Human Development, pp 574–576.)* As people age or retire they can replace their old roles with new roles and activities, concentrate and redirect their energies on the roles and activities that remain, or withdraw. Redistribution of one's energy is the most frequent mechanism of coping with lost roles, activities, or capacities. This usually involves redistributing time and energies among remaining roles and activities. Problems arise, however, with those who have so few roles or activities that there are not enough to absorb the energies freed by the loss. Substitution of new roles and activities is an obvious alternative; however, substitute roles are not always available, especially if there is income decline, physical decline, or little motivation to find a meaningful substitute. Disengagement is a withdrawal from roles or activities and a reduction of activity level or sense of involvement. Disengagement is not inevitable and depends on opportunities, interests, and motivation. A form of differential disengagement, similar to redistribution, is more apt to occur. The degree of disengagement also appears to be related to the degree of perceived threat to the living conditions of the elderly and the attitudes of others toward the elderly. The balance between redistribution, substitution, and disengagement is very dependent on good health. Poor health is more apt to force a person into disengagement. Disorganization is maladaptive and infrequent. So is depression, but it is more frequent than disorganization and is much more severe.

348. The answer is D. *(Hamburg, Selected Perspectives, pp 136–138.)* With the social and biologic trends of earlier menarche, reproductive readiness, and postponed adult roles, the median age for the initiation of sexual activity has dropped from 18 to 16 years. With such social changes as those in female roles, permissive attitudes, legalization of abortion, and change of traditional family patterns, the sexual behavior of adolescents has also changed. Even though the technology and availability of contraceptives have improved, the youngest of the adolescents are less likely than older women to use contraceptives. The abortion rate increased steadily from the Supreme Court decision in 1973 until about 1979, when it began to level off. Of the approximately 1 million adolescent pregnancies each year (which has increased recently), about 400,000 (40 percent) end in abortions. Contrary to conventional opinion, it has been found that an adolescent who has had an abortion is less likely to become pregnant again within 2 years than one who has given birth. Parental involvement in a teenager's abortion does not appear to reduce the probability of subsequent unwanted pregnancies.

349. The answer is D. *(Hazzard, 2/e. pp 116–119.)* Promoting healthy lifestyles has been more effective in the most educated and older groups and less effective in less well educated and lower socioeconomic groups. Poverty also increases the incidence and prevalence of disease. It is significant that Social Security policy in the United States over the past 2 decades has reduced poverty among older adults, thus helping to reduce their vulnerability to disease. Social Security has been less successful for older unmarried women, however, as in 1984, 20 percent of them were still in poverty. In fact, women are two and a half times more likely than men to be poor or near poor. The differential life expectancy between lower and middle classes at birth is 5 years, but by the time they are elderly, the middle-class advantage has expanded to 9 years. The differential for disability-free years is over 13 years.

350. The answer is C. *(Rosen, pp 201–214.)* A person's beliefs are important determinants of preventive health behavior. Even though most patients with hypertension cannot determine when their blood pressure is abnormal, the majority believe they can. They are also more apt to believe that their own reading of symptoms and the fact of feeling better are more valid than their physician's instructions or reassurances. As a result, many patients will stop or change treatment on the basis of their feelings and symptoms. If patients have the belief that they can control their health outcome, they are more apt to try to be more successful in changing such health behaviors as smoking, diet, and exercise to prevent or to cure an illness. Older patients are more apt to believe that they can enhance their health by controlling their emotions (anger, anxiety, and depression) and staying mentally active. Younger people place more value on vigorous exercise to promote health and prevent illness.

351. The answer is A. *(Hazzard, 2/e. p 154.)* The maintenance of social connections and support has an important association with health and well-being throughout the life span. When compared with younger populations, however, elderly people are more apt to experience significant life changes such as death of a spouse and involuntary relocation. Also, the relative importance of specific social relationships may be different in the elderly. For example, marriage decreases the risk of mortality in younger populations, but seems to be less of a protective factor in older populations. Marital status is not a major predictor of mortality in the elderly because not having a spouse is a more normative experience and therefore is considered to be less stressful. The support of friends and other relatives becomes a more powerful predictor of mortality in the elderly group than in younger groups. Older groups are also less likely to maintain extensive contacts with multiple sources and will have more limited networks for support.

352–356. The answers are: 352-C, 353-D, 354-B, 355-A, 356-E. *(Vander Zanden, 4/e. pp 409, 460–465, 467–471, 490.)* An ethnic group is a group distinguished on the basis of socially acquired lifeways. The members are usually biologically related and are related on the basis of common customs or culture (e.g., Italian or Irish).

Prejudice is described as a hostile or aversive attitude toward the members of a group simply because they belong to it and are therefore presumed to have the same objectionable qualities attributed to the group. The basic factors that characterize prejudice in the dominant group are feelings of superiority; the perception that the minority group is inherently different and alien; a claim to power, privilege, or status; and a fear or suspicion that the minority group wants the power, privilege, or status of the dominant group. Also, prejudice has a cognitive component (mental image), an affective component (feelings or emotions), and a behavioral component (predisposition to act).

Discrimination is an arbitrary denial of power, privilege, or status to a group (usually a minority) whose qualifications are equal to those of the dominant group. It is important to note that prejudice may or may not be associated with discrimination.

The authoritarian personality is characterized by rigid and conventional thinking, obsession with power and submission to authority, and highly judgmental values. T. W. Adorno characterized the authoritarian personality as having a mind-set similar to that of a fascist. There does appear to be a link between prejudice and authoritarianism.

A minority group is any racial or ethnic group that has hereditary membership, a consciousness of oneness, and a high degree of in-group marriage and usually suffers oppression from a dominant (majority) segment of a nation or state. The members often find themselves disadvantaged in terms of privilege and status, and the minority is often the source of the dominant group's advantages.

357–361. The answers are: 357-D, 358-E, 359-C, 360-A, 361-B. *(Gatchel, 2/e. pp 174–196.)* The *health belief model* is useful in predicting compliance. Patients' perception of the severity of their condition and the extent to which they perceive themselves as being susceptible play a major role in whether or to what extent they will act to comply with the treatment regimen. Other factors to be assessed are patients' perceptions of the costs and benefits of compliance. The physician can use the beliefs and perceptions of patients to assist in the communication process and to predict when the patient is more apt to follow the recommended treatment.

The *naive health theory* proposed by Leventhal (also called the common-sense model of illness) asserts that many patients identify a medically unrelated symptom as being related to their disorder and they often limit their compliance to the presence of the unrelated symptom. An example would be a patient with hypertension who identifies the occurrence of a headache with the state of the hypertension. Even though objective evidence indicates that patients cannot reliably identify or predict changes in their blood pressure, the naive causal connection is made between the headaches and the blood pressure. The connection is reinforced when the patient develops a headache, measures his or her blood pressure, and indeed sees that it is elevated. The patient then reduces compliance to instances when a headache develops.

The *health opinion survey* measures patients' preferences for more or less active participation in their own health care and their preferences for a more or less informed role. Compliance is related to the degree of involvement and amount of information a patient prefers. Knowledge of these preferences allows the physician to attempt to match patients with the best treatment intervention to enhance compliance.

The *defense mechanism model* links a patient's own psychological defense mechanisms with compliance and recovery. Denial is a particularly important defense mechanism that is often used by the coronary patient. Since denial reduces stress, coronary patients who use denial in the critical care unit will experience less anxiety than those who do not. The moderate use of denial in the early phases of a myocardial infarction has been found to enhance recovery and survival. Those who use denial to an excessive extent, however, can actually endanger their recovery because they are less apt to comply with medical recommendations.

The *health perception model* is based on how patients view the status of their own health or illness. Patients who perceive their health to be poor have lower morale and are less likely to recover as rapidly and to return to work or to their pre-illness activities than are those who perceive their health as relatively good and have an optimistic view of their health. These perceptions of one's health affect compliance and suggest several interventions that can be used to modify patients' perceptions of their health, such as education, instruction, nursing care, brief psychotherapy, and other means of encouraging as realistic and optimistic a view of recovery as possible.

362–365. The answers are: 362-B, 363-A, 364-C, 365-C. *(Linden, pp 13–19.)* The behavioral model of alcoholism states that alcohol consumption and abuse are socially acquired and learned patterns of behavior. Alcoholism occurs as a function of antecedent and consequent events. These events are situational or environmental factors and involve the alcoholic's cognitive and affective states. The proponents of the behavioral model are inclined to neglect the genetic and physiologic variables.

The traditional, or disease, model assumes alcoholism to be a progressive and irreversible disease in which the alcoholic experiences an irresistible craving for alcohol with eventual loss of control over consumption. The pathogenesis is considered to be physiologic or genetic. The traditional or disease view tends to neglect the role of environmental, cognitive, and affective determinants.

Although organismic variables are more frequently cited in behavioral research, they are regarded as important in treatment programs based on both behavioral and disease models. Organismic variables include cognitive, affective, and physiologic factors. Examples of interrelated cognitive processes include the alcoholic's appraisal of his or her coping skills, the alcoholic's expectations regarding the effects of the alcohol, and the alcoholic's identification of the reason or situational factors that led to the event of taking a drink.

Neuropsychological deficits are included in the etiologic and treatment assumptions of both the behavioral and the biologic models. To date, many of the biologic factors tend to be overlooked by behaviorally oriented clinicians. For example, alcohol is neurotoxic and causes specific neuropathologic changes, so chronic abuse of alcohol can produce brain damage, resulting in cognitive impairment and deficiencies in such factors as memory, perception, motor performance, abstraction, learning, and problem solving. Behavioral treatments thus can be severely compromised if one does not consider both the biologic and behavioral components and their interrelatedness.

0- 63, 26 ?

Human Ecology and Disease

DIRECTIONS: Each question below contains five suggested responses. Select the **one best** response to each question.

366. Obesity has been well documented as a primary contributing factor in the development of each of the following diseases EXCEPT

(A) adult-onset diabetes
(B) hypertension
(C) gallbladder disease
(D) arthritis
(E) myocardial hypertrophy

367. Behavioral research on nutrition and obesity has demonstrated that all the following are true EXCEPT

(A) eating is often a response to, compensation for, or defense against tension and frustration
(B) analyzing conditions under which one usually eats facilitates weight control
(C) psychological makeup influences eating behaviors and activity levels
(D) there are consistent, identifiable personality factors common to persons who have difficulty making a satisfactory weight adjustment
(E) weight gain occurs when energy intake exceeds energy output

368. Hospital patients who are well behaved but experience a state of helplessness are

(A) more likely to try to improve their own condition
(B) less apt to withhold information
(C) apt to be more informed about their own condition
(D) invariably happy to leave the hospital
(E) less able to accomplish the transition back to normal life after leaving the hospital

369. Changes in life-style had caused a decline in each of the following diseases before the application of modern medicine and technology EXCEPT

(A) tuberculosis
(B) prostatic carcinoma
(C) rheumatic heart disease
(D) coronary artery disease
(E) stroke

370. Behavioral medicine has demonstrated significant contributions to the treatment of all the following diseases or conditions EXCEPT

(A) hypertension
(B) cardiac arrhythmias
(C) Raynaud's disease
(D) third-degree heart block
(E) asthma

371. The incidence of smoking addiction among high school seniors

(A) is more influenced by caring adults than by peer pressure
(B) can be reduced significantly by caring adults
(C) can be reduced significantly through arousal of fear
(D) exceeds the level of the general adult population
(E) occurs in an upward trend from elementary and junior high school

372. The food aversion paradigm is involved in medicine in all the following EXCEPT

(A) chronic alcoholism
(B) chronic pain
(C) Addison's disease
(D) cancer
(E) chemotherapy

373. Which of the following markers is the LEAST effective predictor of morbidity and longevity?

(A) Gender
(B) Income
(C) Psychological markers
(D) Age
(E) Marital status

374. All the following statements concerning the mechanisms of the development of coronary heart disease are currently held to be true EXCEPT that

(A) repeated excessive heart rate or pressor responses to behavioral stressors can promote arterial injury through turbulence and sheer stress
(B) increased output of catecholamines and corticosteroids is biochemically toxic to coronary arteries
(C) increased circulating catecholamines influence platelet aggregation and the mobilization of serum lipids
(D) acute behavioral stressors can raise thresholds for ventricular fibrillation
(E) disruption of central nervous system control of the heart can initiate arrhythmic activity

375. All the following statements about teenage smoking are true EXCEPT that

(A) the age for beginning smoking is decreasing
(B) the majority of female smokers begin smoking after they are 13 years of age
(C) 12 percent of those 12 to 17 years of age smoke
(D) 26 percent of those 17 to 18 years of age smoke
(E) one-third of all 18 year olds are regular smokers

Physicaly

376. Active versus inactive persons usually report all the following psychological factors EXCEPT

(A) less depression
(B) less anxiety
(C) less type A behavior
(D) more hostility
(E) more self-confidence

377. Which of the following social variables is most closely linked to infant mortality?

(A) Poverty
(B) Education of mother
(C) Education of father
(D) Occupation of father
(E) Marital status of parents

378. Use of drugs by the elderly can be characterized by all the following statements EXCEPT

(A) over-the-counter medications account for 40 percent of drugs consumed
(B) psychotropic agents surpass all other drugs consumed by the institutionalized elderly
(C) over half of patients over age 60 make one or more medication errors during each illness
(D) a high risk factor for adverse drug reactions is being a male
(E) about 25 percent of national drug expenditures is consumed by the elderly

379. General characteristics of life events found to be very important in linking stress and illness include all the following EXCEPT

(A) desirability of an event
(B) reappraisal of a threat
(C) perceived control of an event
(D) effort required for readjustment
(E) frequency of an event

380. Compared with pregnant adult mothers, pregnant adolescent mothers have which of the following characteristics?

(A) Increased rates of toxemia
(B) Fewer placental abruptions
(C) Fewer infections of amniotic fluid
(D) Similar patterns of labor
(E) Similar amounts of cigarette and alcohol use

381. Each of the following statements about sleep problems is true EXCEPT that

(A) the number of people who have a sleep problem is about 50 percent
(B) pain and trouble sleeping are the two most common complaints in medicine
(C) insomnia is the chronic inability to obtain the necessary amount or quality of sleep to maintain adequate daytime behavior
(D) there is little evidence that sleeping medication is effective for more than several days
(E) there is an excessive tendency for poor sleepers to self-medicate and for physicians to overprescribe strong sleeping pills

382. Studies of the links between psychological factors and disease states during and after World War II found all the following EXCEPT that

(A) blood pressure of Londoners increased during the initial phase of bombing
(B) survivors of concentration camps showed greater rates of physical illness
(C) survivors of concentration camps were better able to cope with cancer
(D) survivors of concentration camps showed a higher incidence of premature death following release
(E) survivors of concentration camps showed increased rates of relatively permanent problems of psychological adjustment

383. Which of the following causes a person to use the most calories per hour above basal metabolism?

(A) Bicycling (moderate speed)
(B) Walking (3 mph)
(C) Dancing (fox-trot)
(D) Swimming (2 mph)
(E) Horseback riding (trot)

384. The following statements about alcohol and alcoholism are true EXCEPT that

(A) 10 percent of men and 3 to 5 percent of women develop alcoholism
(B) the homeless or skid-row alcoholic represents over 25 percent of all alcoholics
(C) there is considerable genetic variability controlling a person's response to alcohol
(D) 10 g of ethanol is equal to about 12 oz of beer, 4 oz of nonfortified wine, and 1.5 oz of 80-proof beverage
(E) alcoholics have a carcinoma rate 10 times higher than that of the general population

385. Anorexia nervosa involves concern about all the following EXCEPT

(A) body image
(B) control
(C) achievement
(D) sexuality
(E) dieting out of control

386. Patients with metastatic breast cancer are LEAST likely to live significantly longer if they are

(A) negatively reactive
(B) depressed
(C) married
(D) able to express hostility
(E) active in a social network

387. Empirical findings about patterns of disease and illness include all the following EXCEPT

(A) a large range of symptoms (e.g., headache, upset stomach, and sore muscles) is found in the general population on any given day
(B) a very small percentage of persons experiencing symptoms of disease or illness seeks medical care
(C) individual persons show highly diverse reactions to the presence of many disease symptoms
(D) it is important for physicians to understand how patients interpret their perceived physical signs and symptoms
(E) persons are relatively independent of communication from others in deciding on the meaning of their own unexpected physiologic changes

388. True statements about the placebo effect include all the following EXCEPT

(A) it is useful in the treatment of anxiety
(B) it involves β-endorphins
(C) it is useful in psychotherapy
(D) it is an important factor in bio-feedback
(E) placebos have no effect when used in conjunction with chemically active drugs

389. True statements about alcohol abuse include that

(A) the percentage of families with problem-drinking men increases with age of head of household
(B) alcoholism is the second most frequent form of drug dependence after tobacco use in the United States
(C) the highest mortality from alcohol abuse is from accidents, followed by suicide and cirrhosis of the liver
(D) the annual cost to industry and the economy of alcohol abuse is currently estimated to be less than the cost of tobacco-related disease and death
(E) as a group, heavy drinkers of alcohol contribute more to national alcohol-related problems than does the group of moderate drinkers

390. All the following statements about hyperthyroidism are true EXCEPT that it

(A) may be the cause of a frank psychosis
(B) is more frequent in women than in men
(C) may be precipitated by acute emotional stress
(D) is associated with mental retardation in children
(E) is associated with tension and hyperexcitability

391. Behavioral prodromes of myocardial infarction and sudden death include all the following EXCEPT

(A) emotional exhaustion
(B) disregard of time pressures
(C) feelings of despair
(D) hopelessness
(E) depression

392. During the first year after myocardial infarction, the majority of patients exhibit which of the following responses?

(A) Extensive disturbances in objective state
(B) Very little physical distress
(C) Perception of selves as not handicapped
(D) Depression and anxiety
(E) Perception of selves as having returned to normal

393. Adolescents represent about 17 percent of the population (40 million citizens), yet they account for all the following EXCEPT

(A) over twice as many automobile accidents as adults
(B) 20 percent of all suicides (5000 to 7000 adolescent suicides per year)
(C) over 600,000 pregnancies in unmarried girls per year
(D) the only age group for which the death rate is actually decreasing
(E) an age group of which over 12 percent smoke

394. Research studies support all the following findings about the health consequences of smoking behavior EXCEPT

(A) average life expectancy is decreased by 5 to 6 years
(B) most deaths caused by bronchitis/emphysema are smoking-related
(C) most deaths caused by lung cancer are smoking-related
(D) lung cancer deaths are actually decreasing for women
(E) most deaths caused by cancer of the oral cavity are smoking-related

395. The leading cause of death in the elderly (age 65 and older) is

(A) cancer
(B) cerebrovascular disease (stroke)
(C) suicide
(D) heart disease
(E) chronic obstructive pulmonary disease

396. The antidepressant effects of exercise have been linked with all the following EXCEPT

(A) increased cerebral blood flow
(B) increased levels of epinephrine and norepinephrine
(C) sense of mastery and self-control
(D) cathartic inhibition
(E) positive self-image

397. Studies of birth weight of human infants show all the following to be true EXCEPT

(A) black mothers give birth to small babies (2500 g or less) at a higher rate than do white mothers

(B) the most significant characteristic associated with a poor outcome of pregnancy is low birth weight

(C) babies of low birth weight, when compared with heavier babies, are likely to have a greater rate of developmental problems (epilepsy, cerebral palsy, mental retardation)

(D) the most frequently cited factors contributing to low birth weight are lack of prenatal care, poor nutrition, smoking, stress, and poor physical condition

(E) the geographic regions in the United States achieving lower-than-average birth weights in 1988 were New England and the Pacific region

398. Statistics on adolescent suicide show all the following patterns EXCEPT

(A) boys are three times more likely to commit suicide than are girls

(B) adolescents account for 6000 of the 28,000 suicides committed in the United States each year

(C) boys tend to choose more violent methods for committing suicide than do girls

(D) between 1970 and 1980, the suicide rate for teenage boys decreased

(E) schizophrenia may underlie the suicide

399. In a clinical setting, the diagnosis of alcoholism is made when a patient does all the following EXCEPT

(A) ignores early warning signs that alcohol is causing problems in marriage and moves ahead to separation or divorce

(B) is fired or laid-off as a result of alcohol-related problems

(C) demonstrates evidence of a preexisting antisocial personality disorder

(D) is arrested two or more times for an alcohol offense

(E) demonstrates signs of alcoholic withdrawal

DIRECTIONS: The group of questions below consists of lettered headings followed by a set of numbered items. For each numbered item select the **one** lettered heading with which it is **most** closely associated. Each lettered heading may be used **once, more than once, or not at all**.

Questions 400–403

For each condition, select the factor with which it is most significantly associated in the United States.

(A) Poverty
(B) Aging
(C) Heredity
(D) Religion
(E) Race

400. Sickle cell anemia

401. Phenylketonuria

402. Osteoarthritis

403. Dental decay

DIRECTIONS: The group of questions below consists of four lettered headings followed by a set of numbered items. For each numbered item select

A	if the item is associated with	(A) **only**
B	if the item is associated with	(B) **only**
C	if the item is associated with	**both** (A) and (B)
D	if the item is associated with	**neither** (A) nor (B)

Each lettered heading may be used **once, more than once, or not at all**.

Questions 404–409

(A) Unipolar depression
(B) Bipolar (manic depressive) disorder
(C) Both
(D) Neither

404. Women are affected two or three times more often than men

405. Average age of onset is about 30 years

406. There is recurrence about four times during the next 20 years after it first appears

407. Disturbances of mood, energy, appetite, sleep, and sexual function are seen

408. A detectable psychosocial precipitant usually exists

409. A spectrum of depressive illness is involved

Human Ecology
and Disease

Answers

366. The answer is C. *(Rosen, pp 72–73.)* Obesity increases risks for both physical and psychological disorders. It has been well documented as a primary contributing factor in the development of adult-onset diabetes, hypertension, myocardial hypertrophy, arthritis, gout, menstrual abnormalities, and reproductive problems. It is also a secondary contributing factor in endometrial cancer. It is related to gallbladder disease, but primarily on a correlational basis.

367. The answer is D. *(Wilson, 12/e. pp 411–417.)* Fat will accumulate only when the intake of energy exceeds the output of energy. The major causes of obesity have been found to be social, environmental, psychological, economic, ethnic, cultural, racial, genetic, metabolic, endocrinologic, and nutritional. Although studies have not identified any consistent personality factor common to obese persons, the psychological makeup of obese persons has a definite influence on their difficulty in making a satisfactory weight or diet adjustment. Some behavioral factors include life-style, life adjustment, emotional support, anxiety relief, substitute for love and security, response to or defense against tension and frustration, availability of food, comfortable environment, linking of food and hospitality, eating habits, decreased activity, and conditions under which one usually eats. Analysis of these factors and programs to change these behaviors have been found to facilitate weight control.

368. The answer is E. *(Gatchel, 2/e. pp 163–165.)* Helplessness is based on the belief that one cannot meaningfully affect what happens. Thus, when hospitalized patients feel helpless, they are less likely to try to improve their own condition, they are less informed about their own condition, and they are more apt to withhold information that might even be helpful. As helplessness does generalize, they will be less able to feel that they can cope with the transition back to their normal life out of the hospital. They are often reluctant to leave the hospital, especially after an extended stay. Helplessness will also inhibit decision-making and such patients are often unwilling or unable to make decisions.

369. The answer is B. *(Hazzard, 2/e. pp 129–134, 167–170.)* Medical technology and modern medicine (primarily pharmaceutical) have clearly contributed to the decline of certain diseases, but changes in life-style and, in some instances, environment have had the greatest impact on the major diseases over time. Infectious diseases were already declining decades before the discovery of antibiotics. Tuberculosis declined throughout the century before specific antimicrobial agents were introduced. Rheumatic heart disease was also declining because of better living conditions before penicillin was discovered. The decline of coronary artery disease was effected by life-style changes before acute coronary care and intensive care units, coronary artery bypass surgery, and angioplasty were developed. Likewise, cerebrovascular disease, or stroke, has been declining since about 1915. The life-style changes that have had the most effect on these and many other diseases are those involving diet (e.g., consumption of fats and salt), smoking, exercise, stress, environmental toxins, and the prevention and reduction of hypertension. While carcinoma of the prostate is the third most common cause of cancer mortality in men, its etiology is unknown and treatment seems to have little success on mortality. To date, it has not been associated with life-style, although environmental factors have been implicated.

370. The answer is D. *(Schneiderman, pp 243–249.)* Behavioral methods have been developed to treat both the psychological and physiologic aspects of many diseases that have been formerly regarded as exclusively organic. Of the treatments for cardiovascular diseases, those for hypertension and arrhythmias have successfully benefited from behavioral interventions. In hypertension (particularly mild hypertension), relaxation procedures have been effective in controlling pressure and producing a decrease of 5 to 12 mmHg. Arrhythmias can be regulated by biofeedback and relaxation in some patients, and heart rate can be controlled in most patients. Heart block cannot be controlled, particularly third-degree heart block, in which neural control of heart rate is not possible. However, behavioral intervention can be a judicious adjunct to drugs and other treatments. Raynaud's disease (and migraine headache) can be effectively treated with temperature biofeedback and relaxation procedures. Asthma has been treated in some patients by relaxation, self-control, and stress control. Placebo effects are also helpful. Asthma and hypertension, as well as many other diseases, can be treated effectively with behavioral intervention and conjoint use of drugs and other treatments.

371. The answer is E. *(Rosen, pp 22–30.)* Peer pressure has been found to be more influential than any adult involvement in pre-adult smoking behavior. Even well-intentioned adults are often labeled as adult "naggers." Smoking often begins in elementary school, but most significantly in junior high school, and continues in an upward trend into high school, where by the senior year smoking addiction approaches the level of that in the general adult population. Arousal of fear has not been shown to be very effective in attempts to educate youth against smoking, alcohol use, or drug abuse.

372. The answer is B. *(Kandel, 3/e. pp 1001–1002.)* Food aversion (also called *bait shyness* in animals) is a basic biologic process in which persons learn to avoid poisoned substances. The person develops an aversion to food that is followed by nausea produced by a poison. The food aversion paradigm has been applied to the treatment of chronic alcoholism when alcohol is followed by a powerful emetic such as apomorphine. The same mechanism appears to be involved when a person with Addison's disease becomes conditioned to avoid diets deficient in salt and diets that produce malaise. Certain forms of cancer also produce malaise that induces food aversion and depressed appetite. The nausea following chemotherapy for cancer also produces an aversion to foods tasted before the treatment. Anticipatory nausea can also occur before chemotherapy through conditioning mechanisms, so that the sight of the clinic, smell of the clinic, or even anticipating the visit can induce nausea.

373. The answer is C. *(Rosen, p 8.)* The social and economic characteristics of a population, such as income, education, and marital status, are better predictors of morbidity and longevity than biologic or psychological markers. Sex and age, however, are the exceptions. Over the life span, the frequency of disease and mortality increases. Also, women retain an advantage of approximately 8 years over men in longevity.

374. The answer is D. *(Weiss, Stress, pp 44–54.)* Behavioral factors influence the development of coronary heart disease through the cardiovascular or endocrine correlates of sympathetic-adrenal-medullary and pituitary-adrenal-cortical activity. The following mechanisms are currently considered to be most involved: (1) behavioral stressors can promote arterial injury through hemodynamic forces, such as turbulence and sheer stress caused by repeated physiologic reactions of excessive heart rate and pressor response; (2) biochemical sources of injury may exert toxic influences on coronary arteries through behaviorally caused increases in endocrines such as catecholamines and corticosteroids; (3) increased circulating catecholamines may affect atherogenesis through influences on platelet aggregation and on the mobilization of serum lipids; (4) acute behavioral stressors can lower the thresholds for ventricular fibrillation; and (5) central nervous system control of the heart can initiate arrhythmic activity, potentially precipitating sudden cardiac death.

375. The answer is B. *(Lerner, Experiencing Adolescence, pp 200–202.)* Twelve percent of teenagers 12 to 17 years old smoke, which increases to 26 percent for those 17 to 18 years old. About one-third of all 18 year olds are regular smokers. While the teenage smoking rates appear to be decreasing, it may be that only the older group has leveled off. It is important to recognize that the age for beginning smoking is decreasing, especially for females. Sixty percent of the female smokers begin smoking before they are 13 years of age.

376. The answer is D. *(Rosen, pp 119–120.)* Studies of males involved in aerobic-type exercise and jogging have reported a significant reduction in anxiety, depression, and hostility when these males are compared with sedentary controls. They have also reported greater self-confidence. Type A males also showed a reduction in type A patterns of behavior. Biologic stress-reducing factors that could influence such psychological factors are the usual reduction of circulating catecholamines and the increase in β-endorphins occurring during exercise.

377. The answer is A. *(Last, 13/e. pp 1114–1116.)* Poverty, the most important social variable in infant mortality, is linked to an almost 50 percent greater risk of both neonatal and postnatal death. Other social variables—such as the educational level, occupation, or income of either the mother or father, or whether the parents are married—can influence the risk of infant mortality, but none is as powerful as poverty. Poverty is also a major contributor to adult morbidity and mortality.

378. The answer is D. *(Hazzard, 2/e. pp 201–202.)* Treatment with multiple medications is a major health problem in the elderly and enhances the hazard of complications from those drugs. About 90 percent of the elderly take at least one medication and the majority take two or more. Forty percent are over-the-counter drugs. It has also been found that over half of patients over age 60 make one or more medication errors during each illness. Psychotropic agents surpass all other drugs consumed in long-term care facilities (in 75 percent of institutionalized patients as opposed to 35 percent of ambulatory patients). The highest risk factors for adverse drug reactions, in addition to use of multiple drugs, include being a woman; this risk is most frequently attributed to small body size. Although only 12 percent of the American population is over age 65, this group consumes 20 to 25 percent of the total national drug expenditure. This is expected to increase in the future.

379. The answer is B. *(Gatchel, 2/e. pp 69–72.)* The stress of various life events or changes is known to correlate highly with the development of various illnesses. Not all life events are of equal importance, but three general characteristics of important life events have been identified: desirability of an event, control, and required adjustment. If an event is highly undesirable, it is more stressful. If a person feels very little or no control over the event, it is more stressful. Likewise, an event is more stressful if a great amount of effort is required to cope with it. The frequency of a threatening or stressful event can be linked to an illness, not necessarily through the severity of the threat, but through its chronic or "hassle" effect. Reappraisal is an ongoing process, but not a general characteristic linking the stress of life events to illness.

380. The answer is A. *(Hamburg, Selected Perspectives, pp 134–136.)* More than 1 million adolescents become pregnant each year, and mortality related to childbirth is one of the five leading causes of death for this age group. While it is suspected that physiologic immaturity accounts for some of the increased risk, this has not been demonstrated. There is a clear increase in the rate of toxemia (of unknown cause) and also an increased incidence of infections of amniotic fluid, placental abruptions, and prolonged or precipitous labor. Pregnant adolescent mothers endanger not only their own health in delivery and in their future, but also the intrauteral and future health of their child.

381. The answer is A. *(Kandel, 3/e. pp 805–810.)* The inability to sleep is a hardship that can alter a person's mood and behavior and even disrupt a life by affecting the entire behavioral repertoire. Quantitative surveys have established that about one in five persons has a sleep problem. Physicians report that the two most common complaints in medicine are pain and trouble sleeping. Insomnia is defined as the chronic inability to obtain the necessary amount or quality of sleep to maintain adequate daytime behavior. In reality it is a symptom of a variety of disorders. It is such a public health problem that there is an excessive tendency of poor sleepers to medicate themselves and for physicians to overprescribe strong sleeping pills. The net result is a serious problem of abuse of sleeping medications. Various studies have shown that there is very little evidence that any current sleeping medication is effective for more than several days. A part of the reason for so much overtreatment of sleep complaints is that they are often exaggerated by patients.

382. The answer is C. *(Gatchel, 2/e. pp 39–49.)* During World War II, researchers noticed that Londoners showed increased blood pressure during the early phases of the mass bombings. Also, studies of incarceration in German concentration camps and prisoner-of-war camps found that survivors showed greater rates of physical illness and greater rates of relatively permanent problems of psychological adjustment than people of similar age who were not prisoners. The incidence of premature death was also higher in survivors of concentration camps during the years following their release. One study found that survivors of concentration camps who had developed cancer were poorer at coping than similar patients who had not been in camps. Thus, such survivors may have been more vulnerable to stress associated with cancer.

383. The answer is D. *(Wilson, 12/e. pp 415–416.)* The calories required for physical activity above the needs of basal metabolism depend on the type of activity, the duration of activity, and the size of the person performing it. Some tables show energy expenditures based on the type of activity irrespective of the size of the individual, but allowing for body weight and intensity of the activity is more accurate. In spite of these limitations, tables of energy costs can be useful tools in nutrition and medicine. The energy cost of walking 3 miles per hour is only 2 kcal/kg of body weight above maintenance requirements. Thus, a 60-kg (132-lb) person will burn up 120 calories and a 75-kg (165-lb) person will expend 150 calories. An hour of moderate bicycling will expend about 3.5 kcal/kg (210 calories for the 60-kg person or 260 calories for the 75-kg person). Moderately heavy activity, such as swimming (2 mph), expends 7.0 kcal/kg/h or 420 calories per hour for the 60-kg person and 525 calories for the 75-kg person. Light running will consume 7.5 kcal/kg/h (450 or 562 calories, respectively). Thus, an increase in activity can be another behavioral mechanism for generating a negative energy balance for patients attempting to lose weight.

384. The answer is B. *(Wilson, 12/e. pp 2146–2151.)* It is estimated that 90 percent of people in the U.S. drink alcohol at some time, 40 to 50 percent of men have temporary alcohol-induced problems, and 10 percent of men and 3 to 5 percent of women develop alcoholism. Even light drinking can adversely interact with other medications, heavier drinking can exacerbate most medical illnesses, and alcoholism can masquerade as other medical disorders and psychiatric syndromes. While most information on alcohol applies to the "average" person, there is considerable variability among individuals that depends on genetic factors, other drug use, and existing pathology or disease. It is also little appreciated that the cancer rate with alcoholism is 10 times higher than that in the general population, especially in the head and neck, esophagus, stomach, liver, and pancreas. The homeless or skid-row alcoholic represents only 5 percent or less of all alcoholics. In general, 12 oz of beer, 4 oz of nonfortified wine, and 1.5 oz of 80-proof beverage contain the same amount (10 g) of ethanol.

385. The answer is E. *(Hamburg, Selected Perspectives, p 133.)* Anorexia nervosa is an emotional disorder of adolescent females that is life-threatening.

There is self-imposed starvation that may require hospitalization. The pathogenesis of anorexia is still not completely understood, but it does involve family relations, a disturbed body image, need for overachievement, and a concern for control and sexuality; it also often involves depression. The very difficult treatment of anorexia often involves a combination of modalities, such as hospitalization, medically regulated feeding, behavior modification, antidepressant drugs, and psychotherapy. Anorexia nervosa is a very complex, life-threatening disorder and is not simply a case of dieting out of control.

386. The answer is B. *(Rosen, pp 303–304.)* Although a "cancer-prone personality" has not been identified, the link between behavior and cancer progression is becoming more established, especially for the relationship between the inability to express emotion (e.g., hostility) and cancer. Sandra Levy is finding that negatively reactive patients with metastatic breast cancer live significantly longer than passive patients. Negative reactivity does not imply obnoxious behavior but rather a determination to "fight" the cancer and begin to cope positively versus giving way to apathy, helplessness, or surrender. On the other hand, overly cooperative, bland, and passive cancer patients in the face of stress have a shorter life span. Also, patients with breast cancer who are married or who are a part of an intact social network have an increased survival rate. Depression will act to suppress the immune system and thus will not assist longer survival.

387. The answer is E. *(Last, 13/e. pp 688–694.)* Symptoms of physical illness that might be defined simply as perceived or subjective changes of one's bodily state play a key role in health care. Such perceived changes, combined with observable signs, are the only way that the presence of illness can be detected. An understanding of how these symptoms and signs are interpreted by the average person is important for the practicing physician. The traditional view concerning the frequency of symptoms states that the illness experience constitutes a relatively infrequent or unusual event. In recent years, however, there have been a number of studies of symptom prevalence in normal populations; this evidence shows that there is a sizable number of clinically serious problems reported in supposedly healthy populations. Various empirical studies have reported that a wide range of symptoms—including headaches, upset stomachs, sore muscles, chest pains, nasal congestion, watering eyes, ringing in the ears, racing heart, dizziness, flushed face, sweating hands, and shortness of breath—occurs frequently and that many if not most people experience some of these symptoms much of the time. Behavioral scientists have also found that only a small number of people experiencing such problems ever seek professional care. In most cases, the mere presence of symptoms does not prompt a person to seek professional assistance. Illness becomes an everyday typical experience, and the treated case actually represents only the tip of a clinical iceberg. It is further evident that the experience of unexpected physiologic arousal (symptoms) places a person in a position of needing and seeking information from others to help give meaning to what he or she is experiencing. Thus, when unexpected physiologic changes occur, research findings suggest that we seek out explanations or attributions from our memory and through the advice of others.

388. The answer is E. *(Gatchel, 2/e. p 238.)* A placebo effect is any nonspecific, psychologic, or psychophysiologic therapeutic effect produced by a supposedly inert substance or nontherapeutic treatment. It is most often based on the belief or expectations of patients that the placebo will help them or relieve their symptoms. Historically, the placebo played a major role in medical treatment before the discovery of modern pharmacologic agents. The placebo effect is useful in psychotherapy, especially in the treatment of anxiety, and has also been shown to be an important factor in the biofeedback process. Endorphins (endogenous opiate-like substances in the brain) are involved in the mediation of the placebo effect. There is extensive literature in the research journals verifying the fact that the belief of the patient that a prescribed medication is active (even if it is chemically inert) often leads to significant reduction of symptoms, including a reduction in pain. The placebo also plays a role when used with modern chemically active and inactive drugs.

389. The answer is B. *(Last, 13/e. pp 741–760.)* Alcohol abuse is the second most frequent form of drug dependence after tobacco. It directly affects an estimated 2.5 to 5 percent of the United States population. In addition, their families, employers, and coworkers are directly and indirectly affected. With about half the annual traffic deaths being related to alcohol use and abuse, a major physical health and disability problem is generated. The economic loss associated with alcohol abuse was estimated to be over $100 billion annually (tobacco estimated at $60 billion). Drinking alcoholic beverages has generally become a socially acceptable form of activity, but its adverse effect on health and behavior can be severe. Alcohol use contributes to a number of disease conditions and reduces the efficiency of productive activity. The highest mortality of alcohol abusers is from cirrhosis of the liver, followed by suicide, accidents, and cancer of the upper digestive and respiratory tracts. The average life span of an alcoholic is shortened by 10 to 12 years. The increased use of psychoactive and addictive drugs, especially among the younger age group, has led to a major effort to bring such drug dependence into the mainstream of modern medicine, public health, and medical education. Furthermore, there is a renewed recognition of both the physical and psychological dependence common with the use of alcohol and tobacco. Although alcohol-related problems of the heavy drinker are more frequent, the moderately drinking segment of the population is actually a much larger group and contributes the greater proportion of the problems. Therefore, physicians must be aware of the greater dimension of the problem rather than just focusing on the minority who use alcohol in large quantities.

390. The answer is D. *(Kaplan, 6/e. pp 268, 508.)* Hyperthyroidism (thyrotoxicosis) is a syndrome resulting from a chronic excess of thyroid hormone (thyroxine). It may be precipitated by acute emotional stress and may even develop within hours after an emotional trauma. It is an endocrine disorder and is almost always accompanied by mental changes—the patient may feel tense and hyperexcitable and may be emotionally labile, with inappropriate temper outbursts, crying spells, or euphoria. Distractibility, short attention span, and impaired recent memory may also be present. Severe hyperthyroidism may result in frank psychosis, delirium, coma, and death. Thyroid disorders are seven times more frequent in women than in men; they occur most commonly in women in their third and fourth decades and in men at older ages. In contrast to the tense and hyperexcitable behaviors usually observed, a minority of patients, particularly the elderly, may be depressed, apathetic, and anorectic with chronic hyperthyroidism. Mildly hyperthyroid patients occasionally are misdiagnosed as having anxiety neuroses. Mental retardation in children is frequently associated with *hypo*thyroidism, not *hyper*thyroidism, since normal brain development requires the thyroid hormone.

391. The answer is B. *(Rosen, pp 132–133.)* In the type A pattern of behavior, the joyless striving characteristic is regarded by Friedman and Rosenman as representing a constant struggle for recognition and reward in order to overcome fears of inadequacy and insecurity. As such, emotional exhaustion, feelings of despair, hopelessness, and depression can be recognized as prodromes in type A persons just prior to their myocardial infarction and frequently sudden death. Such chronic striving can represent an attempt to overcome the underlying feelings of depression. Disregarding time pressures would actually be therapeutic, especially for a person with a strong type A personality.

392. The answer is D. *(Steptoe, pp 302–303.)* After myocardial infarction a patient experiences many psychosocial and physical responses, even a full year after the acute attack. The most frequent response is a change in mood, leading to depression and anxiety. Also, a majority report experiencing moderate physical distress, extensive disturbances in subjective states, contradictions between patients and their families in assessing the patient's level of activity, the perception of themselves as handicapped, and personal lives that have not returned to normal. These factors must be recognized in order to achieve a successful rehabilitation.

393. The answer is D. *(Lerner, Experiencing Adolescence, pp 191–225.)* Even though adolescents are relatively free of illnesses and have lower rates of illness and use of health care than children or adults, they account for over twice as many automobile accidents as adults, 20 percent of all suicides, well over 600,000 pregnancies in unmarried girls per year, and a 32 percent pregnancy rate among sexually active, unmarried teenagers. They are the only age group for which the death rate is actually increasing, with a higher death rate than 20 years ago. Seventy percent of all deaths of teenagers are the result of automobile accidents or violence, both of which are increasing in frequency among adolescents while they are decreasing in the general population. The reported smoking rate for 12-to-17-year-old teenagers is 12 percent and the rate increases to 26 percent for the 17-to-18-year-old group.

394. The answer is D. *(Last, 13/e. pp 671–723.)* The health consequences of smoking behavior are well established and clearly understood. The term *smoking behavior* is used because smoking is a behavioral act. Studies show that smokers, especially cigarette smokers, are much more likely than nonsmokers to die from a large number of diseases. Among these are diseases of the heart, bronchitis/emphysema, arteriosclerosis, and cancers of the lung, oral cavity, larynx, pancreas, bladder, esophagus, and kidney. Other diseases and disorders caused or affected by smoking behavior are cancer of the upper gastrointestinal tract, peptic ulcers, and adverse effects on the fetus. Increases in total mortality of cigarette smokers in prospective studies vary from 30 to 80 percent, depending partly on the age groups studied. An overall risk of 60 percent greater than the mortality of nonsmokers is considered a reasonable estimate. This results in a reduced life expectancy of cigarette smokers of 5 to 6 years. The reduction in life expectancy increases directly with the number of cigarettes smoked. Between 1970 and 1985, deaths from lung cancer among women 55 to 74 years of age increased about 7 percent each year compared with a 1 percent increase for men. Since 1987, mortality from lung cancer among women has exceeded that from breast cancer. While there has been a reduction in the number of male smokers, the number of female smokers is still increasing. Lung cancer deaths attributed to smoking addiction appear to have peaked for males. The death rate for females is still climbing rapidly.

395. The answer is D. *(Hazzard, 2/e. pp 150–154.)* Heart disease is the leading cause of death both in the general and the elderly population. Cancer ranks second and cerebrovascular disease ranks third among the elderly. The fourth leading cause of death for persons age 65 and over is chronic obstructive pulmonary disease, followed by pneumonia, diabetes, and accidents. Suicide is an important cause of mortality, especially among elderly depressed males, but it is not among the 10 leading causes of death of persons age 65 and over.

396. The answer is D. *(Matarazzo, pp 496–503.)* Most studies dealing with the effects of exercise on depression have demonstrated significant improvements in the subject's mood state. Exercise was as effective as time-limited psychotherapy, mediation, or group psychotherapy. Exercise fostered a sense of mastery, a positive self-image, an increased peripheral and cerebral blood flow, increased oxygenation, increased levels of catecholamines (norepinephrine and epinephrine), and some cathartic relief. While the studies have been mainly correlational rather than causative and they may have been influenced by a self-selecting bias, the evidence is considered more than suggestive. The expectancy and demand characteristics associated with exercise are very powerful.

397. The answer is E. *(U.S. Public Health Service, pp 1, 60–61.)* Survival is not the sole criterion for evaluating outcomes of pregnancy. Many conditions that may lead to an infant's death also carry potential hazardous consequences when the outcome is not fatal. The most significant characteristic associated with a poor outcome of pregnancy is low birth weight, usually defined as less than 5½ pounds (2500 g). Infants of low birth weight fr ⸱ a fiftyfold greater chance of dying before 1 month of age and are five times more likely to die between 1 month and 1 year of age than are infants of normal birth weight. They are also more likely to have serious congenital anomalies or other severe impairments. Babies of low birth weight are likely to have a greater rate of developmental problems than are heavier babies. The morbidity and mortality of low birth weight are most frequently related to poverty, lack of prenatal care, poor nutrition, smoking, stress, and poor physical condition. In 1988, 6.88 percent of all infants born in the United States were of low birth weight. The incidence of low birth weight was more than twice as high for black infants as it was for white infants (12.7 percent and 5.6 percent, respectively). Nearly all the difference in neonatal mortality between white and black infants can be attributed to difference in the distribution of birth weight. The U.S. average for infants born with low birth weight was 6.88 per 100 live births in 1988. The regions that achieved fewer than the U.S. average for low–birth-weight infants were the Pacific, New England, North Central, and Mountain regions with 5.88, 5.90, 5.81, and 6.65 per 100 live births, respectively. The others ranged between 7.21 and 7.87 per 100 live births.

398. The answer is D. *(Kaplan, 6/e. pp 557–559, 805.)* During adolescence, there is a marked increase in the number of suicides. Adolescents account for 6000 of the 28,000 yearly suicides in the United States. Boys are three times more likely to commit suicide than are girls, and boys typically choose more violent acts than the more passive methods used by girls. Suicide is the third leading cause of death among adolescents, exceeded only by accidents and homicides. It is thought that suicide attempts represent an adolescent's final call for help and attention. These attempts are all too often successful. During the period between 1970 and 1980, the rate of suicide for adolescent males increased 40 percent and is still rising. The suicide rate for females is also continuing to rise. Studies show that 60 percent of adolescents who commit suicide live with only one parent. Suicide risk is also associated with depression, with families in which one or more members has a chronic illness, with a family history of suicide, and with long-standing family and social problems throughout childhood. Suicide can be precipitated by another suicide in a peer group, by a loss of a loved one, and by an adolescent suicide seen on television. A substrate of psychopathology generally exists.

399. The answer is C. *(Wilson, 12/e. pp 2148–2149.)* The diagnosis of alcoholism is difficult. General criteria include four situations: when a person ignores early warning signs such as alcohol-related problems in marriage and then goes on to an alcohol-related marital separation or divorce; when a person is fired or laid off because of an alcohol-related problem; when there are two or more arrests related to alcohol; or when there is evidence that alcohol has harmed one's health, such as cardiomyopathy, cirrhosis, or alcoholic hepatitis, including signs of alcohol withdrawal. If a person has alcohol-related problems during an episode of mania or related to a preexisting antisocial personality disorder, then the alcohol problem is likely to be secondary to the primary disorder and not alcoholism per se.

400–403. The answers are: 400-E, 401-C, 402-B, 403-A. *(Wilson, 12/e. pp 242–243, 1475–1479, 1544–1547, 1870–1871.)* Sickle cell anemia is a congenital hemolytic anemia seen most frequently among, and hence characterized as a condition of, the black population. About 0.15 percent of black children in the United States have sickle cell anemia. It has a lower prevalence in adults because of decreased life expectancy.

Phenylketonuria is an autosomal recessive metabolic disorder. It is associated with severe mental retardation and, less frequently, with other neurologic manifestations such as psychomotor symptoms. No abnormalities are apparent at birth, but treatment in early infancy may prevent retardation.

Osteoarthritis, known also as *degenerative joint disease,* is most often an affliction of advancing years. Wear-and-tear processes seem to be the major causative factor; certain occupations and hobbies, particularly those involving joint trauma, appear to be causally related to the development of osteoarthritis. Forty million Americans have radiologic evidence of degenerative joint disease, including 85 percent of persons over the age of 70.

Although dental decay has links with heredity and a direct relationship to age, the most important factor associated with tooth decay at every age is lack of attention and poor oral hygiene, most frequently occurring in poverty or lower socioeconomic situations. Unless treated, this infection of enamel and underlying dentin in due course extends to involvement of the dental pulp and frequently results in loss of the affected tooth.

404–409. The answers are: 404-A, 405-A, 406-A, 407-C, 408-D, 409-C. *(Kandel, 3/e. pp 869–880.)* Major unipolar depression and bipolar (manic depressive) disorders are affective disorders that involve a disturbance of mood or feeling tone. Both are related to an intrinsic regulatory defect involving, at least in part, the hypothalamus, which is involved in regulation of mood, sexual drive, sleep, and autonomic and motor activity.

For unipolar depression, the average age of onset is about 30 years and the incidence for women is about two to three times greater than for men. It also tends to recur about four times during the next 20 years. The depression usually lasts 4 to 12 months, and it is estimated that about 4 percent (8 million people) of the U.S. population suffer from it. Unipolar depression is probably several disorders.

Bipolar (manic depressive) disorder causes both manic and depressive episodes and affects men and women about equally. The typical age of onset is about 20 years, and the depression is clinically similar to unipolar depression. The manic phase lasts about a week or longer. The episodes of depression and mania occur about twice as often over a 20-year period as do episodes of unipolar depression. A patient may switch episodes quite rapidly.

Neither unipolar nor bipolar depression can be related to significant psychosocial precipitating factors in at least 60 percent of the episodes, and both are relatively unresponsive to conventional psychotherapy and environmental change. Treatment with medication is frequently effective. There also appears to be a strong genetic predisposition for both unipolar and bipolar depressions. Genetic studies have shown them to be not completely distinct but probably part of a spectrum of depressive illness; the unipolar depression may represent a milder form and the bipolar depression the more severe form of the same disorder. Chromosome number 11 has been demonstrated to be related to bipolar depression, but the genetic components are more complex than a single gene.

$0-77,27\ \%$

Behavioral Risk Factors and Disease

DIRECTIONS: Each question below contains five suggested responses. Select the **one best** response to each question.

410. The single most significant source of preventable morbidity and premature mortality is

(A) environmental pollution
(B) crime and homicide
(C) auto and home accidents
(D) poor nutrition
(E) cigarette smoking

411. Alcohol consumption in pregnant females is associated with all the following risks for the infant EXCEPT

(A) fetal alcohol syndrome in 1 per 1000 live births
(B) decreased birth weight
(C) mental retardation
(D) increased spontaneous abortion
(E) poor sucking ability

412. True statements regarding adolescence include all the following EXCEPT

(A) mortality is generally higher for males
(B) accidents are positively correlated with affluence
(C) accidents are the leading cause of death among males
(D) at least half of motor vehicle accidents involve alcohol
(E) suicide is the leading cause of death among females

413. The most effective behavioral intervention for hypertension is

(A) biofeedback
(B) relaxation
(C) learning to discriminate sources of stress
(D) developing alternative reactions to stressors
(E) diet

414. All the following social and cultural factors have been found to be related to the development of hypertension EXCEPT

(A) stress
(B) personality
(C) obesity
(D) dietary salt
(E) compliance with medical treatment

415. Duodenal ulcer activity is exacerbated by all the following EXCEPT

(A) expression of a characteristic personality
(B) chronic anxiety
(C) alcohol consumption
(D) psychological stress
(E) cigarette smoking

416. It has been found that there is a higher incidence of stress-related coronary heart disease among

(A) women working outside the home in general than among housewives
(B) childless women working outside the home than among housewives in general
(C) working women with control over decisions than working women with little input on decisions
(D) clerical workers than among housewives
(E) housewives with several children than among women working outside the home with fewer children

417. Human immunodeficiency virus (HIV) is spread primarily by all the following EXCEPT

(A) exchange of bodily fluids during sex
(B) sharing of needles or other drug paraphernalia
(C) blood transfusion
(D) fomites contaminated by respiratory infection
(E) perinatal contact of an infected mother with her infant

418. Chronic alcohol consumption by a pregnant woman can produce fetal alcohol syndrome with all the following symptoms EXCEPT

(A) retardation of intrauterine growth
(B) defective cerebral development
(C) microcephaly
(D) premature birth
(E) reduction in number of fingers and toes

419. True statements related to AIDS and ARC (AIDS-related complex) include

(A) the minority of intravenous drug users share needles regularly
(B) the time needed for reported cases to double has increased modestly with increased public education
(C) the manner in which AIDS is transmitted can be characterized as primarily behavioral
(D) the spreading of AIDS into the heterosexual community has recently begun to level off
(E) the only existing palliative treatment is AZT

420. Risk factors for problem behaviors in adolescence can be identified. All the following personal or personality factors have a major influence EXCEPT

(A) unconventionality
(B) rebelliousness
(C) high risk-taking
(D) low value on achievement
(E) low value on autonomy

421. An adolescent has an increased risk of becoming a smoker if all the following are true EXCEPT that he or she

(A) is employed outside the home
(B) has a high level of achievement in school
(C) has parents who smoke
(D) has friends who smoke
(E) has adult role models who smoke

422. The component of the type A pattern of behavior most pathogenic for coronary heart disease is

(A) physiologic reactivity to social stress
(B) impatience
(C) vigorous speech
(D) hostility
(E) competitive drive

423. College students are considered to be at risk for AIDS because of all the following EXCEPT

(A) frequent sexual contact
(B) a sense of invulnerability
(C) the belief that only homosexuals and drug users get AIDS
(D) the belief that educated people are not apt to get AIDS
(E) a lack of knowledge about risks

424. Correct statements about insomnia include all the following EXCEPT

(A) the most common causes of insomnia are psychological and emotional disturbances
(B) anxiety is positively correlated with difficulty in falling asleep
(C) depression is positively correlated with frequency of early awakenings
(D) the most frequent emotional cause of insomnia is anxiety
(E) anticipation of poor sleep is the cause in about 15 percent of cases

425. Which of the following actions would most powerfully reduce the incidence of cardiovascular disease?

(A) Reduction of salt intake
(B) Reduction of excess weight
(C) Exercise
(D) Reduction of type A behavior
(E) Cessation of cigarette smoking

426. Failure to cope with psychological stress has been found to contribute rather consistently to the pathogenesis of all the following illnesses EXCEPT

(A) coronary artery disease
(B) hypertension
(C) gastrointestinal problems
(D) cancer
(E) alcohol abuse

427. Research findings on the use of alcoholic beverages show all the following EXCEPT

(A) the alcoholic's life span is shortened by 10 to 12 years
(B) alcohol is considered to be a contributory cause in half of all deaths resulting from automobile accidents
(C) current rates of use of alcohol are higher for young adults (18 to 25 years of age) than for older adults (26 years of age or older)
(D) behavioral treatment of problem drinking and alcoholism has shown that total and permanent abstinence is considered the only treatment objective
(E) the usual public policy response to alcohol-related health problems is to increase treatment services

428. What percentage of the mortality from the 10 leading causes of death in the United States can be traced to life-style?

(A) 10
(B) 20
(C) 30
(D) 40
(E) 50

429. Behavioral factors associated with enhancing tumor growth include all the following EXCEPT

(A) bereavement
(B) consumption of alcohol
(C) exercise
(D) stress
(E) lack of close personal ties

430. Most of the major health problems of adolescents

(A) have a genetic basis
(B) have a sexual basis
(C) involve sensory deficits
(D) are self-inflicted
(E) involve bacterial and viral infections

431. Great potential for health promotion exists in all the following strategies EXCEPT

(A) changing the typical stance of dependence in the relationship with professionals
(B) development of more healthful patterns of daily living
(C) mitigating and eliminating risk factors
(D) more effective adaptation to the presence of chronic illness
(E) increased use of physician services

432. *Life style* refers to those individual and societal patterns of behavior that are at least partly under individual control and that demonstrably influence personal health. True statements regarding health status and life-style behaviors include all the following EXCEPT

(A) the major causes of death, serious illness, and disability in the United States today are chronic disease and violence
(B) behind most chronic disease, disability, and premature death are many life-style factors that are potentially amenable to change
(C) a few life-style patterns (e.g., smoking, drinking alcohol) constitute the major behavioral risk factors involved in chronic disease and severe disability
(D) educational techniques that modify life-style patterns can improve both preventive and curative medical practices
(E) changing one's life-style is very little different from changing one's treatment regimen

433. True statements about the health consequences of smoking include all the following EXCEPT

(A) the overall mortality risk is 60 percent greater for smokers than for nonsmokers
(B) the risk of dying of lung cancer is between 8 and 15 times higher in a cigarette smoker than in a nonsmoker
(C) life span is shortened by about 5.5 min for each cigarette smoked
(D) children whose parents smoke have a higher incidence of respiratory infections and impaired function than those whose parents do not smoke
(E) while more women than men are initiating smoking, more women are quitting smoking than men

434. The best predictor of health and longevity is

(A) income level
(B) education level
(C) life-style
(D) marital status
(E) religious participation

435. All the following statements about obesity are true EXCEPT

(A) obesity increases the risk of developing diabetes approximately fourfold
(B) obese persons are more likely to die in automobile accidents than are members of the population in general
(C) obesity increases the severity of most health problems
(D) obesity is the leading cause of hypertension
(E) obesity has been linked to complications from surgery and infections

436. Exercise has been demonstrated to aid in the prevention of all the following EXCEPT

(A) chronic obstructive lung disease
(B) abnormal body weight and composition
(C) osteoporosis
(D) coronary heart disease
(E) hypertension

437. The major cause of death among adolescents and young adults is

(A) homicide
(B) suicide
(C) motor vehicle accidents
(D) infections
(E) illicit drug abuse

438. All the following are highly ranked health problems and concerns as expressed by adolescents EXCEPT

(A) colds
(B) depression
(C) venereal disease
(D) personal problems
(E) acne

439. True statements regarding exercise of moderate intensity include all the following EXCEPT

(A) 30 min of exercise will generally result in an energy expenditure of 300 kcal
(B) the metabolic rate remains elevated for several hours after exercise
(C) exercise helps to retain lean body mass in the elderly
(D) when exercise is combined with calorie restriction, a greater weight loss of muscle tissue is accomplished
(E) increased metabolism from exercise combined with restricted calories increases loss of adipose tissue

440. Which of the following statements about smoking is true?

(A) The most effective deterrent to substance abuse is arousal of fear
(B) The major influence on teenagers to smoke comes from their parents
(C) The social context is the excuse, not the reason, for maintaining a smoking habit
(D) The most rapid increase in smoking is among teenage females
(E) Social inoculation strategy in prevention has not been effective

441. All the following statements about Down's syndrome are true EXCEPT

(A) most affected persons have 47 chromosomes
(B) the incidence of Down's syndrome is related to maternal age
(C) amniocentesis can detect the presence of Down's syndrome before birth
(D) it accounts for approximately 30 percent of retarded children in the United States
(E) most infants born with Down's syndrome die at an early age

442. All the following are risk factors for cardiovascular disease EXCEPT

(A) physical inactivity
(B) cigarette smoking
(C) obesity
(D) personality type
(E) moderate alcohol consumption

443. Stress leading to the risk of psychosomatic disorders can be best measured by the

(A) Friedman and Rosenman structured interview
(B) Luria-Nebraska battery
(C) Minnesota multiphasic personality inventory
(D) Holmes and Rahe rating scale
(E) Rorschach test

444. Essential hypertension has been frequently associated with all the following EXCEPT

(A) repressed anger
(B) acutely stressful events
(C) familial history of hypertension
(D) decreased sympathetic nervous system activity
(E) decreased parasympathetic inhibition

445. Behavioral factors appear to be crucial to all the following aspects of cigarette smoking EXCEPT

(A) initiation of the smoking habit
(B) maintaining abstinence
(C) day-to-day fluctuations in smoking
(D) nicotine addiction
(E) choice of cigarette brands

446. The importance of psychosocial factors in the etiology of schizophrenia is correctly illustrated by
each of the following statements
EXCEPT

(A) lower socioeconomic status correlates with a higher incidence
of schizophrenia
(B) family psychosocial factors are
about equal to biologic factors
(C) the stress-diathesis model has
linked biologic vulnerability
with induction of stress
(D) there is no schizophrenia-prone
personality type
(E) there is a developmental deficit
in the vulnerable individual

Behavioral Risk Factors and Disease

Answers

410. The answer is E. *(Last, 13/e. pp 724–726.)* Each U.S. Surgeon General's report since 1964 has emphasized that the single most significant source of preventable morbidity and premature mortality is cigarette smoking. The excess annual toll is estimated to exceed 350,000 people, more than all American lives lost in all wars during the twentieth century. Environmental pollution, crime and homicide, auto and home accidents, and poor nutrition are all significant sources of preventable morbidity and premature death, but smoking is considered the most significant.

411. The answer is A. *(Hamburg, Frontiers of Research, pp 43–45.)* Fetal alcohol syndrome is a danger in those women who drink heavily during pregnancy. It is characterized by certain morphological abnormalities and is frequently associated with mental retardation. Fetal alcohol syndrome occurs in about 1 per 700 live births, which is more frequent than Down's syndrome (1 per 1000). Even two drinks daily of alcohol during pregnancy can also result in significantly decreased birth weight, and consumption levels as low as two drinks twice a week can increase the spontaneous abortion rate. Other adverse effects implicating alcohol consumption during pregnancy are lowered viability at birth, abnormalities of heart rate, poor sucking ability, and other behaviors associated with poor functioning of the central nervous system. Cigarette smoking combined with alcohol consumption during pregnancy results in an increased and potentiated risk.

412. The answer is E. *(Hamburg, Selected Perspectives, pp 130–132.)* Among adolescents, the mortality is higher for males than for females. Motor vehicle accidents are the leading cause of death among males, followed by suicide and homicide. Accidents are linked with affluence and frequently related to alcohol consumption. Among females, especially those below the age of 18, the leading causes of death are complications of pregnancy, childbirth, and the puerperium.

413. The answer is B. *(Kaptein, pp 115–123.)* Relaxation training is the most frequently used and the most effective behavioral therapeutic technique for essential hypertension. Of course, relaxation is most effectively used in combination with antihypertensives, but it has demonstrated some lowering of blood pressure, especially in mild hypertensives. Relaxation exercises reduce sympathetic activation and have proved superior to nontreatment, blood pressure self-monitoring, and biofeedback. Learning to discriminate sources of stress, developing alternative reactions to stressors, and diet have all demonstrated some positive effect, but the combination of pharmacotherapy and relaxation training often allows the physician to reduce the medication and also gets the patient involved in the therapeutic process. Relaxation has also been used effectively for prevention.

414. The answer is E. *(Gatchel, 2/e. pp 114–119.)* Fifteen percent of the population (more than 35 million people) in the United States have hypertension. Risk factors for hypertension constitute complex interactions between behavioral, physiologic, and genetic factors. Age, race, and family history have been the standard risk factors, but they are not modifiable. More recently behavioral and environmental factors have been documented to play a significant role in the pathogenesis of hypertension. Of these behavioral risk factors, eating behaviors related to high intake of dietary salt and obesity are most relevant, followed by stress and personality factors, which are again related to a person's coping mechanisms. The complex interaction of these behavioral factors over time is most significant. Compliance with medical treatment is crucial after hypertension has developed, but not in its pathogenesis.

415. The answer is A. *(Wilson, 12/e. pp 1232-1237.)* Duodenal ulcer is chronic and recurrent in 6 to 15 percent of the population. It can also exist with or without symptoms. Hence, it is difficult to establish biologic and behavioral etiologies. Formerly, a personality exhibiting oral-receptive characteristics and unmet oral needs was thought to be a dominant causative factor, but such a personality designation has not been substantiated. Psychosocial and behavioral factors—particularly chronic anxiety, psychological stress, cigarette smoking, and diet (including alcohol and coffee)—do play a role in the exacerbation of ulcer activity. No difference in frequency of duodenal ulcers has been identified among different socioeconomic classes or occupation groups.

416. The answer is D. *(Gatchel, 2/e. pp 100–102.)* Occupations with high psychological demands and low control over decisions are associated with increased cardiovascular risk for both men and women. Data from the Framingham Heart Study showed that when working women (employed for more than half of their adult years outside the home) are compared with housewives, in general they were not at significantly higher risk, but clerical workers and working women with children were more apt to develop coronary heart disease. Furthermore, the incidence of coronary heart disease increased linearly with the number of children for working women, but not for house-wives with multiple children. Working women whose bosses were nonsupportive were also at greater risk.

417. The answer is D. *(Gatchel, 2/e. p 139.)* The human immunodeficiency virus (HIV) affects the immune system by decreasing T lymphocytes, some types of immunoglobulins, T-helper lymphocytes, and lymphocyte responsiveness to antigens, thus disrupting cellular immunity and increasing susceptibility to opportunistic infections. HIV is spread primarily through exchange of body fluids during sex, the sharing of needles or other drug paraphernalia, blood transfusion, and perinatal contact of an infected mother with her infant. Spread through fomites has not been documented. Other intimate exchanges of body fluids have been implicated but not yet documented, except in cases of contact with open lesions. While fairly rare, infections of health care workers with HIV by accidents with contaminated needles and blood have been documented.

418. The answer is E. *(Wilson, 12/e. p 2057.)* Fetal alcohol syndrome can occur as the result of chronic heavy drinking by a pregnant woman. Symptoms may include severe retardation of intrauterine growth, premature birth, microcephaly, and other deformities such as congenital eye and ear problems, heart defects, extra fingers and toes, and patterns of disturbed sleep. It is the most prevalent cause of defective cerebral development. Most recent research suggests a 10 percent risk of this syndrome if the pregnant woman drinks as little as 2 to 4 ounces of hard liquor daily. It is estimated that 6000 infants a year suffer from the effects of fetal alcohol syndrome.

419. The answer is C. *(Gatchel, 2/e. pp 138–142.)* The incidence of AIDS has increased rapidly since 1978. It is estimated that three-fourths of AIDS cases occur among gays or bisexuals, followed by intravenous drug users, recipients of transfusion (including hemophiliacs), and children born to mothers infected with HIV. AIDS is increasingly being spread into the heterosexual community, and the time needed for reported cases to double has been decreasing steadily. It has been found that the majority of intravenous drug users share needles regularly. The transmission of AIDS is considered to be potentially controllable using strategies of behavioral change and technologies. There is no cure for AIDS, but powerful drugs and behavioral strategies and technologies can extend life and improve the quality of life.

420. The answer is E. *(Hamburg, Selected Perspectives, pp 140–141.)* Health-damaging behaviors of adolescents are very complex and involve some underlying influences and motivations that can be termed *risk factors* for problem behaviors. In general, these risk factors can be categorized as personal or personality factors, social or interpersonal factors, and cultural or environmental factors. While social or interpersonal and cultural or environmental factors are extremely important in understanding or predicting health-damaging behaviors, the personal and personality factors underlie the cognitive and emotional perceptions and reactions of each adolescent's behavior. The major personal or personality factors that underlie and influence the risk factors for problem behaviors are unconventionality, rebelliousness, high risk-taking behavior, a low value on achievement in both school and job performance, and a high value on being or attempting to appear autonomous.

421. The answer is B. *(Lerner, Experiencing Adolescence, pp 200–204.)* Smoking is a behavior determined by multiple factors; however, a number of environmental factors have been found to place individual adolescents at greater risk of becoming regular smokers. Adolescents employed outside the home are more apt to start smoking (females having twice the risk); if both of their parents smoke they have twice the risk—less if one parent smokes; the greater the number of friends who smoke, the greater risk, especially if one's best friend smokes; adult role models (teachers, television stars, adult friends) who smoke increase the risk of the teenager's smoking. Positive-image and action-oriented advertising also increases the risk, as well as individual rebelliousness, not participating in organized school and community activities, low school achievement, impatience in assuming an adult role, and need for a sense of identity.

422. The answer is D. *(Gatchel, 2/e. p 119.)* The type A pattern of behavior has been linked to the risk of coronary heart disease. The specific behavioral factors have been identified as competitiveness, impatience, vigorous speech, hostility, and time urgency. Also, physiologic reactivity to occupational and social stress is a more recently identified component. The hostility component of the type A pattern of behavior has been found to be the most pathogenic of all the behaviors. Hostility, interacting with the other behaviors and stresses, may in effect drive the physiologic reactivity to produce the physiologic and pathologic damage.

423. The answer is E. *(Gatchel, 2/e. pp 139–142.)* AIDS did not spread initially among college students, but they are now considered increasingly to be at risk. College students feel that the campus is a protected environment; however, they are at risk because of their frequent sexual contact. Also, they are less apt to practice "safe sex" because they still have a sense of invulnerability that was characteristic of their adolescence and because of their belief that their partners will let others know if they have AIDS. Some also believe that only homosexuals and drug users get AIDS. They need to know that AIDS cuts across all educational levels and that educated people do get AIDS. Some studies show that college students already have the knowledge about risks, but that their beliefs in the safety of the campus, in their student colleagues, and in their own invulnerability prevent them from practicing safe behavior.

424. The answer is D. *(Kandel, 3/e. p 806.)* A recent study showed that emotional problems were the cause of 70 percent of the cases of insomnia. Depression, which is characterized by early-morning awakening, was the most frequent cause of insomnia. Anxiety, positively correlated with difficulty in falling asleep, was also a frequent cause of insomnia. The most frequent presenting complaint was insomnia, not depression, and hence the problem was often treated initially with sleeping pills. The perception of insomnia is self-reported and can be quite independent of the actual number of hours slept. One study of 127 insomniacs observed a sleep duration of 7 h. Physiologic events (e.g., leg twitches, restless leg syndrome) do keep about 30 percent of insomniacs awake. Most insomniacs maintain higher core body temperatures during sleep, perhaps associated with an autonomic hyperarousal on a decreased deep slow-wave sleep. Anticipation of poor sleep can also cause insomnia (about 15 percent of cases).

425. The answer is E. *(Gatchel, 2/e. pp 97–102.)* There are many physiologic, environmental, and behavioral variables that interact in the development of cardiovascular disease. Age, sex, and family history cannot be controlled, but behavioral and environmental risk factors can be modified by changing a person's life style. Lowering salt intake, reducing excess weight, increasing exercise, and reducing type A behavior will each assist in lowering the risk, but cessation of smoking has a more powerful effect because it will reduce the severe pathophysiologic effects of smoking.

426. The answer is D. *(Gatchel, 2/e. pp 71–73.)* Inability to cope with psychological stress has a direct physiologic effect and over time can cause damage to most systems of the body. The most frequently cited illnesses related to failure to cope with stress include coronary artery disease, hypertension, and gastrointestinal problems. Coping style and life-style are very important since they help determine the reaction to stress and they lead people to adopt behaviors and habits that can predispose them to illness. Cancer can be aggravated by psychological stress but the initial pathogenesis appears to be more dependent on other factors. Stress is increasingly considered to be a major factor in the prognosis of cancer.

427. The answer is D. *(Last, 13/e. pp 741–760.)* Research findings on the use of alcoholic beverages show that the life span of an alcoholic is on the average shortened by 10 to 12 years. Alcohol is considered to be a contributory cause in half of all deaths resulting from automobile accidents. The current rate of use of alcohol is 70 percent for young adults in the age range of 18 to 25 years and 55 percent for adults 26 years or more in age. Recent research on the behavior and educational treatment of problem drinking and alcoholism has shown that total and permanent abstinence is no longer considered the only treatment objective. The total abstinence treatment was based on the belief that alcoholism is a physical disease characterized by craving for alcohol and loss of control over drinking during periods of intoxication. The disease model justified abstinence because one cannot allow a sick person to have access to the agent that causes the sickness. Abstinence was also an exquisitely simple treatment goal to define and monitor. Although total abstinence is appropriate in some instances, more recent empirical studies of the drinking behavior of alcoholics support the use of the social learning model for selected individuals. Various behavioral therapies are employed, such as the use of rewards rather than punishments and the pursuit of controlled social drinking rather than total abstinence as a therapy goal. The degree of addiction and dependence on alcohol is an important underlying factor. Heritability must also be assessed. The usual response of health policy makers and governments to alcohol-related health problems has been to think only in terms of increasing treatment services, which leaves the root causes essentially unaddressed. One of these root public policy issues is the complicated number of conflicting policies. Unlimited treatment facilities and services would be beyond all financial resources and still would not deal with the biologic, psychosocial, cultural, religious, and legal issues. An important first move may be that of the recommendation that alcohol consumption be reduced to 2 gallons per person per year (from 2.54 gallons in 1987) as proclaimed as a health objective for the U.S. by the year 2000.

428. The answer is E. *(Hamburg, Frontiers of Research, pp 35–51.)* Lifestyle is a term used to refer to single and collective aspects of individual behavior, especially long-term patterns of behavior that characterize a person's general habits of living, adapting, coping, and achieving. The United States Department of Health and Human Services has estimated that 50 percent of the mortality from the 10 leading causes of death can be traced to one's lifestyle. Major known behavioral risk factors are cigarette smoking, certain dietary habits, reckless driving, violence, use of illicit drugs, excessive consumption of alcoholic beverages, insufficient exercise, nonadherence to medication regimens, maladaptive responses to social pressures and stress, and obesity.

429. The answer is C. *(Gatchel, 2/e. pp 127–138.)* Bereavement from the loss of a loved one has been found to reduce the responsiveness of lymphocytes to mitogens. The same reaction occurs as a result of certain life-style factors, such as cigarette smoking and alcohol consumption. Psychological and social stress not only suppresses the immune system, but also suppresses DNA synthesis and DNA repair. Lack of close personal or family ties has been associated with reduced immune competence and with tumor growth. Environmental, physiologic, and psychosocial factors are thought to trigger the development and growth of cancer by suppressing the "surveillance" function of the immune system, which protects the body from invasion of alien cells and viruses. Exercise improves normal bodily functions, so the usual defense mechanisms should help protect against rather than enhance tumor growth.

430. The answer is D. *(Hamburg, Frontiers of Research, pp 247–256.)* Although most American adolescents judge their own health to be very good, many adolescents take actions that produce self-induced health problems resulting in physical or behavioral disability or death. Most of these have to do with behaviors associated with accidents, drug and alcohol abuse, tobacco use, and poor eating habits. Accidents are the leading cause of death in the adolescent years, and their incidence appears to be increasing at a rapid rate. Homicide is the second leading cause of death, and suicide is the third. Drug, alcohol, and tobacco use usually begin during adolescence or even during preadolescence. Since these activities are all behaviorally related, there is at least the potential that behavioral intervention can make the greatest impact on the health of youth.

431. The answer is E. *(Last, 13/e. pp 701–711.)* Research studies of behavior in illness and relationships with medical professionals clearly show the need for increased competency of the patient in adapting to and coping with conditions of illness and injury. This runs counter to the frequent appearance of dependency of the patient on the physician to manage and prevent an illness. Thus, the largest potential for promoting health will result from social action directed to the development of more healthful patterns of living, rather than increased use of physician services. Eliminating risk factors and attempting to modify patterns of behavior are important strategies for improving the health status of specific population groups.

432. The answer is E. *(Last, 13/e. pp 687–697.)* The major causes of death, serious illness, and disability in the United States today are chronic disease and violence. Chronic diseases account for 75 to 80 percent of all deaths. Accidents, suicide, and homicide account for another 10 percent. Another measure of the relative impact of various diseases and lethal forces is the concept of "potential years of life lost," which highlights the loss to society as a result of youthful or early death. The most recent life expectancy tables indicate that three categories—diseases of the circulatory system, cancer, and accidents and violence—account for about 72 percent of the potential years of life lost in the United States. Two chronic disease categories—diseases of the circulatory and musculoskeletal system—account for 38 percent of conditions causing disability and limitations of major activity. Behind most chronic diseases, disabilities, and premature deaths are many environmental and behavioral factors that are potentially amenable or susceptible to change or prevention. Although the etiology is usually multidimensional, it is now recognized that environmental threats and individual behavior play a major role. It is estimated that about 80 percent of all cancer among men and 75 percent among women is attributable to environmental or behavioral factors or a combination of both. This percentage represents a great potential for prevention. The individual and societal life-style patterns and behaviors that constitute the major behavioral risk factors involved in chronic disease and severe disability include cigarette smoking, alcohol and other drug abuse, poor nutrition, lack of adequate physical activity, irresponsible use of motor vehicles, irresponsible use of guns and other manifestations of violence, the apparent decline of family health and social supports, sexual promiscuity or carelessness about contraception, and excessive television viewing. Information alone is insufficient for change, so health education must be directed at devising the most effective strategies for changing and then maintaining the individual and group behavior that promotes health and prevents disease. In spite of the apparent simplicity with which behavior is sometimes regarded, it is nevertheless one of the most difficult attributes of human beings to change, and one of the most complex issues is attempting to understand the biopsychosocial components and mechanisms of behavior. Yet most behavior is learned, and if something can be learned, then it should be possible to unlearn it and substitute and practice a more health-promoting behavior. A component of behavioral change that is often ignored is the environmental context under which a specific behavior is learned, the environmental context that maintains the behavior, and the changes that must be made in the environmental context if the behavior is going to be changed. Behavioral and risk profiles are important, but so is the environmental context within which a person lives.

433. The answer is E. (*Last, 13/e. pp 715–728.*) Intensive scientific studies begun in the 1940s have clearly established the health hazards associated with the use of tobacco products, particularly cigarettes. The overall mortality risk for smokers compared with nonsmokers is 60 percent greater. Each cigarette smoked shortens the smoker's life span by about 5.5 min. Studies in the 1950s showed that smokers were much more likely than nonsmokers to die from a large number of diseases. Lung cancer, cardiovascular diseases, and emphysema are three of the more significant diseases associated with smoking. The risk of dying of lung cancer, for example, is between 8 and 15 times higher in cigarette smokers than in nonsmokers. More recent studies have led to the realization that there is a serious impact of smoking pollution on the health of nonsmokers. For example, children whose parents smoke have a higher incidence of respiratory infections and impaired function than those whose parents do not smoke. In 1989 there were 142,000 deaths from lung cancer with 83 percent attributed to smoking. More women than men are initiating smoking and the rate of mortality for women is increasing more rapidly than for men. In 1985, smoking initiating rates were 34.6 percent for women and 33.4 percent for men, and fewer women (39.8 percent) were quitting than men (49 percent).

434. The answer is C. *(Gatchel, 2/e. pp 290–296.)* A remarkable number of studies have found that life-style, schooling, marital status, income level, and even religious participation are good predictors of health and longevity. While all of these factors are important, life-style represents a combination of all the behavioral factors upon which health risks and prevention are based and has a central role in the etiology and treatment of most diseases. Of course genetics is also a major factor, but one's life-style can have a direct effect on the expression of particular genes or predispositions. Education is associated with income, life changes, life-style, habits, knowledge, self-esteem, and other factors, all of which affect health. Marriage favors men, but both men and women gain significantly relative to unmarried or divorced persons. Religious participation generally is related to conventionality of life-style, and more positive health behaviors in respect to smoking, drinking, and other risks.

435. The answer is D. *(Wilson, 12/e. pp 411–417.)* Maintaining a lean body is conducive to good health and a long life. Actuarial studies have shown that obesity is associated with a diminished life expectancy. A 50-year-old man who is 50 pounds overweight has half the remaining life expectancy of a normal-weight man of the same age. Excess weight can aggravate existing health problems, causing more severe symptoms or accelerating the appearance of a disorder earlier in life than might otherwise occur. Experts in heart disease estimate that at least one-fourth of our problems with cardiovascular disease are attributable to obesity, which makes the heart and lungs work harder than normal. Hypertension is twice as common among the obese as among lean persons. Although obesity is not the leading cause of hypertension, it does contribute to hypertension, which in turn can cause death from heart and kidney disease and stroke. Many people with high blood pressure are able to bring their pressure down to normal levels without drugs by losing weight and reducing their consumption of salt. Obesity also increases the risk of developing diabetes about fourfold and is associated with heart disease, blood clots, varicose veins, gout, respiratory disease, gastrointestinal disorders, gallbladder and liver disease, and arthritis of weight-bearing joints. Overweight people appear to be more clumsy, react to unexpected events more slowly, and are more likely to have accidents than normal-weight people. Compared with the general population, overweight people are more likely to die in automobile accidents. They have also been shown to be more susceptible to complications of surgery, infections, and delayed healing of wounds.

436. The answer is A. *(Rosen, p 112.)* There are many claims of health benefits from exercise, but the greatest scientific evidence supports the prevention of coronary heart disease, the maintenance of optimal body weight and body composition, and the normalization of fat and carbohydrate metabolism. There is also good support for the prevention of hypertension, osteoporosis, and low back pain and for improved psychological status. While exercise has not been shown to prevent such diseases as type I diabetes, chronic obstructive lung disease, renal failure, or arthritis, it has been shown to result in clinical improvement of these and other diseases after they have become manifest.

437. The answer is C. *(Lerner, Experiencing Adolescence, pp 195–207.)* Motor vehicle accidents are the major cause of death among adolescents and young adults. Physicians consider them to be of epidemic proportion among adolescents—in whom they account for 36 percent of all deaths. Homicide is the second leading cause of death; 25 percent of homicides occur in the 15-to-24-year-old group. Suicide is the third leading cause of death and is increasing for this age group, while it is decreasing for the general population. Infections and illicit drug abuse account for a relatively small number of deaths in this age group.

438. The answer is C. *(Lerner, Experiencing Adolescence, pp 194–195.)* An extensive study by Korlath showed the following incidences of health concerns of adolescents: colds (70 percent), depression (48 percent), dental problems (43 percent), personal problems (42 percent), flu (40 percent), family problems (35 percent), acne (34 percent), eye trouble (31 percent), headaches (27 percent), weight problems (26 percent), nervousness (25 percent), and difficulty sleeping (25 percent). Thus, socioemotional problems equal or exceed physical problems, and all were ranked higher than such physical problems as menstrual disorders and sexual problems (e.g., birth control, urinary infections, vaginal infections, venereal disease, and pregnancy). Also, physical problems such as acne, dental problems, headaches, and obesity have prominent behavioral components, and socioemotional problems such as depression, personal and family problems, nervousness, and sleeping difficulties have related physical components. Physicians must take a broader perspective, considering and integrating biologic, psychological, social, and situational factors in response to health perceptions and concerns.

439. The answer is D. *(Rosen, pp 117–118.)* Exercise has a major effect on the amount of fat in relation to lean tissue and body weight. Exercise of moderate intensity can result in an increase in energy expenditure of 300 kcal for 30 min of activity. Also the metabolic rate remains elevated for several hours after physical activity, which further increases the contribution of exercise to weight loss. Exercise is important in the elderly as it helps retain muscle mass. Exercise also contributes to general weight loss, especially when combined with calorie restriction, as it causes a greater proportion of weight loss to be from adipose tissue.

440. The answer is D. *(Lindzey, 3/e. pp 809–810.)* Social context and peer pressure are most important both in acquiring a habit of substance abuse and in maintaining it. The social context has been shown to be of primary importance in maintaining a habit of substance abuse, even for addicted heroin users. Substance abuse includes such addictive behaviors as smoking, drug abuse, and alcohol abuse. Peer pressure is especially effective with teenagers in initiating, terminating, and avoiding substance abuse, especially with cigarette smoking. The percentage of teenage smokers is still increasing, especially among teenage females. Attempts by such pioneers as Richard Evans to use peer pressure through social inoculation to prevent smoking among teenagers have been relatively effective. Becoming a teenage smoker has some immediate value, such as being accepted by one's peers, feeling more mature or adult, and defying authority figures. Arousal of fear and traditional methods of health education have had very limited effects on smoking and other addictive behaviors.

441. The answer is E. *(Last, 13/e. pp 967–968, 986.)* Down's syndrome (mongolism) is caused by a chromosomal aberration. Most sufferers have 47 chromosomes instead of 46. The risk of Down's syndrome increases dramatically with maternal age, especially after age 35. The general incidence is about 1:700 live births, varying from about 1:2000 live births in early childbearing age to about 1:400 at age 35 and about 1:100 at age 40. About 80 percent of Down's syndrome infants will have standard trisomy, about 15 percent will have the translocation form, and 5 percent will have the mosaic form. About one-third of the translocation cases are inherited and detectable in one or the other parent. Amniocentesis can detect the presence of Down's syndrome, but the procedure requires surgical skill, is not free from hazard, and, if the test is positive, introduces ethical and religious considerations of potential induced abortion. Down's syndrome accounts for about 30 percent of the retarded children in the United States. Although some sufferers have a relatively normal IQ, most IQs are between 40 and 60. Most children used to die early, but with antibiotics and other scientific advances, those who live to the preschool age can now be expected to live to the average age of 40.

442. The answer is E. *(Hamburg, Frontiers of Research, pp 124–133.)* Most of the characteristic risk factors for cardiovascular disease are behavioral. The usual factors of hypertension, cholesterolemia, and cigarette smoking have basic behavioral bases, particularly in terms of stress, diet, and behavioral addictions, but others such as obesity, personality type, and physical inactivity are also behaviorally based. Advanced age, male sex, and diabetes are less behaviorally related (but still have behavioral components). A high concentration of glucose without overt diabetes is both behaviorally (via diet) and metabolically related. A small amount of alcohol consumption appears to decrease risk, but excessive amounts increase risk, especially when combined with smoking behavior and type A personality.

443. The answer is D. *(Kaplan, 6/e. pp 141–142.)* Thomas Holmes and Richard Rahe developed a social readjustment rating scale that includes 43 life events that can cause varying amounts of stress and disruption in the lives of normal people (e.g., death of a spouse, separation or divorce, death of a close friend, changing or losing one's job, moving to a new location, retirement). Each stressful life event was assigned a unit score. They found that if one accumulated a certain number of stress or life-change units in a single year, the vulnerability to and incidence of psychosomatic disorders increased. Recent data show that persons who face these life-event readjustments optimistically rather than pessimistically are less apt to develop psychosomatic disorders or will recover from them more rapidly. The mechanism is still being explored, but a series of life-change events and a person's coping skills, values, and personality may combine to generate or "drive" physiologic correlates to influence genetically predisposed or vulnerable persons to develop a psychosomatic disorder. The Holmes and Rahe scale is being revised to incorporate the variability of individual values and social and physical status.

Friedman and Rosenman defined type A and type B personalities and developed a structured interview to identify the specific personal components in a type A or type B person. The Luria-Nebraska neuropsychological battery assesses a wide range of cognitive functions, e.g., dyslexia and dyscalculia, in addition to brain dysfunction and the localization of various cortical zones. The Minnesota multiphasic personality inventory (MMPI) is an objective, self-report test for assessing personality, and the Rorschach is a projective test originally designed to identify patterns of thinking and association and particularly various thought disorders.

444. The answer is D. *(Hamburg, Frontiers of Research, pp 126–129.)* One of the earliest psychosocial hypotheses in the etiology of hypertension was that it was anger directed inward because of an inability to express anger properly. While it has been demonstrated that hypertensive persons do tend to avoid involvement and confrontation, additional relevant factors are involved. Acutely stressful events have been related to hypertension, and it has been demonstrated that persons with a familial history of hypertension have an increased response to environmental and behavioral stressors compared with normotensive controls. Increased sympathetic nervous system activity and diminished parasympathetic inhibition result in increased blood pressure, which suggests a possible disturbance of central autonomic regulation with possible increased sensitivity to stressors.

445. The answer is D. *(Hamburg, Frontiers of Research, pp 99–107.)* Cigarette smoking is a powerful addiction; it is estimated that about 60 percent of smokers have tried to quit and another 30 percent want to quit. While nicotine may be the major pharmacologic reinforcer and behavioral factors play a role in the reinforcement of the addiction, behavioral factors have been demonstrated to play a major role in the initiation of the smoking habit itself, the day-to-day fluctuations in smoking, and the difficulty of maintaining abstinence after one has quit. Behavioral factors also play a major role in the situations in which smoking occurs and in the choice of cigarette brands. Of the estimated 30 million smokers who try to quit each year, only about 3 million achieve long-term abstinence. A physician's advice has a low 1-year abstinence result, except for patients recovering from a recent heart attack, in whom the 1-year abstinence is about 50 percent.

446. The answer is B. *(Wilson, 12/e. pp 2128–2131.)* Twin, family, and adoptive studies have shown that schizophrenia has a significant and primary genetic basis. Even though psychosocial factors are regarded as secondary, the stress-diathesis model incorporates a host of stressful factors that may precipitate a psychotic state in a person at high risk. The stress can be the result of specific illnesses, social or psychological, environmental, or chemical (such as that from use of PCP or amphetamines). Also, specific hallucinogens may precipitate a psychotic episode that is indistinguishable from schizophrenia. There is no specific schizophrenia-prone personality type, even though a small percentage of persons with a schizoid and paranoid personality disorder seem to be more vulnerable to developing schizophrenic disorders. Lower socioeconomic status does correlate with a higher incidence of schizophrenia. The onset of schizophrenia is generally related to a developmental or intrapsychic deficit in the vulnerable individual.

0-72,9 %

Health Care Systems

DIRECTIONS: Each question below contains five suggested responses. Select the **one best** response to each question.

447. Patients seek the services of "nonscientific," in preference to "scientific," systems of healing primarily because these services are

(A) less costly
(B) more available
(C) more efficacious
(D) more supportive
(E) none of the above

448. Native-American healers are responsible for discovering and using all the following EXCEPT

(A) the cure for scurvy
(B) oral contraception
(C) the use of antibiotics
(D) nearly 50 drugs now officially listed in the *National Formulary*
(E) an appreciation of the integration of humans and nature

449. Which of the following health professions had the highest percentage of women enrolled in 1989?

(A) Medicine
(B) Dentistry
(C) Pharmacy
(D) Optometry
(E) Veterinary medicine

450. A health maintenance organization is characterized by all the following key principles EXCEPT

(A) provision of comprehensive medical care to its enrolled members
(B) emphasis on efficiency and economy as well as medical care
(C) strong emphasis on preventive health services
(D) members who pay only for the services received
(E) reduction of time spent in the hospital

451. The statistics for 1990 show that intravenous drug users accounted for what percentage of the infections with human immunodeficiency virus (HIV) among men?

(A) 7
(B) 11
(C) 22
(D) 33
(E) 44

452. Correct characterizations of the elderly in the health care system include all the following EXCEPT

(A) 15 to 20 percent of the noninstitutionalized elderly have limitations in activities of daily living
(B) 5 percent of the elderly reside in nursing homes or institutions
(C) only 15 percent of the functionally limited elderly are receiving needed help from the formal medical or nonfamily system
(D) most elderly initially consult a health care provider in a health crisis
(E) there are twice as many disabled elderly being cared for by their families as by institutions

453. Long-term care for elderly widowed parents is most often provided by

(A) health professional caregivers
(B) nursing homes
(C) sisters or brothers
(D) daughters
(E) long-time friends

454. True statements about the nursing profession include all the following EXCEPT

(A) nearly three-fourths of all working registered nurses are employed in hospitals and nursing homes
(B) only 80 percent of the potentially employable registered nurses in the United States are working full-time
(C) hospitals report a very high turnover rate, often as high as 50 percent of the nursing staff annually
(D) there are more than 1.5 million registered nurses in the United States
(E) nurses are the largest single group of health professionals in the United States

455. The folk medical care system employed by many Mexicans and Mexican-Americans is known as

(A) *medico*
(B) allopathy
(C) voodoo
(D) soma
(E) *curanderismo*

456. The principles of the hospice movement include all the following EXCEPT

(A) acceptance of death as a logical part of life
(B) self-determination
(C) importance of family support
(D) control of pain only when severe
(E) direction of services usually by the primary care physician

457. The form of treatment that most resembles *curanderismo* in its techniques of therapy is

(A) allopathy
(B) homeopathy
(C) osteopathy
(D) chiropractic
(E) spiritual healing

458. Studies of the economics of health care show that all the following statements are true EXCEPT

(A) between 1940 and 1990, the percentage of gross national product spent on health tripled
(B) per capita expenditures for health care increased nearly tenfold between 1950 and 1977
(C) government expenditures for health care have increased nearly 2000 percent since 1950
(D) current health expenditures by the federal government represent 13 percent of the total federal budget
(E) the federal government contributes 72 percent of the funds in the total health care field

459. In the United States since 1900,

(A) cancer deaths have increased 50 percent
(B) gastrointestinal infections have increased
(C) life expectancy for both men and women has increased by 50 percent
(D) heart disease has been reduced to pre-1900 levels
(E) the number of AIDS cases reached a peak in 1989 and leveled off

460. Economic benefits of health promotion programs to the employer are seen in all the following areas EXCEPT

(A) company pension fund costs
(B) worker absenteeism
(C) worker morale
(D) life and disability insurance costs
(E) cessation of smoking

461. International statistics on the per capita consumption of absolute alcohol in liters show which country to rate the highest?

(A) Finland
(B) United States
(C) Russia
(D) Spain
(E) France

462. Between 1950 and 1985, the greatest total percentage increase in per capita consumption of alcoholic beverages was in

(A) Finland
(B) France
(C) the former German Democratic Republic (East Germany)
(D) Netherlands
(E) United States

463. All the following statements about the early history of medical education in the United States are correct EXCEPT that

(A) the first medical school in the United States was established in 1783 at Harvard University
(B) the American Medical Association (AMA) at its founding in 1847 had as a primary goal the reform of medical education
(C) the Association of American Medical Colleges (AAMC) was organized in 1876 as part of the effort to improve the quality of medical education
(D) in 1902, the *Journal of the American Medical Association (JAMA)* began publishing medical school failure statistics on state licensing board examinations
(E) in 1905, only five medical schools required any college preparation for admission

464. Medicare expenditures are correctly characterized by which of the following statements?

(A) Ten percent of Medicare enrollees account for over 70 percent of all Medicare expenditures
(B) Over 50 percent of Medicare expenditures are for care in the last year of life
(C) Fifteen percent of all Medicare enrollees have no reimbursable expenses in a given year
(D) Only 5 percent of Medicare enrollees over age 85 have no reimbursable Medicare expenses
(E) The 6 percent of Medicare patients who die each year consume over 50 percent of all Medicare expenses

465. All the following statements concerning health care for the elderly are true EXCEPT

(A) demands on the health care system are expected to increase for the over-65 age group
(B) acute diseases are expected to increase in all segments of the over-65 age group
(C) mortality among the elderly has shown a decline over the past 15 years
(D) the sex differential in human longevity is the cumulative result of excessive male mortality throughout the life span
(E) females have been the heaviest users of the health care system

466. True statements regarding the deinstitutionalization of patients in state mental hospitals since 1955 include which of the following?

(A) It has been attributed to the improved treatment (drug) programs in state mental hospitals
(B) It provided a last resort for one class of society's rejected mentally ill population
(C) It resulted in an initially decreased public investment in mental health and a subsequent increase in the 1980s
(D) It resulted in local, state, and federal agencies taking comprehensive responsibility for psychiatric and social services for the chronically mentally ill
(E) Both private and public hospitals are now required to take severely mentally ill patients without insurance

467. Which of the following is the leading consumer of health care dollars?

(A) Cardiovascular disease
(B) Cancer
(C) Gastrointestinal disease
(D) Respiratory disease
(E) Accidents

468. During the early and mid-1980s the number of

(A) registered nurses (RNs) decreased
(B) physician assistants (PAs) decreased
(C) midwives increased
(D) licensed practical nurses (LPNs) increased
(E) nurse practitioners (NPs) decreased

DIRECTIONS: Each group of questions below consists of lettered headings followed by a set of numbered items. For each numbered item select the **one** lettered heading with which it is **most** closely associated. Each lettered heading may be used **once, more than once, or not at all**.

Questions 469–472

For each health care plan described, select the payment plan with which it is most closely associated.

(A) Medicare
(B) National health insurance
(C) Medicaid
(D) Blue Cross
(E) Blue Shield

469. A compulsory hospital insurance plan whose cost is shared by employees and employers through Social Security payroll taxes

470. A prepayment insurance plan providing limited coverage of hospital costs on a nonprofit basis for individuals or groups

471. A grant-in-aid program whose costs are shared by the federal and state governments for all low-income persons

472. A prepayment supplementary medical insurance program to pay physicians' fees in hospitals, surgery, and emergency care

Questions 473–475

Match the descriptions below with the appropriate medical problem.

(A) Neoplasms
(B) Circulatory disorders
(C) Mental disorders
(D) Musculoskeletal disorders
(E) None of the above

473. The greatest number of Social Security disability awards for women

474. The greatest number of Social Security disability awards for men and women combined

475. The most rapidly increasing rate of Social Security disability awards

Questions 476–479

For each approximate percentage change in mortality between 1970 and 1988, select the disease with which it is associated.

(A) Disease of the heart
(B) Malignant neoplasm
(C) Chronic obstructive pulmonary disease
(D) Cerebrovascular disease
(E) None of the above

476. Increased by 3 percent

477. Increased by 45 percent

478. Decreased by 35 percent

479. Decreased by 55 percent

Health Care Systems
Answers

447. The answer is D. *(Twaddle, 2/e. pp 155, 165–182.)* Although cost and availability may contribute to a patient's decision to seek "nonscientific" health care, the main attraction of such treatment is that it more often serves a patient's psychological needs than do "scientific" systems of health care. "Scientific" medicine frequently contradicts patients' cultural beliefs and expectations and ignores their psychological and social plight. The nontraditional system recognizes that healing also occurs within the intimate context of family, community, and religion.

448. The answer is D. *(Twaddle, 2/e. pp 176–179.)* Native-American health care systems have contributed more to Western scientific medicine than any other cultural healing art. The ethnocentricity of Euro-Americans with respect to medicine has prevented our recognition and appreciation of this contribution. In so doing, we have ignored a large and important part of our cultural heritage. Native-American tribes discovered cures for scurvy, herbal oral contraception, the use of antibiotics, and more than 200 drugs that are now officially listed in the *United States Pharmacopeia* since its first edition in 1920. It is not generally realized that knowledge and other benefits did not flow exclusively from our scientific Western culture into the so-called lower cultures of Native-American civilizations. In fact, the advice of Native-American healers was much sought after by white patients and physicians alike. In addition to the herbs and healing techniques, Native-American healing systems relied heavily on a reverence for all forms of natural processes and were designed to preserve or reestablish the integration of humans and nature, i.e., harmony or balance between all living things and objects.

449. The answer is C. *(U.S. Public Health Service, p 172.)* The number of women enrolled for training in the health professions has continued to increase over the past decade. Pharmacy has the highest with 59.2 percent, followed by veterinary medicine with 57.2 percent, allopathic medicine with 35.2 percent, and optometry with 39.3 percent. Osteopathic medicine has 30.0 percent women enrolled, followed by dentistry with 33.0 percent. Over the past decade, podiatry had an increase from 6.8 to 25.7 percent, followed by optometry with an increase from 13.4 to 39.3 percent, and dentistry with an increase from 11.2 to 33.0 percent. Veterinary medicine increased from 27.3

to 57.2 percent and pharmacy increased from 36.8 to 59.2 percent. Enrollment of women in medicine increased 35 percent (24.7 to 35.2 percent) and nursing has decreased from 95.3 to 93.8 percent women.

450. The answer is D. *(Williams, SJ, 3/e. pp 144–147.)* Physicians affiliated with health maintenance organizations (HMOs) have a strong financial incentive to provide medical care to enrolled members in a manner that emphasizes efficiency and economy. Prepayment for maintenance of health dictates minimal expenditures for patient care in order to maximize income. Means of accomplishing this include reducing the time patients spend in the hospital, doing as much diagnosis and therapy as possible on an outpatient basis, detecting disease early, and emphasizing preventive services. The HMOs have provided comprehensive services with greater economy and containment of costs than traditional fee-for-service arrangements.

451. The answer is C. *(U.S. Public Health Service, pp 111–112.)* As of 1990, intravenous drug users accounted for 22 percent of the HIV cases among men. Men who are both intravenous drug users and homosexual accounted for an additional 5 percent of the HIV cases. Adult and adolescent homosexual and bisexual men accounted for 57 percent of the HIV cases. Among women with HIV, 48 percent acquired their infection through intravenous drug use. Heterosexual contact accounted for 30 percent of the HIV infections among women. As of 1990, approximately 87 percent of all HIV infections occurred among adult or adolescent men, 12 percent among adult or adolescent women, and 2 percent among children under 2 years of age. Increases are occurring in intravenous drug users and heterosexuals, as well as in total number of infections.

452. The answer is D. *(Hazzard, 2/e. pp 232–233.)* It is important to recognize that most of the elderly are able to function independently even though most have at least one chronic health condition. A survey by the U.S. Department of Health and Human Services found that 18 percent of the elderly population have limitations in activities of daily living, but only 5 percent of the elderly are residents of nursing homes or other institutions. Only 15 percent of the elderly with functional disabilities receive the help they need from the formal medical or nonfamily health care system. The vast majority of the elderly initially consult a relative or friend in a health crisis rather than a medical health care provider. There are twice as many elderly being cared for by their families as are being cared for by institutions. Daughters, and in some cases daughters-in-law, are the principal caregivers in the family. This will become an increasing problem with the increase of middle-aged women in the work force.

453. The answer is D. *(Hazzard, 2/e. pp 232–233.)* When elderly parents are widowed, most of the long-term care is given by their adult children, primarily by a daughter. Contrary to the modern myth, adult children are not alienated from their aged parents and they make strenuous efforts to avoid institutional placement of the elderly. These middle-generation women are under increasing stress, however, because their traditional roles as wives, homemakers, parents, grandparents, and parental caregivers are now being increasingly expanded as women join the labor force. Sixty percent of women between the ages of 45 and 54 are employed, and more than 40 percent of women between the ages of 55 and 64 are now employed. This remains an increasing trend.

454. The answer is B. *(Williams, SJ, 3/e. pp 326–332.)* There are more than 5 million people employed in health-related occupations. One-half of these are in nursing or related services, and they constitute the largest single group of health professionals in the country. Nursing remains a largely hospital-based profession. Nearly 75 percent of all nurses employed work in hospitals and nursing homes, and only 13 percent work in private physicians' offices and similar work places. The number of registered nurses in practice has grown since 1977, when it was 978,000, to 1,404,000 in 1983. Many hospitals report very high turnover rates in their nursing staffs. A rate of 50 percent turnover in a year is not unusual for many community and teaching hospitals in the United States. With more than 1.5 million registered nurses in the United States, less than half of the employable nurses are working full-time. Increased demand will come from acute-care hospitals, long-term care, home-based care, and preventive care. Also, the nursing profession has been attempting to increase and enhance its role and responsibility, especially over the past 2 decades.

455. The answer is E. *(Twaddle, 2/e. pp 175–176.)* *Curanderismo* is a very popular and widely used system of folk medicine. It is a blend of Native-American medicine, Mexican folk medicine, African folk medicine, and European medieval medicine. This health care system is an important source of cultural solidarity and pride for practitioner and client alike. Indeed, the social and cultural aspects of *curanderismo* may well overshadow the practical concerns of actually getting well.

456. The answer is D. *(Hazzard, 2/e. pp 354–360.)* The hospice movement is an attempt to provide care for the dying person progressing along the journey of life toward death. It deals with some of the major psychological and social conflicts encountered by patient, family, and health care provider when patients are dying. The basic principles of the movement are self-determination, acceptance of death as a logical part of life, and the importance of family support. These are accomplished through providing inpatient, outpatient, and home services under the direction of the primary care physicians; using the concept of the health care team; providing most primary care roles through family, hospice staff, and volunteers; early control of symptoms through aggressive and innovative approaches to pain, fear, and stress; support for family before and after patient's death; and support for the staff and caregivers. Most often the patient is kept at home and as comfortable as possible until death.

457. The answer is D. *(Twaddle, 2/e. p 175.)* Curanderismo, like chiropractic, stresses manipulation and massage of body parts as a major part of its therapeutic technology. However, *curanderismo* also enlists the aid of various medicines and poultices, including mood-changing drugs. Manipulation and massage are important in helping to establish rapport between physician and patient. Indeed, the importance of "laying on" of hands is recognized by virtually all effective systems of the curative arts.

458. The answer is E. *(Last, 13/e. pp 1074–1078.)* Health care costs in the United States are increasing at an alarming rate, with health expenditures representing an increasingly larger portion of family and governmental budgets. Current health expenditures by the federal government represent 13 percent of the total federal budget, with the federal budget contributing 40 percent of the funds for all health costs. Between 1940 and 1990 the percentage of GNP spent on health care tripled from 4.1 to 12.1 percent. Per capita expenditures for health care increased from $78 in 1950 to $1365 in 1980. The causes of the rise in health care costs are multiple. General inflation has contributed to this to a great extent, along with the dramatic shift in the federal government's role of providing third-party payment for significant segments of the population, the increase in technology, and subspecialization. As these costs increase without apparent limit, legislators and other public officials are looking increasingly to prevention, in general, and life-style change, in particular, to bring these cost increases under control.

459. The answer is C. *(Gatchel, 2/e. pp 5–6.)* With the advent of vaccinations and antibiotics to treat and prevent infectious illnesses and with the changes in health care and health behavior practices, the life expectancy for both men and women has increased by 50 percent. The high incidence of death from diseases such as influenza, pneumonia, diphtheria, tuberculosis, and gastrointestinal infections has been reduced to less than 5 percent of 1900 levels. These infectious diseases have now been replaced by many other diseases caused by life-style and behavior. Increased numbers of deaths are now caused by or facilitated by preventable behavioral factors such as smoking, poor diet, substance abuse, lack of exercise, and stressful conditions. A reduction in heart disease has been made over the past few decades, but levels have not yet reached those of 1900. The number of AIDS cases has continued to increase over the past 15 years, with the greatest increases occurring in the heterosexual and adolescent populations.

460. The answer is A. *(Rosen, pp 239–247.)* Recent analyses of the economic benefits of most health promotion programs in the work place show benefits in such areas as savings through smoking-cessation programs, less worker absenteeism, improved worker attitude and morale, decreased life and disability insurance costs, less use of medical care services, and increased recruitment value. All of these savings, however, appear to be overshadowed by the increased costs and demands on the company's pension fund. In effect, the prevention programs would prolong the lives of former workers in their economically nonproductive years. The question being debated by employers now is who will pay for the longer and better lives of the workers.

461. The answer is E. *(Last, 13/e. pp 745–750.)* The highest per capita alcohol consumption by regions is in Australia and New Zealand, North America, and Europe. These regions are the most economically developed, share similar cultural heritages, and have a long history of acceptance and use of alcohol. France has the highest per capita consumption of alcohol (13.3 L) and Spain is third with 11.8 L per capita. The U.S. ranks sixteenth with 8.0 L per capita per year, Finland thirty-sixth with 6.9 L, and Russia fiftieth with 5.2 L per capita. Other countries with the highest per capita consumption include Barbados, Luxembourg, Argentina, and Portugal. In the past 10 years, France has shown a significant decrease in per capita consumption and seven other countries have shown a small decrease. This has been attributed to changes in some consuming populations, economic trends, recent efforts of governments to deal with alcohol problems, and an increased awareness of health-related risks.

462. The answer is C. *(Last, 13/e. pp 745–760.)* Since World War II, there has been a general trend of increased production and consumption of alcohol. Major per capita consumption increases have been recorded in Europe, North America, Australia, and New Zealand. The countries with the greatest per capita increases between 1950 and 1985 were the German Democratic Republic (758 percent), the Federal Republic of Germany (272 percent), the Netherlands (305 percent), Finland (282 percent), and Poland (133 percent). Other countries with over a 100 percent increase were Denmark, Hungary, and Czechoslovakia. The U.S. has shown a 60 percent increase while France has shown a 23 percent decrease. Of interest is that each of the top eight countries showing the greatest increase has increased at a faster rate each decade, while France, Austria, Portugal, Yugoslavia, Ireland, and Britain have experienced a slight decrease, especially since 1976. The World Health Organization has expressed concern that the conduct of international trade and marketing in alcoholic beverages constitutes a serious international public health problem.

463. The answer is A. *(Last, 13/e. pp 1065–1073.)* Today's physician receives vastly different training from the practitioner in eighteenth- or nineteenth-century America. Today's medical practitioner has pursued a rigorous course of study in clinical practice under the close supervision of faculty who are typically at the forefront of the field of academic medicine. In colonial America, there were very few physicians. The first medical school was established in 1756 at the College of Philadelphia (later, University of Pennsylvania). The second school was founded at King's College (later, Columbia University) in 1768. At the time of the Revolutionary War, there were estimated to be 3500 practitioners in the colonies of which only 400 had received any formal training. Apprenticeship to a practicing physician was the most common approach to training for a long period of time. The American Medical Association was founded in 1847 with the reform of medical education as a primary goal. In 1876, 22 medical schools organized the Association of American Medical Colleges as part of an effort to improve the quality of medical education. Beginning in 1902, *JAMA* published medical school failure statistics on state board licensing examinations, a form of exposure that could not help but embarrass and lead to institutional reform. In 1905, only five schools required any college preparation for admission. Ten years later, 85 schools prescribed a minimum of 1 or 2 years of college preparation. By 1932, every recognized medical school and most of the state licensing boards required at least 2 years of college work. Many required 3 years, and several required a college degree.

464. The answer is A. *(Hazzard, 2/e. p 160.)* The distribution of Medicare expenditures for those over age 65 is highly skewed, especially for care in a nursing home, less for hospital care, and less for physician and drug costs. This skewness is because only 10 percent of Medicare patients account for over 70 percent of all Medicare expenditures. On the other hand, it is important to recognize that about 35 percent of Medicare enrollees have no reimbursable expenses in any given year. Even 20 percent of persons over age 85 have no reimbursable expenses in a given year. The last year of life is often very expensive, so that the 6 percent of Medicare patients who die each year consume nearly 30 percent of all Medicare expenditures. Thus, a relatively small number of older persons consume the major portion of Medicare expenditures.

465. The answer is B. *(Hazzard, 2/e. pp 157–164.)* The elderly use a dispro-portionate amount of health care resources. With the estimated increase in the 65-and-over age group from 24 million (11 percent) to 38 million (14 per-cent), there will be an increased demand for health care services between now and the year 2000. Also, with the shift of health problems from acute illness to more chronic and debilitating conditions, there will be additional need to increase continuing and long-term health care. Data show women to be heav-ier users of services than men. With the increase in the elderly and with the female population progressively outnumbering the male population, the need for health care and help with social and economic problems in elderly females is expected to increase. The greater part of the sex differential in human lon-gevity is considered to be the cumulative result of excessive male mortality throughout the life span. This is because of increased risk behaviors and hab-its that increase the vulnerability of males to health problems. The decline in mortality of the elderly over the past 15 years is partly due to the reduction in mortality from cardiovascular disease, improvements in medical science, and a shift in the population toward gathering more information and having more concern about their own health behaviors.

466. The answer is A. *(Last, 13/e. pp 956–958.) Deinstitutionalization* is a term used to describe the continuous decline in numbers of patients in state mental hospitals. It began about 1955 partly as the result of improved drug treatment programs. Policy and legislative changes 10 years later resulted in geographic decentralization and removed much of the power for involuntary commitments away from the mental hospitals (patients the hospitals had to accept). Thus, the state hospitals, which had provided a last resort for one class of society's rejected population (the chronically mentally ill), reduced their census and transferred much of the financial responsibility to the state and local communities. The public investment in mental health increased ini-tially with federal funds supporting the decentralization. However, the federal support was gradually withdrawn during the 1980s and the state and local agencies have been unable to take responsibility for the comprehensive psy-chiatric and social services needed by the chronically mentally ill. Private hospitals treat more patients from the upper socioeconomic classes. Severely mentally ill patients without insurance generally are not accepted at private hospitals, so they must be admitted to public hospitals.

467. The answer is A. *(Matarazzo, pp 862–863.)* About 900,000 Americans die annually from cardiovascular diseases, about 700,000 from heart attack and 200,000 from stroke. This accounts for more than half of the deaths each year, and another million people become disabled each year by cardiovascu-lar disease. In 1977, the cost was about $80 billion (about $54 billion in indirect costs and $26 billion in direct medical care spending)—10 percent of the nation's medical costs—and this cost has increased tremendously since. Hypertension is a major risk factor, increasing risk threefold for developing heart disease, sixfold for congestive heart failure, and sevenfold for stroke, yet hypertension can be effectively treated through pharmacologic and behavioral interventions.

468. The answer is C. *(Williams, SJ, 3/e. pp 326–331.)* The number of registered nurses (RNs) has actually doubled over the past 30 years, so that by 1983 there were about 1.4 million employed licensed registered nurses. By 1986 the number of RNs had increased to 1.6 million. Yet a shortage remains because of the need for more personnel to operate new technology and to care for sicker patients. In addition, inferior wages and working conditions (short staffing, perceived lack of respect and authority) dissuade some prospective nurses. Licensed practical nurses (LPNs) have decreased from over 267,000 in 1982 to fewer than 205,000 in 1986. LPNs are assuming more and more duties in hospitals, but they have little upward mobility as RN nursing programs refuse to allow transfer credits. The number of physician assistants (PAs) has increased since their inception in 1966 to about 18,000 in 1985. About 75 percent work with physicians in primary care settings and others in internal medicine and surgery. Their number in hospitals is also increasing. Nurse-midwives have increased in number from 300 in the mid-1960s to 2700 certified nurse-midwives in 1983. Most work in hospitals and rural areas where they provide care for women who do not have private physicians, but a growing number are entering private practice, where they refer high-risk problems to physicians. In 1960, 83 percent of nursing graduates were trained in hospitals, but by 1980, 83 percent were trained in college and university programs. Nurse practitioners (NPs) are registered nurses who have completed advanced programs preparing them for expanded roles and responsibilities (e.g., health histories, physical examinations, formulating and managing care for acute and chronically ill patients). By 1980, there were about 16,000 NPs with 2000 additional graduates each year.

469–472. The answers are: 469-A, 470-D, 471-C, 472-E. *(Williams, SJ, 3/e. pp 345–378.)* Medicare has two basic components. Part A is a compulsory hospital insurance plan for persons 65 years or older who are entitled to benefits under the Social Security or Railroad Retirement Acts. Social Security payroll taxes provide the funds for inpatient diagnostic studies, hospital room and board costs, and some home care and extended care services. Part B is a voluntary supplementary insurance program that pays for a major part of outpatient visits, diagnostic studies, doctors' fees, home health services, and certain medical equipment. Costs are shared between the individual and the

Federal General Revenue Fund, except for a deductible charge that is steadily increasing.

Blue Cross is a prepaid, limited "nonprofit" commercial medical insurance plan to cover hospital costs. It has grown rapidly with the burgeoning costs of hospital care. It also has become increasingly burdensome as a negotiated health care benefit between industry and labor.

Blue Shield is the same kind of payment mechanism as Blue Cross, extended to cover physicians' fees in hospitals as well as surgery and emergency care. Blue Cross, Blue Shield, Medicare, and Medicaid reimburse physicians and hospitals on a "reasonable cost" basis, which has continued to increase dramatically, and limit decision-making responsibilities of physicians and hospitals.

The federal and state governments share the costs of Medicaid, although the program is administered by the states. The program provides medical care for low-income people of all ages and can complement some of the provisions of Medicare if the patient is without funds and if the health care provider will accept Medicaid patients. Medicare and Medicaid are providing limited and decreasing care. In spite of the four major payment plans discussed above, the major problems of equity, effectiveness, and economy still exist and are worsening. A very large segment of the population has no medical insurance coverage.

There is no national health insurance program at the present time; however, with the increasing number of citizens with no health insurance or affordable health care, and the constantly increasing costs of health care, health technology, and commercial insurance, there are strong political pressures toward a national health insurance or single-payer health care system available to all citizens.

473–475. The answers are: 473-C, 474-C, 475-D. *(Rosen, pp 390–399.)* Social Security disability awards are highest for mental and musculoskeletal disorders with back pain disabilities increasing at a rate more than ten times the growth of our population. The greatest number of Social Security disability awards for women are for mental disorders. The greatest number of awards for men and women combined are also for mental disorders. Of the various kinds of disability, back pain and mental disorders are most affected by the external contingencies of eligibility for wage replacement funding (WRF), duration of benefits, and percentage of WRF. These contingencies all influence the persistence of disability.

476–479. The answers are: 476-B, 477-C, 478-A, 479-D. *(U.S. Public Health Service, pp 78–99.)* Heart disease is still the leading cause of death in the U.S. It reached a peak before 1950, but has continued to decline since then.

Between 1970 and 1988 the death rate for heart disease decreased by 35 percent (from 253.6 to 166.3 deaths per 100,000 population). The rate for white males decreased 37 percent compared with 24 percent for black males. The rate for white females decreased 32 percent, but that for black females decreased only 29 percent.

Malignant neoplasms increased about 3 percent between 1970 and 1988, from 129.9 per 100,000 population in 1970 to 132.7 in 1988. Lung cancer increased 17 percent for white males, but this was accompanied by a 120 percent increase in lung cancer for white women. In 1988 the incidence of lung cancer in women exceeded the incidence of breast cancer (formerly the highest form of cancer in women), and lung cancer is expected to continue to increase over the next decade because of the increased smoking behavior of women.

Mortality from chronic obstructive pulmonary disease has increased by 45 percent (from 13.2 to 19.4 deaths per 100,000 population). This has primarily resulted from smoking behaviors. It has now become the fifth leading cause of death in the U.S., and it is increasing most rapidly in women (a 45 percent increase in men versus a threefold increase in women).

Mortality from cerebrovascular diseases declined by 55 percent between 1970 and 1988. It is still the third leading cause of death in the U.S. The present rate is 29.7 deaths per 100,000 population, down from 66.3. The annual rate of decrease has been about 5 percent per year since 1970 for both sexes and major race groups. Better control of hypertension and healthier cardiovascular systems are given as explanations. However, the death rate for black males and females is almost twice that for white males and females.

The suicide rate has held rather constant with 11.6 deaths per 100,000 population in 1970 and 11.4 in 1988, although it has varied within subgroups such as adolescents and the elderly. It is the second leading cause (after accidents) of death among those 15 to 24 years of age. The youth suicide rate more than tripled between 1950 and 1980. White males committed the majority of suicides in all age groups. The male-to-female ratio was 5 to 1, and the white-to-black ratio was almost 2 to 1. Homicide is the second leading cause of death for black children, with a death rate 3 to 4 times the rate for any other group. The homicide rate for black adolescents continues to rise.

0-54,54 %.

Behavioral Statistics and Design

DIRECTIONS: Each question below contains five suggested responses. Select the **one best** response to each question.

480. In studying human development, the remeasurement of a cross-sectional sample of people after a given fixed interval of time has passed is called

(A) time-lag design
(B) sequential design
(C) multivariate design
(D) cross-sectional design
(E) longitudinal design

481. If one is conducting research that requires comparisons of content and material gathered for certain patients by different interviewers, the best format to use would be one that is

(A) projective
(B) structured
(C) unstructured
(D) analytical
(E) none of the above

482. The revised third edition of the *Diagnostic and Statistical Manual of Mental Disorders (DSM III-R)* offers an improvement over earlier psychiatric classifications. Its major advantage is that it

(A) identifies mental illness as a disease
(B) deals with predisposing factors
(C) confirms and supports the nosologic system
(D) is an all-inclusive classification system
(E) is a multiaxial classification system

483. Which of the following statements best describes the Likert technique of attitude measurement?

(A) Subjects indicate on five-point scales the extent of their agreement with a set of attitude statements

(B) Subjects indicate whether they agree with each of a series of attitude statements, which are equally spaced along an attitude continuum

(C) Subjects' responses to an open-ended interview are coded by content analysis

(D) Subjects judge a particular concept on a series of bipolar semantic scales

(E) Subjects check all acceptable items in a set of statements arranged in order of "difficulty of acceptance"

484. A sample of a population selected so that each observation or unit has an equal chance of being included is called a

(A) random population parameter
(B) systematic sample
(C) systematic random sample
(D) selected sample
(E) simple random sample

485. Two drugs were administered in several different doses, and the effects were measured and recorded. The data were subjected to regression and correlation analyses. The computed regression lines and correlation coefficients are presented below. Which of the following statements is true?

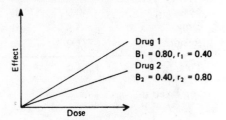

(A) In general, the strength of the causal relationship between two variables is indicated by the square of the correlation coefficient

(B) The proportion of variation in response to Drug 1 accounted for by dose is $(0.80)^2$

(C) The data indicate Drug 1 is more effective than Drug 2

(D) The data indicate Drug 1 is more potent than Drug 2

(E) There is more variability in responses to Drug 1 than to Drug 2

486. Two sedative-hypnotic drugs are being compared for relative efficacy in promoting sleep and also for possible differences in their effects on men and women. The results of a two-way analysis of variance are presented below. Of the following figures, which is the most plausible graphic representation of the observed effects?

Source of Variation	Sum of Squares	df	Mean Square	F	Significance
Drug	571.2	1	571.2	17.2	$p<0.01$
Sex	340.9	1	340.9	10.3	$p<0.01$
Drug × sex	63.3	1	63.3	1.9	NS
Residual	531.2	16	33.2		
Total	1506.4	19			

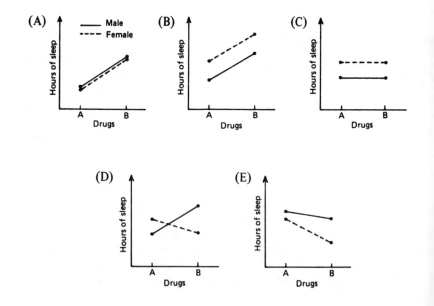

DIRECTIONS: Each group of questions below consists of lettered headings followed by a set of numbered items. For each numbered item select the **one** lettered heading with which it is **most** closely associated. Each lettered heading may be used **once, more than once, or not at all.**

Questions 487–492

For each description below, choose the correct term.

(A) *F* distribution
(B) Power of a test
(C) Correlation coefficient
(D) Meta-analysis
(E) Validity
(F) Reliability
(G) Standard deviation

487.   All values begin at zero and range upward to positive infinity

488.   A measure of the degree or strength of association between two variables

489.   The degree to which an instrument measures what it is supposed to measure

490.   The probability that your findings will be able to reject a false hypothesis

491.   A quantitative assessment of the results of a group of studies of a given topic

492.   The degree to which results are consistent on a repeat measurement

Questions 493–496

For each experimental design, select the term with which it is most closely associated.

(A) Randomized block design
(B) Completely randomized design
(C) Completely randomized factorial design
(D) Split-plot or repeated measures design
(E) Latin square design

493.

	treatments	
T_1	T_2	T_3
P_{11}	P_{12}	P_{13}
P_{21}	P_{22}	P_{23}
P_{31}	P_{32}	P_{33}
P_{41}	P_{42}	P_{43}
P_{51}	P_{52}	P_{53}
$\overline{P}_{.1}$	$\overline{P}_{.2}$	$\overline{P}_{.3}$

15 patients, randomly assigned to T_1, T_2, or T_3

$\overline{P}_{.1}$ $\overline{P}_{.2}$ $\overline{P}_{.3}$ = treatment means

(P_{21} = patient 2, treatment 1)

494.

	treatments			ward means
	T_1	T_2	T_3	
ward 1	P_{11}	P_{12}	P_{13}	$\overline{P}_{1.}$
ward 2	P_{21}	P_{22}	P_{23}	$\overline{P}_{2.}$
ward 3	P_{31}	P_{32}	P_{33}	$\overline{P}_{3.}$
ward 4	P_{41}	P_{42}	P_{43}	$\overline{P}_{4.}$
ward 5	P_{51}	P_{52}	P_{53}	$\overline{P}_{5.}$
treatment means	$\overline{P}_{.1}$	$\overline{P}_{.2}$	$\overline{P}_{.3}$	$\overline{P}_{..}$ = grand mean

3 patients from each of 5 wards, randomly assigned to T_1, T_2, or T_3

(P_{21} = patient from ward 2 in treatment 1)

495.

	age groups			
	20-40	41-60	61-80	weight means
weight <120	P_{112}	P_{121}	P_{133}	$\bar{P}_1..$
121-190	P_{213}	P_{222}	P_{231}	$\bar{P}_2..$
>191	P_{311}	P_{323}	P_{332}	$\bar{P}_3..$
age means	$\bar{P}._1.$	$\bar{P}._2.$	$\bar{P}._3.$	grand mean = $\bar{P}...$

(left label: weight groups)

} 9 patients, each categorized according to 2 nuisance variables, with treatment T_1, T_2, or T_3 assigned and specified by the 3rd subscript

treatment means $T_1 = (P_{121} + P_{231} + P_{311})/3 = \bar{P}.._1$
$T_2 = (P_{112} + P_{222} + P_{332})/3 = \bar{P}.._2$
$T_3 = (P_{133} + P_{213} + P_{323})/3 = \bar{P}.._3$

(P_{213} = patient from weight group 2, age group 1, treatment 3)

496.

	treatment A			
	T_{A1}	T_{A2}	T_{A3}	treatment B means
T_{B1}	P_{111} P_{112} P_{113}	P_{121} P_{122} P_{123}	P_{131} P_{132} P_{133}	$\bar{P}_1..$
T_{B2}	P_{211} P_{212} P_{213}	P_{221} P_{222} P_{223}	P_{231} P_{232} P_{233}	$\bar{P}_2..$
T_{B3}	P_{311} P_{312} P_{313}	P_{321} P_{322} P_{323}	P_{331} P_{332} P_{333}	$\bar{P}_3..$

} 27 patients, randomly assigned to all combinations of 2 treatments, each with 3 levels

treatment A means $\bar{P}._1.$ $\bar{P}._2.$ $\bar{P}._3.$ $\bar{P}...$ = grand mean

(P_{123} = treatment B1, treatment A2, patient 3)

Questions 497–500

For each outline of an experiment, select the form of statistical analysis that is most appropriate.

(A) Analysis of variance
(B) One-tail t-test
(C) Two-tail t-test
(D) Linear regression
(E) Chi-square

497. Does the inhibition of dopamine-sensitive adenylate cyclase have predictive value in assessing the potency of antipsychotic drugs? The data for each of 20 currently available antipsychotic drugs include an inhibition constant (K_i) that represents the drug concentration required to produce 50 percent inhibition of dopamine-stimulated cyclic AMP formation and an average clinical dose as a measure of potency

Drug	K_i (nM)	Approximate Equivalent Daily Dose (mg)
Chlorpromazine	50.0	100
Thioridazine	137.0	93
Fluphenazine	4.3	11
Trifluoperazine	18.0	6
•	•	•
•	•	•
•	•	•

498. Are black people who undergo a common surgical procedure more likely to be treated by a less experienced surgeon than are white people? The data represent hospital records from 340 patients undergoing gallbladder or hernia-repair operations in 10 randomly selected hospitals and include the patients' race (only black and white patients have been retained in the sample) and the status—resident or staff—of the surgeon

Race of Patient	Status of Surgeon	
	Staff	Resident
Black	31	63
White	31	215

499.   Methylphenidate often is used in the management of a childhood syndrome known as *hyperactivity,* or *minimal brain dysfunction.* Does the drug also retard the growth of children? The data, which are from 15 children who have taken methylphenidate for at least 2 years and 15 unmedicated controls matched for age and sex, consist of each child's change in height over a 2-year period

Hyperactive, with Methylphenidate Δ Height (in)	Hyperactive, Unmedicated Δ Height (in)
3	5
7	4
4	8
5	2
•	•
•	•
•	•

500.   Drug companies often claim that a particular aspirin preparation provides greater relief from arthritic pain than other apparently similar products. Are all aspirins alike? Two hundred subjects suffering from arthritis were randomly assigned to receive one of five aspirin preparations. The data are measures of increase in hand-gripping strength after treatment

Change in Hand-Gripping Strength (lb)

		Treatment		
1	2	3	4	5
10	8	4	3	6
8	2	9	2	2
3	4	4	5	8
7	9	7	5	7
•	•	•	•	•
•	•	•	•	•
•	•	•	•	•

Behavioral Statistics and Design

Answers

480. The answer is B. *(Lerner, Psychology, pp 171–179.)* The four research designs for studying human growth and development are longitudinal, cross-sectional, time-lag, and sequential. In the longitudinal design, the same group of people are observed at more than one time. The cross-sectional design studies age groups at one time. The time-lag design allows a researcher to see differences in behavior associated with particular ages at various times in history. Instead of focusing on one cohort or one time of measurement, a time-lag design considers only one age level at different times of measurement, say 1950, 1960, 1970, and 1980. The sequential design combines features of longitudinal and cross-sectional designs so that the researcher may assess differences between groups owing to age, cohort, or time of testing. The sequential design involves the remeasurement of a cross-sectional sample of people after a given fixed interval of time, obtaining repeated measures from each of the different cohort groups included in a given cross-sectional sample, and obtaining data from retest control groups to assess the effects of retesting.

481. The answer is B. *(Gatchel, 2/e. pp 200–203.)* The clinical interview is effective in obtaining data on concerns, feelings, problems, and history, but it tends to vary depending on the clinical and theoretical orientation of the interviewer, e.g., behavioral versus psychoanalytical. If one must compare the data gathered by different interviewers, interviewer bias can be reduced by using a rather highly structured interview of predetermined questions with specific categories of analysis or by using an existing standardized test, questionnaire, or rating scale. An audiotaped analysis could be designed so that a quantitative analysis would allow comparisons using different interviewers, but if the interviews were unstructured, comparisons of content would not be valid. Projective techniques are unstructured because they allow the subject to "project" his or her feelings, attitudes, or interpretations of an ambiguous stimulus or situation. Comparisons of different interviewers would not be valid.

482. The answer is E. *(Gatchel, 2/e. pp 197–200.)* DSM III-R is the official classification schema of mental disorders. Serious problems of validity and reliability were associated with *DSM I* and *DSM II*. The major advantage of *DSM III-R* is that it allows for a multiaxial classification. Earlier classifications were one-category systems, with the patient receiving only one diagnostic label or category. *DSM III-R* provides the possibility that a patient with several disorders can be scored or classified with multiaxial diagnoses. The broad dimensions or axes are as follows: I. Clinical psychiatric syndromes and other conditions; II. Personality disorders (adults) and specific developmental disorders (children and adolescents); III. Physical disorders; IV. Severity of psychosocial stressors; and V. Highest level of adaptive function during the past year.

483. The answer is A. *(Vander Zanden, 4/e. pp 176–177.)* In the Likert "method of summated ratings" relating to attitude measurement, subjects indicate on five-point scales the extent of their agreement with a series of attitude statements. These ratings are then summated to yield a single attitude score. This technique is less laborious than the Thurstone technique (choice B of the question), in which statements are first sorted by a group of judges into 11 equally spaced categories. The Guttman scalogram (choice E) differs from both of these techniques in that it involves a series of items assumed to be cumulative—that is, acceptance of one statement is assumed to imply acceptance of all other less extreme statements. Whereas Guttman assumes unidimensional concepts, C. E. Osgood argues for multidimensionality. His "semantic differential" (choice D) uses a series of seven-point bipolar scales (e.g., good-bad, strong-weak, active-passive) that are answered with respect to a single word or concept.

484. The answer is E. *(Duncan, 2/e. pp 54–55.)* When a mean and a standard deviation are calculated by using the data from the entire population, they are called *population parameters*. When they are calculated from a sample of that population they are referred to as *sample statistics*. In choosing a sample, the objective is to select observations or units that are truly representative of the total population being studied. If the sample is selected so that each observation or unit has an equal chance of being included in the sample, it is called a *simple random sample*. Randomness does not mean haphazardness, selecting something without intentional bias, having someone else choose, or using some general techniques, such as drawing from a hat, "randomly" pointing one's finger, or dart throwing. Using a table of random numbers or some mechanical means is considered best. An example of using a systematic sample would be interviewing every third person. Every possible source of sample bias must be explored.

485. The answer is E. *(Duncan, 2/e. pp 115–127.)* The only data available about the two drugs presented in the question are the regression coefficients (*b*) and the correlation coefficients (*r*) for a particular dosage range. Thus, one may conclude that the proportion of variation in responses to Drug 1 and Drug 2 accounted for by dose in that range is $r_1^2 = 0.16$ and $r_2^2 = 0.64$, respectively, or that there is more variability in response to Drug 1 than to Drug 2. There is no justification, however, for extrapolation in this context—the curves may even cross at higher doses. Finally, causal inferences from regression or correlation analyses are never justified.

486. The answer is B. *(Kirk, 2/e. pp 134–143.)* The results in the analysis of variance table indicate that both main effects—drug and sex—were significant, but there was no interaction. Graphically, this means there should be two lines (one for men, one for women), the lines should not be horizontal (Drug A was different from Drug B), and the lines should be parallel (there was no interaction). Choice C is an example of a sex effect but no drug effect or interaction; choice A represents a drug effect with no sex effect and no interaction; and choices D and E both illustrate significant main effects *with* an interaction. Choice B is only one of several possible correct representations, however, because the data presented do not disclose which drug was the more effective or whether both drugs were more effective with men or with women. Thus, other plausible figures would include:

487–492. The answers are: 487-A, 488-C, 489-E, 490-B, 491-D, 492-F. *(Rosenthal, pp 46–48, 60–61, 140–141, 276–278, 324–326, 439–440.)* In *F* distributions all values begin at zero and range upward to positive infinity. Statistical tests that employ the *F* distribution as the theoretical model are called *parametric tests* because they compare parameters estimated from sample distributions rather than the distributions themselves. Consequently, most of the assumptions concerning their use—normally distributed populations, continuous variables, and equal population variances—act to preserve the accuracy of the estimated procedures. There is the additional restriction that the observations must be independent because the computed *F* test value is a ratio of explained to unexplained variance. Any correlation between the observations would make such a ratio meaningless.

Power is the probability of rejecting the null hypothesis when the null hypothesis is false. Your hope, according to your hypothesis, is that you will be able to reject the null hypothesis. The sample size can be increased if the preliminary calculations indicate that the power is inadequate. Power can also be increased by reconstructing the experimental design to provide a more precise estimate of the treatment effects and smaller error effects.

A correlation analysis is used to obtain a measure of the degree or strength of association between two variables under study. The degree of association between X and Y is provided by r, the coefficient of correlation. It is important to observe several precautions: (1) the relationship between variables must be linear, (2) there is a real danger of making inferences beyond the range of actual observations or measurements on which the analysis is based, and (3) it must always be remembered that correlation does not necessarily mean causation. A significant correlation is an indication that the two variables, X and Y, tend to be associated. The problem is that a third variable may be affecting the relationship, thus causing both X and Y to vary together.

A meta-analysis is the quantitative analysis of the results of a group of studies of a given topic, i.e., an analysis of analyses. It is a widely used set of statistical procedures for comparing and combining results from different studies. One of the advantages of meta-analysis is that by combining the results of a number of studies we can increase the power of the statistical analysis, thus allowing us to identify effects that might escape our notice in a single study.

Reliability is the degree to which the results of one measurement are consistent (stable) upon repetition of the measurement or experiment. The term *reliability coefficient* refers to the degree to which what you have measured is relatively free of measurement fluctuations. Reliability coefficient would tell us about the objectivity or repeatability of our observations, judgments, or ratings.

Validity tells us the degree to which a test or questionnaire is measuring what it is supposed to be measuring. It is the most important consideration in test evaluation. We would have to have evidence in four categories: (1) content-related validity (e.g., Does the test contain items from the appropriate content areas?); (2) criterion validity, or the degree to which the test correlates with the outcome criteria (e.g., those things a medical student should know); (3) concurrent validity, which is a correlation of the results of the test with the concurrent performance or task being assessed; and (4) predictive validity, a correlation of the extent to which the test predicts the outcome or future performance (e.g., graduation).

493–496. The answers are: 493-B, 494-A, 495-E, 496-C. *(Kirk, 2/e. pp 12–19.)* Choosing the appropriate design for an experiment is crucial because the design involves a plan for assigning subjects to treatment groups, it expresses the relation being tested between the dependent and independent variables, and it organizes the effects of nuisance variables so that they can be tested and considered accordingly. The simplest experimental design is the completely randomized design. As the name implies, random assignment of subjects to treatments is essential if inferences drawn are to be logically valid. The hypothesis tested by this design—that all group means are equal—is evaluated with an F ratio.

The randomized block design, although very similar to the completely randomized design, tests the additional hypothesis that grouping the subjects according to one other variable, usually a background variable, will account for some variance previously left in the error term. This design and the others discussed below also employ an F ratio to test their hypotheses.

Subjects in a Latin square design are grouped according to two background or blocking variables in order to reduce further the error variance. If it can be assumed that there is no interaction between the two blocking variables, and if there are an equal number of treatment levels, rows, and columns, treatment levels can be randomly assigned to the cells such that each treatment occurs in each row and each column exactly once. The random assignment of treatment levels to cells reduces the sample size considerably from that which would be required if all treatment levels were given to all cells.

The completely randomized factorial essentially is a completely randomized design for two independent variables or factors. Again, all subjects must be randomly assigned to all cells. This design permits the simultaneous testing of two main treatment effects as well as any interaction effect between the two treatments.

497–500. The answers are: 497-D, 498-E, 499-B, 500-A. *(Goldstein, pp 51–53, 63–64, 102–104, 129–131.)* The experiment in the first question is designed to investigate the possibility that a linear relationship exists between an inhibition constant and the potency of antipsychotic drugs. This is a curve-fitting (as opposed to a difference) hypothesis, and a parametric procedure is justified because the data are continuous, ratio-level variables (choice D).

The experiment in the second question compares a set of counts in a contingency table with the expected distribution, given the unequal proportions of black and white patients. This is not a two-way analysis of variance, however. The data in the four cells are not means of randomly sampled, ordinal-level, or better variables; they are counts of binary variables (in a cell or not in a cell). The chi-square test (choice E) is designed for such enumeration data, regardless of the number of categories or the sample size.

The experiment in the third question is a test for differences between two groups measured with continuous, ratio-level variables. A one-tail t-test (choice B) is the best choice because the experiment is not concerned with whether methylphenidate retarded or accelerated children's growth, just whether it retarded growth. Both the two-tail t-test and the analysis of variance are inappropriate because they test two-tailed hypotheses.

The experiment in the fourth question is similar to that in the third: both test for differences between groups measured with continuous, ratio-level variables. An analysis of variance (choice A) is the best choice here, however, because this experiment tests a two-tailed, not a one-tailed, hypothesis, and there are more than two groups to compare.

Bibliography

Ader R, Felton DL, Cohen N (eds): *Psychoneuroimmunology,* 2/e. New York, Academic Press, 1991.

Carlson NR: *Physiology of Behavior,* 4/e. Boston, Allyn & Bacon, 1991.

Conger JJ: *Adolescence and Youth: Psychological Development in a Changing World,* 4/e. New York, Harper & Row, 1991.

Duncan RD, Knapp RG, Miller MC: *Introductory Biostatistics for the Health Sciences,* 2/e. New York, John Wiley & Sons, 1983.

Feuerstein M, Labbe EE, Kuczmierczyk AR: *Health Psychology: A Psychobiological Perspective.* New York, Plenum, 1986.

Gatchel RJ, Baum A, Krantz DS: *An Introduction to Health Psychology,* 2/e. New York, Random House, 1989.

Goldstein A: *Biostatistics: An Introductory Text.* New York, Macmillan, 1964.

Hamburg DA, Elliott GR, Parron DL (eds): *Health and Behavior: Frontiers of Research in the Biobehavioral Sciences.* Washington, DC, National Academy, 1982.

Hamburg DA, Sartorius N: *Health and Behavior: Selected Perspectives.* New York, Cambridge University, 1989.

Hazzard WR, et al: *Principles of Geriatric Medicine and Gerontology,* 2/e. New York, McGraw-Hill, 1990.

Kammeyer KCW: *Marriage and Family.* Boston, Allyn & Bacon, 1987.

Kandel ER, Schwartz JH (eds): *Principles of Neural Science,* 3/e. New York, Elsevier, 1991.

Kaplan HL, Sadock BJ: *Modern Synopsis of Comprehensive Textbook of Psychiatry,* vol 4, 6/e. Baltimore, Williams & Wilkins, 1991.

Kaptein AA, et al (eds): *Behavioral Medicine: Psychological Treatment of Somatic Disorders.* New York, John Wiley & Sons, 1990.

Kirk RE: *Experimental Design: Procedures for the Behavioral Sciences,* 2/e. Belmont, CA, Wadsworth, 1982.

Last JM (ed): *Maxcy-Rosenau Public Health and Preventive Medicine,* 13/e. East Norwalk, CT, Appleton & Lange, 1992.

Lerner RM, Galambos NL: *Experiencing Adolescence: A Sourcebook for Parents, Teachers, and Teens.* New York, Garland, 1984.

Lerner RM, Hultsch DE: *Human Development: A Life-Span Perspective.* New York, McGraw-Hill, 1983.

Lerner RM, et al: *Psychology.* New York, Macmillan, 1986.

Linden W (ed): *Biological Barriers in Behavioral Medicine.* New York, Plenum, 1988.

Lindzey G, Aronson A (eds): *The Handbook of Social Psychology,* vol 2, 3/e. New York, Random House, 1985.

Martin PR (ed): *Handbook of Behavior Therapy and Psychological Science: An Integrative Approach.* Elmsford, NY, Pergamon, 1991.

Matarazzo JD, et al (eds): *Behavioral Health: A Handbook of Health Enhancement and Disease Prevention.* New York, John Wiley & Sons, 1984.

Plomin R, DeFries JJ, McClearn GE: *Behavioral Genetics: A Primer,* 2/e. San Francisco, WH Freeman, 1990.

Ragland DR, Branch RJ: Type A behavior and mortality from coronary heart disease. *N Engl J Med* 318: 65–69, 1988.

Rosen JC, Soloman LJ (eds): *Prevention in Health Psychology.* Hanover, NH, University Press of New England, 1985.

Rosenthal R, Rosnow R: *Essentials of Behavioral Research: Methods and Data Analysis,* 2/e. New York, McGraw-Hill, 1991.

Schneiderman N, Tapp J: *Behavioral Medicine: The Bio-Psychosocial Approach.* Hillsdale, NJ, Lawrence Erlbaum, 1985.

Schuster CS, Ashburn SS: *The Process of Human Development: A Holistic Approach,* 2/e. Boston, Little, Brown, 1986.

Simons RD (ed): *Understanding Human Behavior in Health and Illness,* 3/e. Baltimore, Williams & Wilkins, 1985.

Steptoe A, Mathews A: *Health Care and Human Behavior.* New York, Academic Press, 1984.

Suinn RM: *Fundamentals of Abnormal Psychology.* Chicago, Nelson-Hall, 1984.

Tryon WW (ed): *Behavioral Assessment in Behavioral Medicine.* New York, Springer, 1985.

Twaddle AC, Hessler RM: *A Sociology of Health,* 2/e. New York, Macmillan, 1986.

U.S. Public Health Service: *Health United States, 1990,* PHS No. 91–1232. Washington, D.C., U.S. Department of Health and Human Services, 1991.

ЪЂЪЂ

Vander Zanden JW: *Social Psychology,* 4/e. New York, Random House, 1987.

Weiss SM, Herd JA, Fox BH (eds): *Perspectives on Behavioral Medicine,* vol 1. New York, Academic Press, 1981.

Weiss SM, et al (eds): *Stress, Reactivity and Cardiovascular Disease,* NIH No. 84–2698. Washington, DC, U.S. Department of Health and Human Services, 1984.

Williams RB: *Perspectives on Behavioral Medicine: Neuroendocrine Control and Behavior,* vol 2. New York, Academic Press, 1985.

Williams SJ, Torrens PR: *Introduction to Health Services,* 3/e. New York, John Wiley & Sons, 1989.

Wilson JD, et al (eds): *Harrison's Principles of Internal Medicine,* 12/e. New York, McGraw-Hill, 1991.